CULTURESHOCK!

A Survival Guide to Customs and Etiquette

MOROCCO

Orin Hargraves

Marshall Cavendish
Editions

This edition published in 2006, reprinted 2008, by:
Marshall Cavendish Corporation
99 White Plains Road
Tarrytown, NY 10591-9001
www.marshallcavendish.us

Other Marshall Cavendish Offices:
Marshall Cavendish International (Asia) Private Limited. 1 New Industrial Road,
Singapore 536196 ■ Marshall Cavendish Ltd. 5th Floor, 32–38 Saffron Hill,
London EC1N 8FH, UK ■ Marshall Cavendish International (Thailand) Co Ltd.
253 Asoke, 12th Flr, Sukhumvit 21 Road, Klongtoey Nua, Wattana, Bangkok
10110, Thailand ■ Marshall Cavendish (Malaysia) Sdn Bhd, Times Subang,
Lot 46, Subang Hi-Tech Industrial Park, Batu Tiga, 40000 Shah Alam, Selangor
Darul Ehsan, Malaysia

Marshall Cavendish is a trademark of Times Publishing Limited

ISBN 10: 0-7614-2502-0
ISBN 13: 978-0-7614-2502-1

Please contact the publisher for the Library of Congress catalog number

Printed in China by Everbest Printing Co Ltd

ABOUT THE SERIES

Culture shock is a state of disorientation that can come over anyone who has been thrust into unknown surroundings, away from one's comfort zone. *CultureShock!* is a series of trusted and reputed guides which has, for decades, been helping expatriates and long-term visitors to cushion the impact of culture shock whenever they move to a new country.

Written by people who have lived in the country and experienced culture shock themselves, the authors share all the information necessary for anyone to cope with these feelings of disorientation more effectively. The guides are written in a style that is easy to read and covers a range of topics that will arm readers with enough advice, hints and tips to make their lives as normal as possible again.

Each book is structured in the same manner. It begins with the first impressions that visitors will have of that city or country. To understand a culture, one must first understand the people—where they came from, who they are, the values and traditions they live by, as well as their customs and etiquette. This is covered in the first half of the book.

Then on with the practical aspects—how to settle in with the greatest of ease. Authors walk readers through how to find accommodation, get the utilities and telecommunications up and running, enrol the children in school and keep in the pink of health. But that's not all. Once the essentials are out of the way, venture out and try the food, enjoy more of the culture and travel to other areas. Then be immersed in the language of the country before discovering more about the business side of things.

To round off, snippets of basic information are offered before readers are 'tested' on customs and etiquette of the country. Useful words and phrases, a comprehensive resource guide and list of books for further research are also included for easy reference.

CONTENTS

ACKNOWLEDGEMENTS

My first debt of gratitude is to the directors of the International Meditation Center USA, and especially to Craig and Charlotte Storti, who have accommodated me in every sense of the word while I was writing this book.

I salute the US Peace Corps who provided me the opportunity to experience Morocco the first time. I am also grateful for the Peace Corps' robust and extensive grapevine, which I have used in tracking down resources and information in Morocco. I hope that in writing this book, I have made some contribution towards the Peace Corps' third goal of enlarging knowledge and understanding about the developing world.

Many people in Morocco went out of their way to help me find information that would have been otherwise much more difficult to ferret out. Among them, I thank Badia Bakkali, Bettina Brunner, Khalil El Harim, Hakim Illi, Criss Juliard, Joe Kitts, Latifa Louraoui, Jim and Heidi Lowenthal, Alexander Moll and Stephanie Sweet. I must also mention Fatima Meskina, who over the years has opened many doors in Morocco to me that most foreigners never get to see beyond.

In London, I thank Mr Bennis of the Moroccan Embassy. In the United States, I say thank you very much to the ladies of the Westminster Branch of the Carroll County Public Library, including those who work in interlibrary loan. If there are libraries in heaven, surely they work like this one does.

Finally, I record my deep appreciation of Maati Ouarraki, my friend of 15 years who has kept my Arabic alive through his tireless correspondence, provided a home for me whenever I have visited Morocco and showed me an enduring example of loyalty and faith in friendship that I shall always treasure.

MAP OF MOROCCO

PORTUGAL

SPAIN

MEDITERRANEAN SEA

N O R T H   A T L A N T I C   O C E A N

● RABAT

MOROCCO

CANARY
ISLANDS

ALGERIA

WESTERN
SAHARA

A Moroccan man stares pensively into the distance, perhaps wondering what the future has in store for the people of Morocco.

FIRST IMPRESSIONS

'When I meet fellow Americans travelling about in North Africa, I ask them, "What did you expect to find here?" Almost without exception, regardless of the way they express it, the answer, reduced to its simplest terms, is a sense of mystery. They expect mystery, and they find it.'
—Paul Bowles, *Morocco*

LIVING ABROAD:
THE DREAM AND THE REALITY

The prospect of packing up and setting off for a prolonged stay in a faraway country is one of the most exciting things on offer for us humans. It satisfies the parts of us that crave stimulation, discovery, novelty and change. After all, what could better answer any discontent in our lives than a wholesale change to an environment where we can make a completely fresh start?

But implicit in our yearnings for novelty and change is an element that may go unnoticed, namely that part of us that we gleefully expect to experience all of the wonder, diversion and exotic encounters that a foreign culture offers. We call this part of us 'I' or 'me'. Sadly, perhaps this is the least portable of all the things we might take with us on that journey to another country, and it usually doesn't survive intact for more than a couple of months.

What happens? Are our personalities so fragile that they can't be transplanted overseas? Is our sense of self really so dependent on familiar surroundings? If you have spent long periods abroad before, then you probably know already that the answer to these questions is closer to yes than no. Like all organisms, we thrive on stasis and predictability; in fact, our very survival often depends on them. Through a lifetime of experience, we become very adept at maintaining a constant and often predictable relationship with our environment that ensures we will not only survive, but thrive in it. Indeed, we often do everything in our power to 'keep on an even keel', and it is universally thought desirable to do so. So it should come as no surprise that a complete change of our mental and physical environment, such as when we get into another culture, comes as quite a shock to our system.

We are shocked even further when we take our lifetime of learning to another culture and put it to work. Two major and, up to now, dependable products of our experience, what we might call our world view and our coping mechanisms, may go belly up right away. They no longer work, because the experience on which they are founded—our aggregate interpretation of people and what they're about—doesn't hold up in another country. The people are different, and not only on the outside, in ways we can see such as language, gestures, clothing and looks. Our inability to understand—much less predict—what they may say and do very soon leads us to the conviction that these foreigners are also different on the inside, in ways we can't see, and this is unnerving. It makes us question not only who they are, but before long it makes us question who *we* are, because a lot of what we always took for granted about others and ourselves now suddenly looks like it's up for grabs. The well-oiled machine that we call 'I' may appear to be founded on shakier ground than we had ever before imagined.

WHERE AM I GOING FROM HERE?

So does this mean there's an identity crisis waiting for you on the other side of the airport immigration officer? Ultimately, the answer is probably no, because in the end, the chances are pretty good that you will come to an understanding of the culture you're in and perhaps a new understanding of yourself that hasn't completely thrown over the old. The going isn't always easy though, and the process of getting to a place where you are comfortable, functional and even happy in another culture is what most people understand as the various stages of culture shock.

The process of adapting to a foreign culture is mostly about change, and the change must occur in you. If you are to function happily and productively in a culture foreign to you, then you have to meet that culture on its own terms, because it's not going to meet you on yours. All the people you deal with—and in the end it is people that you have to adapt to—also have their own lifetime of experiences, but they may have come to very different conclusions than you have about matters both great and small. And here in their own country, it is their rules and their views that prevail, not yours. Your relations with and expectations of others have to be grounded in an understanding of who the others are and what makes them tick, and a great deal of what makes them tick is not what makes you tick.

HOW DO I KNOW IF I'VE GOT CULTURE SHOCK?

Culture shock usually occurs in several stages. Let's look at how these stages might manifest themselves as you prepare to go to Morocco, and what may happen when you get there.

Anticipation

We can't really say that culture shock begins before you even reach the country, but your expectations about what you will find there may have a great influence on how you respond later. It is probably safe to say about Morocco, as about any other country, that many expectations are founded on the flimsiest of evidence or even on wishful thinking, so that the fewer expectations you have, the better. You may, for instance, have met some Moroccans in your own country and formed an impression of the people on that basis. But remember, you're not seeing them in their native environment. Moroccans you know may well be going through a culture shock of their own, or they may have made some adaptation to your culture that tells very little about what they are like at home.

In the English-speaking world, the film *Casablanca* is renowned as a romantic portrait of Morocco during World

War Two. In fact, none of it was filmed there, and you would search far and wide to find anything like Rick's Café in Casablanca today. Similarly, a popular song of the 1970s called 'Marrakesh Express' painted a charming picture of the carefree pleasures of hippie tourists in Morocco. But in fact, the trains into and out of Marrakech run at speeds that hardly anyone would think of as 'express', and though there are people there 'charming cobras in the square', you won't get within viewing distance of them without being approached by every variety of con artist looking for a way to part you from your hard currency. So you would be well advised to evaluate carefully anything you hear or read about Morocco in advance, and wait for your own experience there to decide what's real and what's not.

Good Times

Unless something dreadful happens upon your arrival in Morocco, chances are that you will thoroughly enjoy the beginning of your stay. It is after all a sunny, friendly, hospitable country where the food is delicious, the scenery fantastic, transportation easy and prices are low. This is what tourists come for, and when you first arrive, you will very likely have that experience too. Many of your pleasurable expectations about the country may in fact be borne out, especially as you get the first taste of the exotic and foreign aspects of Morocco. If this is what you came for, you won't be disappointed. Morocco is geared up and ready to show you a good time.

What's Wrong with This Picture?

But chances are also good that before long, little things—frustrations, irritations, misunderstandings—will start to build up. If you don't speak Arabic or French, you may find that communication is a serious problem. If you are a woman, you may be mystified and disturbed by all the aggressive attention you receive from men when you're not aware of doing anything to invite it. If you've begun your job, you may be frustrated that what people say will happen and what actually happens seem to have no relation to each other at all. And if you're just plain human, you may be very uncomfortable with the fact that people seem to stare at you wherever you go. These incidents are all different ways in which Morocco is knocking at the door of your mind. Will you let it in?

Initially, you probably won't. Even with the best of intentions, the changes that are brought on by planting yourself in the heart of a foreign culture come too thick and fast for anyone to take them on at once. So you may start to selectively block things out, or respond to them in ways that don't quite feel right. For example:

- You start to avoid or strictly limit your contact with Moroccans, because every social or personal encounter ends with you not really understanding what just happened.
- You imagine that people are conspiring to make sure you pay twice as much for everything as a Moroccan would because they think you're rich.
- You react angrily to a situation before it even happens, because you feel it has already happened too many times before: being cut in front of in a queue, or being addressed obsequiously in French, or being

unceremoniously nudged out of the seat you have chosen in a taxi.

- You feel unduly depressed about something which wouldn't have been so significant at home: someone not showing up for an appointment, a few days without a letter from a loved one, being unable to find something in the market you want to buy.

Along with events such as these, there may be any number of other symptoms that have everything to do with culture shock: physical symptoms of stress such as insomnia, headaches, illness or stomach trouble, irritability, homesickness, feeling helpless and alienated, being obsessive about doing or checking something. Face it! Your system is overloaded, you're using all the coping mechanisms you know, and for the moment, things seem to be getting worse rather than better.

THE BEATEN PATH AND THE ROAD LESS TRAVELLED

If you are at this point in your adaptation to Morocco, you are in fact at a fork in the road.

In one direction, you will see the established expatriate community. They have been here a long time, and they have all the answers. They have 'figured out' this culture, and even though they seem to have little directly to do with it nowadays, they are quite confident about the conclusions they have reached. You can see them at their lawn party, where the absence of Moroccans is quite conspicuous (except those serving, of course). They know how you feel. They are holding out a cocktail to you and smiling. They are ready to confirm all of your uncomfortable observations and deepen your misunderstanding about the culture, if you will only join them. Sadly, perhaps, most people do. It requires no effort, and enables you to stop where you are now and get back that old but now endangered sense of 'I' which was always so comfortable at home. This is the path of least resistance, but it is essentially a dead end as far as your progress in Morocco is concerned. Think twice before you take that cocktail!

Down the other, less travelled fork, the road ahead is a little more difficult to see. In fact, you can't see much of anything on it, except that there are more Moroccans there than people from your own country. Initially, it is a little lonelier than the first road, but down a little further, it opens up to a broader view that at the moment you can't even imagine, because you're not there yet. If you take this road, there is a little more work to be done, but the rewards are worthwhile. You will learn a lot about Morocco and Moroccans; you will probably learn even more about yourself; and you will find a way of living and working in Morocco that brings out the best in it and in you.

WHAT GOOD IS THIS BOOK?

You will find this book quite useful whichever road you choose, because how you use the book is up to you. If you want to become an expat armchair expert on Moroccan culture, the facts are here. If you want to make a sincere attempt to cross the bridge to Moroccan culture and be at home in the country, this book will help to get you there.

Please be aware of one thing: this book does not tell you how to adapt successfully to life in Morocco, because that is something that only you will be able to figure out for yourself. This book is not trying to sell you a particular view on Moroccan culture, though it occasionally takes one. This book reflects the experience of many people, but, it is hoped, the presentation of their experience will allow you to draw your own conclusions in time, on the basis of your experience.

The intentions of this book are threefold: to provide a handy reference guide to many aspects of Moroccan culture; to help you avoid some obvious and subtle pitfalls as you set about making a life for yourself here; and to give you the benefit of many other people's experiences, as points of comparison with your own.

HOW TO SUCCEED

How then do you carry off a successful adaptation to life in Morocco? If there was an easy formula, everyone would be using it. Nonetheless, here are a few hints that, combined with a lot of effort, have not been known to fail:

- Study the natives: what makes them react the way they do? If it isn't clear, it doesn't hurt to ask questions.
- Study yourself: what makes you react the way you do? Can you see how your conditioning causes you to respond one way, and a Moroccan another, in the same situation?
- Learn the language: if you speak only English, life in Morocco will very often be a struggle. Learning French levels the playing field. Learning Arabic will have innumerable benefits.
- Make a friend: Moroccans are very friendly and social people, so chances are you won't want for companionship. But make the effort to find a friend of your own sex whom you trust, and in whom you can confide. A good Moroccan friend can be your ticket to a much happier life in Morocco.
- Study your fellow countrymen: people from your own culture in Morocco can be a very useful resource to aid your understanding. Find out how they have coped with various situations that confront you. Investigate whether the point they've arrived at is where you want to end up.
- Take it easy and be patient: Morocco happens to you only a moment at a time, and that is the best way for you to experience it. There is no reason to imagine a dreadful future based on the experiences of a bad day. No one adapts to a culture overnight, and some people might not really find their wings for a couple of years.
- Don't expect the world: life can be pretty good in Morocco, but it won't be perfect, and it may in the end be a lot less perfect than where you came from. Morocco is a poor country and in many ways still developing. Not everything is possible here, and there will be days when it seems that nothing is possible at the time you want it.
- Take time for yourself: wherever you are from, it's unlikely that you will require more companionship than Morocco offers, because it offers it almost continuously. Don't hesitate to detach from others when you need to, take

stock of yourself, and evaluate where you want to go from where you are.

In a nutshell, living happily in Morocco is a balancing act among three activities: spending time alone, spending time with Moroccans and spending time with your compatriots and other foreigners in Morocco. Each of these is enriching and sustaining in completely different ways, but too much of any one of them can throw you off balance and detract from your ability to enjoy and benefit from the others.

Note on Languages

Arabic and French words appear throughout this book. Guidance for French pronunciation is widely available and so there is no attempt to give any here. A guide for the Moroccan pronunciation of Arabic words and an explanation of the system of transliteration used in this book can be found in Chapter 8: Communication on page 216.

GEOGRAPHY AND HISTORY

'The born traveller—the man who is without prejudices, who sets out wanting to learn rather than to criticise, who is stimulated by oddity, who recognises that every man is his brother, however strange and ludicrous he may be in dress and appearance—has always been comparatively rare.'
—Hugh and Pauline Massingham, *The Englishman Abroad*

AL-MAGHRIB AL-AQSA: AN OVERVIEW

An orientation to Morocco must begin with geography. For hundreds of years, Morocco has been shaped by forces that derive from its unique location in the world. Those who argue that geography is destiny could well use Morocco as an object lesson.

WHERE'S MOROCCO?

Morocco covers the north-west corner of Africa and so is intrinsically African, yet separated from what most people think of as African by the vast Sahara. The image that comes to mind when we think of an African probably doesn't look very much like most Moroccans, but traffic across the great desert has gone on since time immemorial and thousands of black Africans travelled on one-way tickets to Morocco as slaves, concubines or military conscripts. Thus, the influence of sub-Saharan Africa is still everywhere in Morocco: in faces on the street, in music and dance, in dress, language and folklore.

Morocco is only 13 km (8 miles) from Europe across the Strait of Gibraltar, ever on the doorstep of the West but never really getting inside. Morocco once even applied for membership in the European Union. The application was rejected, but Morocco is an associate member of the EU. Its colonial past and its present economic ties ensure that Morocco will always have a close relationship with its neighbours to the north.

Finally, Morocco stands at the western end of the Mediterranean, whose eastern tides lap the shores of the Middle East. It is from there Morocco inherits the basis of its language, its religion and the main-stream of its culture. An Arabic name for Morocco, *al-Maghrib al-Aqsa*, means the extreme west, and attests to Morocco's place in the Arab world. The king, along with many others in Morocco, claims descent from the prophet Mohammed, the founder of Islam.

As we will see shortly, the history of Morocco is a catalogue of the opportunism of invaders from all the lands that border it. The strangers came, they saw, they liked what they saw, and most of them stayed for a long time. Morocco today is an amalgam of the various cultures, languages, religions and values left behind by yesterday's invaders. And the process hasn't ended yet: Morocco continues to open up to the influence of the West, and the emerging world culture transmitted via today's high-technology communications filters daily into the Moroccan psyche. The arrival in recent years of satellite television and the Internet in Morocco may well be the greatest single influence on Moroccans' way of thinking in modern times.

THE LAY OF THE LAND AND ITS PRODUCTS

What we might call Morocco's microgeography, its physical terrain, has also played an important role in shaping the country into the way it is today. In one way or another, most Moroccans make their living off the land, either by working it directly or in the trade of the bounty it produces. So when we look at the lay of the land in Morocco, we are also looking at the foundation of its economy. It is a land rich in natural resources that, except for the deposits of phosphates, have been little exploited by modern technology. Farming methods were perhaps more modern and developed during the colonial period than they are today, although irrigation is increasing and modern farming equipment and technology are becoming more widely available. Many of Morocco's resources are used in a sustainable, low-technology fashion that has not changed for thousands of years.

The principal features of the Moroccan landscape are the mountains, the desert, the rivers, the plains and the sea. Each of them, with the labour of Moroccans, makes a contribution to the growing economy.

Mountains

Four major mountain ranges cross Morocco, running roughly south-west to north-east, starting in the north with the Rif. Though not rising above 2,100 m (6,890 ft), in some places, the cliffs of the Rif drop quite sharply to nearly sea level, making the entire region relatively inaccessible to modern transportation. The Rif are home to the Rifi Berbers, one of the major distinct linguistic groups in Morocco. This part of the country has many citrus groves and is also known for the growing of *kif* (cannabis), which is smoked or processed into hashish.

Just south of the Rif, and separated from them at one point by only a narrow stretch called the Taza Gap, are the Middle Atlas, the northernmost of the three ranges of Atlas Mountains. The highest peaks are just barely over 3,000 m (9,850 ft). The fertile mountain valleys of this area are used intensively for agriculture; the mountainsides and plateaus for grazing sheep, cattle and goats.

The High Atlas rise south of the Middle Atlas and are roughly parallel to them. These are Morocco's highest mountains, with some peaks reaching over 4,000 m (13,130 ft), including Mount Toubkal, Morocco's highest, at 4,165 m (13,670 ft). These two ranges of mountains are together home to the Amazigh Berbers, another of the major linguistic groups.

South of and parallel to the High Atlas, with peaks reaching just 2,400 m (7,880 ft), are the Anti-Atlas. The Soussi Berbers—another linguistic group—come from this part of the country, which is hot and dry most of the year and produces most of Morocco's crop of dates. The sparse population is concentrated along the rivers whose waters flow intermittently, depending on rainfall and snowmelt in the spring.

The interior of Morocco is dominated by mountains, and the mountains are dominated by Berbers. These two facts figure prominently in the history of Morocco, as we will see.

Desert

The word 'Sahara' is from Arabic and merely means 'desert'; so to say Sahara Desert is a bit redundant, but perhaps not so if we think of the Sahara as the desert of deserts. Morocco has only a corner of it, the north-western part, from where it stretches across the breadth of Africa. Nevertheless, the reality of the desert is thoroughly woven into Moroccan folklore and history. The Arabs, whose culture and language dominate Morocco, are themselves desert people from the desert of the Arabian peninsula, and many of their traditions have found a second home in the deserts of Morocco.

Trade across the Sahara also delivered many indigenous desert traditions to Morocco, via the rather small population of desert nomads. The town of Sijilmasa, which now lies in ruins on the banks of the river Ziz near Rissani, was once one of the pre-eminent cities of North Africa, serving as a trading post for those travelling across the Sahara dealing in gold, salt and slaves. The influence of nomadic peoples with roots in the Sahara can be found today in all parts of Morocco,

In the arid south of Morocco, life clings to the oases, like this one in Tinerhir.

and the language, dress and customs of the desert peoples remain distinct from those in other geographical areas.

Rivers

Though none is navigable, the rivers of Morocco play an important part in agriculture, since rainfall is rarely adequate for many crops. Irrigation from rivers and dams now covers about 14 per cent of arable land. Four principal rivers rise in the Middle Atlas, of which three empty into the Atlantic: the Sebou—Morocco's largest—ends at Kenitra, the Bou Regreg empties at Rabat and the Oum r-Rbiâ (which means mother of spring) empties north of El Jadida. The Moulouya, also rising in the Middle Atlas, flows northward into the Mediterranean. Further south, the Tensift, the Sous and the Drâa empty into the Atlantic, and the Ziz and Rheris flow into the desert.

The Plains

Between the Atlantic coast and the mountains, and in between the mountain ranges, lie several flat and relatively featureless plains which nevertheless figure prominently in

Morocco's economy. The plains are cultivated with a variety of crops including grain, tobacco, citrus, olives, sugar beets and other fruits and vegetables; some of these are processed for export. The phosphate plain, in west central Morocco, is the base for a large phosphate mining and processing industry. Morocco has the largest reserves of phosphates in the world, and they are its chief earner of export revenue.

The Sea

Morocco has more than a thousand miles of coastline, divided between the Atlantic and Mediterranean shores. Despite this, it has historically not been much of a seafaring nation, though it enjoyed some notoriety in the past for its role in piracy and the seaborne slave trade. It has, however, often been a destination for other seafaring nations which staked out claims of varying authenticity and duration. From the 15th to the 17th centuries, England, Spain and Portugal set up several enclaves along the coasts, and vestiges of these—both physical and cultural—are still evident. In fact, two Spanish enclaves, Ceuta and Melilla, still exist in Morocco.

Today, Morocco's shores are the basis of its fishing industry, which provides both for local consumption and export. Many anchovies and sardines sold in countries around the world are packed into cans in Morocco. Tourism, one of the biggest industries in Morocco, also makes use of the seaside, and there are beach resorts of all sizes on both the Atlantic and Mediterranean coasts.

WHAT'S THE WEATHER LIKE

For a small country, Morocco has a very wide variety of weather patterns and climates, making generalisations difficult. But as a whole, it enjoys a pleasant climate, which means that on any given day, the weather is bound to be good somewhere. Its size, moreover, makes it easy to get out of one kind of weather and into another. Most of inhabited Morocco lies between the 30th and 35th parallels of north latitude. The seasonal variation in temperature and length of day can be compared to those of Perth, Sydney, Capetown, Los Angeles, Dallas or Atlanta, to draw examples from the English-speaking world. There are four general climates, but even these fluctuate widely from year to year, and the physical boundaries between them are indistinct. We start with the most predictable.

Desert

Here, it's hot all the time and it rarely rains. What relief there is comes with some cool, even cold winter nights, especially at higher elevations. If rain does fall, it will likely come in late autumn or late spring. Life tends to revolve around escaping the punishing rays of the sun, and making the most of scarce water resources.

Mediterranean

Here, the term Mediterranean describes a climate rather than a place, and a climate esteemed the world over by those who have experienced it. Winters can be rainy but are relatively mild and temperatures stay above freezing; summers are occasionally hot, but the temperature is usually moderated by the proximity of the sea. The coasts and coastal plains of Morocco, extending roughly north from Essaouira and to all of the Mediterranean Coast, enjoy this climate.

Low Mountains and Plateaus, Inland Valleys

At lower mountain elevations, summers are hot and dry, but with occasional thunderstorms; cool evening breezes are a welcome feature. Winters are cold and may have snow but rain is more likely. Night-time temperatures may dip below freezing, but a sunny day usually warms things up appreciably. A general greening trend from the rains starts in about November and carries through early June. Much of the Rif and Middle Atlas regions enjoy this climate.

High Mountains

High in the mountains, winters are cold and snow is common. To the surprise of many people, Morocco has a number of ski resorts, the most renowned being at Toubkal and at Ifrane in the Middle Atlas. Summer days are hot and dry with some thunderstorms, but nights are regularly cool or even cold. Rains may start in September, turning to snow in December and January, tapering off in April.

MOROCCAN HISTORY: A RIDE IN THE FAST LANE

We will take a look now at the high points of Morocco's tumultuous past, with a view to understanding how it influences the present. We will be travelling so fast that at most points, we will only discern rough outlines, but we will stop occasionally for the scenic overviews. If you want to slow down for some parts to take in a little more detail, have a look at the bibliography in the back of this book. But for now, fasten your seatbelt!

The Berbers

First, there were the Berbers. It should never be forgotten that they are the indigenous people of Morocco as far back as there is any need to look. Their origins are probably in south-west Asia, and they are thought to have migrated to North Africa—perhaps in separate contingents—beginning in the second millennium BC. They are a people of mixed racial stock who picked up many features of the groups they encountered on their way to North Africa, and they are united more by linguistic than by identifiable genetic features. Moroccans calling themselves Berbers today may have the dark skin, eyes and hair of sub-Saharan Africans, or they may have the fair features normally associated with Europeans, but the majority fall about in the middle, mostly as a result of centuries of mixing with the more homogenous Arabs.

The Berbers are a tribal people with an apparent affinity for life in the mountains. After thousands of years, the mountains are still the domain of the Berbers, and are the only places in Morocco where the language of the street is as likely to be a Berber dialect as Arabic. And though the importance of tribal links is somewhat diminished today, particularly for urban Berbers, they are still the basis for much of the administration of daily life in the mountains.

In early times, life in the mountains and the all-embracing tribal identity precluded the need for the Berbers to have any form of government that extended beyond immediate ties: family, clan (a group of related families) and tribe (a group of clans, perhaps descended from a single ancestor). Thus, no government of any kind reached farther than from one valley to the next, and there was no need for one.

Two things gradually brought on this need: intertribal wars and—more significantly—invaders from the outside.

Wars led to the formation of various confederations of tribes, and occasionally one tribe or another gained enough control to form what could be called a kingdom, but these did not endure. Invaders, over the centuries, were legion and often compelled the Berbers as a whole to unite against them. Indeed, over the last two millennia, invaders largely determined the course of history in Morocco.

Phoenicians and Romans

Several classical historians described the Berbers, but it was probably the Phoenicians who had the first appreciable contact with them. The contacts were mostly for trading, and took place along the coasts. Primitive Punic customs and religion may have penetrated inland to some degree, but did not reach the mountains where the main concentrations of Berbers were settled.

The Romans, after their fashion, set up shop in a more organised way, and annexed what is now northern Morocco—roughly from the Bou Regreg and the Middle Atlas northwards—in AD 40. For 500 years, this part of Morocco was administered by Rome as the province of Mauretania Tingitana, and today it bears the faint imprint also found in other outposts of that empire, mostly ruins of their buildings. The most interesting and well-preserved of these are at Volubilis, just north-west of Meknes. Roman Morocco was Christianised in the 2nd century, and it is thought that the first Jews also came to Morocco during the Roman period as well, although some may have arrived earlier with the Punic traders.

Situated on the southern and western extreme of the empire, Morocco was never a principal concern of Rome, and it was one of the first parts of the empire to fall away. Roman influence did not extend much beyond the provincial borders anyway, and the Berbers of the High Atlas and beyond continued to live the pastoral life that they had enjoyed for centuries, enlivened only by occasional skirmishes with their neighbours.

Up to this time, the influence of outsiders on the Berber way of life had been minimal and ephemeral. Berbers

A guide demostrates how the Roman baths were used, in the ruins at Volubilis.

accepted the protection offerred by invaders against the predations of other Berbers where it was expedient, and they paid tributes as necessary. They formed trading links with whoever passed their way. They also absorbed, temporarily at least, the various religious tenets arriving on their soil from time to time, but always mixed them with the vivid, intense and personal aspects of their own forms of worship.

The Arabs

Following the death of Mohammed in 632, Islam began its rapid expansion outwards from the Arabian peninsula. Within a single generation, North Africa as far west as Tripoli in Libya had been conquered. By the end of the 7th century, the marauding Arab armies had arrived in Morocco, intent on bringing more lands and people into the *Dar al-Islam* (the House of Islam, or world community of Muslims) and generally pursued whatever means were necessary to carry this off.

The Berbers, as they had done with earlier invaders, accepted the protection offered by the new arrivals where it was needed. They also embraced the new religion, again modifying it to suit their needs, and, as with others before them, they traded with the Arabs freely. The arrival of the Arabs, however, began a new era in the history of the Berbers. The Arabs arrived in greater numbers and over a longer period of time than their predecessors, and they came to stay, not merely to trade, exploit or administer from a distance. Thus, they were destined to make a bigger splash in the Moroccan Berber gene pool than any of those who had come before.

Arab migration to Morocco continued over a period of 500 years, beginning roughly in AD 700. Southern Spain was also brought under Islam at around the same time, and a Caliphate (domain of a Caliph, a putative successor to Mohammed in matters of religious authority) was established in Cordoba, Spain, in 756. This date is usually associated with the foundation of Moorish culture, which flourished from the 10th to the 15th centuries. While much of Europe stumbled through the Dark Ages, Moorish civilisation developed to become the pre-eminent influence in the area, extending across North Africa as far east as present-day Libya, and covering the southern half of the Iberian peninsula. A mixture of Arabs, Berbers, Spaniards and Jews, combining elements of Islam, Christianity and Judaism, the Moors made innovations in architecture and music that are still evident today. Both Spain and Morocco retain some fine examples of Moorish architecture, but Morocco alone keeps alive the Andalusian musical tradition that dates from Moorish times. Writers even into the 20th century have referred to Moroccans as Moors.

Berber Resistance

From time to time during the lengthy expansion of Arab dominance in Morocco, Berber tribes from the mountains organised resistance to the Arabs, who remained predominantly urban flatlanders. Ironically perhaps, these resistance movements were ostensibly as much about religion as conquest, always having the purpose of re-establishing a purer, stricter Islam in place of the supposedly corrupted forms of it that had arisen among the Arabs. The three major movements, which enjoyed prominence between the late 11th and the late 15th centuries, were, in order of their fleeting appearance, the Almoravids, the Almohads and the Merinids. Each left traces behind in Morocco and southern Spain, and students of architecture are able to distinguish among buildings from each period. But in a larger historical context, these Islamic revivalist attempts were neither significant nor successful. They did, however, keep alive a Berber identity as distinct from an Arab one, and helped to maintain the divide between mountain Berber and urban Arab that persists today, though in a much more muted form.

Also during this period, a distinction arose both of land and of people that was to persist for centuries in Morocco: *blad l-makhzen* and *blad s-siba*. The terms might best be rendered as governed land and renegade land respectively. They refer to the regions and people that were under the control of *makhzen* (some form of civic authority), and those that were *siba* (without civic authority). The mountains of Morocco made it difficult for any but the largest and most organised of invading forces to gain an advantage, and in any case, it was not often thought worthwhile to bring areas under domination that did not promise some economic advantage. Thus, many Berber tribes continued to experience little hostility from the outside world, and successfully rebuffed it when they did. They formed the backbone of the *blad s-siba*, from which no *makhzen* army was able to extract obedience or taxes. The *blad l-makhzen*, on the other hand, was the more regularly administered area of Morocco under the control of organised, Arab-dominated authority.

Sherifian Dynasties

There persists in Muslim countries a tradition of reverence for those thought to be directly descended from Mohammed.

Such persons are collectively called *Sherfa*, and are believed to possess some of the holiness and spiritual power of their ancestor. In Morocco, their influence was perhaps greatest in the *blad s̲-s̲iba*, where no civic authority was recognised, and thus Sherifian tribes and clans had opportunities to exploit their position to attain leadership and political power, becoming the recognised religious authority and—in the absence of any other—the de facto civil authority. A short-lived sherifian dynasty, the Saadis, arose in the 16th century; in the mid-17th century, the Alawi dynasty came to power, and this family of leaders still rules Morocco today.

As a geopolitical entity, Morocco was still in its infancy at this point, and so to say that a dynasty came to power means merely that the family achieved political hegemony in their area: in the case of the Alawis, the oasis around Tafilalt, in the south-east of Morocco. The goal of any aspiring dynasty, however, had to be the control and expansion of the *blad l-makhzen*, the governed land, for the shifting fortunes of rule and authority in the *blad s̲-s̲iba* were nothing to stake an empire on. Accordingly, the Alawis spread outwards, extending their influence by conquest and doing so in the name of superior religious authority. By the 18th century, they ruled over lands that included virtually all of the coasts, the Rif mountains and a large area around their original stomping grounds in the south-east.

The Alawis, however, were not rising to power in a vacuum. They made regular concessions to dominant tribes in the *blad s̲-s̲iba* to keep them in abeyance, achieving a kind of peaceful coexistence with them. The borders between governed and renegade land were very fluid, and often shifted depending on the success or failure of any given tax-gathering foray on the part of the *makhzen* army, or the success of Berber raids on outlying governed settlements; what was *blad l-makhzen* one day could become *blad s̲-s̲iba* the next. Nevertheless, the Alawis were beginning to acquire the trappings of real leadership, taking on the title of sultan (Arabic for absolute ruler) for the leader in power, and setting up various royal capitals at different times in Marrakech, Meknes and Fez.

European Interest

At the same time, Europeans were waking up to the economic potential of their southern neighbour, and were using their superior technology and organisation to carve out niches there. Starting in the 15th century, Spain, Portugal and England all set out to control various coastal areas of Morocco, and France soon followed suit. Given the general chaos that prevailed outside the governed areas of Morocco, the sporadic and unpredictable violence that erupted between the governed and the ungoverned and the widespread decadence and corruption that grew up under the Alawis and others, it was relatively easy for savvy outsiders to gain influence. Additionally, the Alawi sultans were often besotted by European envoys, mesmerised by technical gadgets they brought with them and dazzled by the fawning recognition the clever Europeans paid them. As a result, the many concessions granted to European interests paved the way for the wholesale economic—and later, political—exploitation of Morocco.

By the 19th century, Europeans essentially controlled Morocco. It remained nominally independent only because the main European players of the day—Britain, France, Germany and Spain—wanted to avoid the conflict among themselves that would result if any one of them tried to wrest complete power in Morocco from the others. There was also a kind of foresighted political correctness in their taking the view, publicly at least, that it was not their business to govern Morocco. So there was an air of cooperation among the Europeans in sharing their interests, but privately, each manoeuvred to get the biggest piece of the Moroccan pie.

Finally, the French

Two European powers in the end edged out the others in the competition to control Morocco. Spain, whose ties went back to the Moorish civilisation, gained control of a northern strip of Morocco along the Mediterranean, which it kept until 1956. In 1912, France, outsmarting its neighbours, established a protectorate in the remainder of Morocco, along borders roughly as they are delineated today. The reigning Alawi sultan of the time, Moulay Hafid, made the protectorate official by signing the Treaty of Fez, which stipulated that France, in the interest of maintaining its own security, could establish civil order in Morocco, but that in all other concerns, Morocco would retain its laws and other viable civil institutions. The sultan had little choice in the matter, as he was by that time beholden to the French army for saving him and his court from the deadly predations of raiding Berber tribes.

As it turned out, 'protectorate' was merely a high-sounding name for 'colony'. Whether by original design or not, the French government gradually usurped and supplanted virtually all civil authority in Morocco, as well as taking in hand its foreign and economic policy. This was partly in response to the lack of competence and stability in the existing Moroccan institutions, and partly in response to the demands of French *colons*, or immigrants, who arrived in droves and demanded protection from their government.

Berber Resistance, Encore

In devising the protectorate, France was actually taking control of the same rather fluid *blad l-makhzen* that had existed for about 300 years. There were still shifting alliances among various independent Berber tribes and areas in the mountains where the power of the Alawi sultans had never penetrated. It took fully 20 years of occupation, but roughly by 1930, France had finally subdued all of the *blad s-siba*. Ironically perhaps, it was the French reaction to continuing Berber resistance that ultimately resulted in a single administration for the whole of Morocco for the first time in its history; and the administration was not a Moroccan one, but French.

The Time of the Christians

The word in Moroccan dialect for the colonial period is *waqt n-nsara*, or the time of the Christians. This phrase aptly describes the theme of the period, for though there was never any systematic attempt to Christianise the Moroccans, the Christian Europeans established authority in all spheres of Moroccan life except for the private practice of the Muslim religion. By the mid-1930s, there were 200,000 Europeans living in Morocco, of whom three-quarters were French. And the French were never people to set up a colonial lifestyle by half measures. The face of Morocco, particularly in the cities, was transformed. New towns with grand boulevards and buildings in stylish architecture went up in all the major cities, usually in areas adjacent to the *medinas*, or walled cities of the Arabs. A comprehensive system of roads, which remains one of the best in Africa, was laid out across the length and breadth of the country, complete with milestones. A system of railroads, already begun in the 19th century, was extended further into the interior. Agriculture was modernised, a topological survey was conducted, ports were built and mineral and timber wealth were assessed with a view to exploitation. In short, the French had moved in—and brought France with them.

The Movement Towards Independence

As with colonised peoples the world over, the Moroccans soon grew tired of their masters. Now that they were used to living under a formalised government, they began to think how nice it would be if it was their *own* government. Several factors influenced the growing nationalism.

As early as the 1920s, a university-based Islamic fundamentalist movement arose in Fez. Its aim was to revive in Morocco a more respectable form of Islam, which was seen as having degenerated under French rule. Though primarily an intellectual movement, the activists in these early efforts to get out from under the French had contacts with liberal thinkers in France and with other nationalist movements elsewhere in the Arab world, where colonialism was generally regarded as antithetical to Islam. The Moroccan nationalists were ready to mobilise when the time was right.

The French had been fairly successful with their policy of 'divide and conquer' among the Moroccans—it seemed easy when the Moroccans were so often divided of their own accord—but when the colonial government tried in 1930 to promulgate a law that would have institutionalised the rift between Arabs and Berbers, it backfired. There were demonstrations against the law in cities across Morocco, and this prompted the French to arrest nationalist leaders. The effect of this action was to galvanise the various factions that had articulated the nationalist sentiment in Morocco.

World War Two further exacerbated relations between Moroccans and their already unwelcome rulers. Most of the French administration in Morocco was only too happy to cooperate with the Vichy government when it supplanted the legal government in France. But the Moroccans were not impressed that one aggressive European power was preferable to another, and what is more, they were unwilling to cooperate in the systematic persecution of Jews (then quite numerous in Morocco) that the Vichy government insisted upon. Allied troops liberated Morocco in 1942, and a year later, Western leaders—including Winston Churchill and Franklin D. Roosevelt—met privately with Sultan Mohammed V, who up till then had been a puppet of the colonial government. The Western leaders seemed sympathetic to his wish for an independent Morocco, further strengthening the independence movement.

Tensions continued to mount between the rulers and the ruled throughout the 1940s and early 1950s. The French, fearing they were losing their grip on the colony, grasped tighter. French troop strength was raised to a level surpassing that used to subdue the Berber resistance 20 years earlier. In 1953, the French deposed their puppet sultan Mohammed V. Significantly, this wasn't accomplished single-handedly; government troops had the help of a powerful Berber chieftain, Thami el-Glawi, who had mobilised his own followers to aid the French. The sultan and his family were arrested and sent to exile on Madagascar, which proved to be a deeply unpopular action and brought matters to a boiling point. Random terrorism against French colonists and officials became commonplace. The French had miscalculated in thinking that Berbers might unite with them against the Arabs. In August 1955, Berber tribesmen descended on the village of Oued Zem, gathering reinforcements on the way and summarily slaughtered every French person in the town.

Everyone saw that the violence had to end, and finally independence was granted. Mohammed V returned from exile, after first visiting Paris where he was grandly honoured under the auspices of a French leadership suddenly repentant about colonialism and foreign domination. Sovereignty was restored to the sultan in 1956, at the time of independence. Spanish Morocco reverted to home rule in a separate agreement later in the same year, and Morocco was for the first time in its history an independent, united country.

The Kingdom of Morocco

Early leaders and thinkers in the nationalist movement and the political parties that grew up around it had envisioned a country with at least the nominal forms of republican government. The returning sultan, however, was a very popular figure and enjoyed the triple distinctions of being royalty, religious leader (by virtue of his putative descent from the prophet Mohammed) and hero of the independence movement. He consolidated his position and took the title 'king' in 1957, when he began to rule the country without much opposition.

In 1957, he named his son Hassan crown prince, and when the king died in 1961, the prince became His Majesty Hassan II. He ruled Morocco until his death in July 1999. His reign was not always smooth—there were two attempted coups plotted by leaders in the military, which the king survived only by a combination of quick wits and good fortune— but in general, the king enjoyed widespread popular support, especially among the poor and uneducated who made up the biggest single block of his subjects.

MOROCCAN GOVERNMENT TODAY

After the death of King Hassan in 1999, his son Mohammed ascended the throne as Mohammed VI. He inherited the constitutional monarchy of his father. Although the constitution under his rule provides all the democratic institutions expected in a republic, there is no question that the king has absolute power, and that he will not hesitate to use it, even if it means overriding the procedures that normally prevail in the machinery of government. In some ways, this can actually be beneficial to the country because its various government institutions are often seen as inept, corrupt and abusive.

The king is officially the head of state, and he also carries the title 'Commander of the Faithful' (*amir l-muminin*), in recognition of his religious authority. The prime minister, whom he appoints, is the head of government. The king also appoints a Council of Ministers, which is effectively a cabinet. On the other hand, the Chamber of Representatives (*majlis n-nu'ab*) is made up of elected candidates whose legislative authority is mostly limited to criminal, civil and commercial law, and who serve, in effect, as a rubber stamp for the king's decrees. The Chamber, often referred to as the Moroccan Parliament, can be disbanded by royal decree, and has been on several occasions.

Below the National Level

The administration of Morocco is further divided into 43 provinces, 9 local administrations, 22 prefectures and over a thousand communes. Authorities in each of these are a mixture of representative councils and government appointees. The historic Arab/Berber, urban/rural divide is reflected today in the make-up of the various subnational governmental institutions, with interrelated Arab families dominating the power structure in most cities, and various Berber tribes and clan alliances dominating the countryside.

The Western Sahara

Before we alight from our historical phaeton, we will take a quick glance at a dominant issue in Moroccan politics and life: the matter of the Western Sahara, a still unfinished episode of Moroccan history. Since the mid-1970s, the Moroccan government has been trying to establish sovereignty over a section of land to its south, the former Spanish Sahara, now called the Western Sahara. Because it has considerable phosphate reserves and is adjacent to rich fishing areas in the Atlantic, the stakes are high. The government has spent a

crippling proportion of its foreign reserves conducting a war against the Polisario, a guerrilla movement which claims to represent the natives of the area. The Polisario until recently has been funded largely by Algeria, which thought the investment worthwhile for access to the phosphate reserves and Atlantic ports.

The Moroccan government also conducts a never-ending propaganda war in the domestic media to ensure that the desert is never far from the minds of the people, and to drum up support for the idea that the region it calls the 'Saharan Provinces' properly belongs to Morocco. It also serves a useful political purpose in uniting Moroccans of all persuasions behind a common cause—and behind the king. At present, Morocco effectively controls the useful parts of the area and administers all civic institutions. The king has agreed in principle to a UN-sponsored referendum in the area to determine whether its people prefer independence or annexation to Morocco (no other countries lay claim to the area at present), but the Moroccan government has always found a way of postponing the referendum, and it has yet to be held.

Morocco left the Organisation of African Unity over the issue of the Western Sahara, but it has not alienated any of its allies in the industrialised world over the issue. No other country has officially recognised Morocco's claim to the area, and except for the government's own figures, demographic statistics about Morocco from any source do not reflect information about the Western Sahara. However, maps of Morocco in international print media increasingly show it as including the Western Sahara. Official annexation of the Western Sahara would roughly double Morocco's size, but add less than a tenth of a percent to its population, as the area has few inhabitants. About 200,000 live there today, more than half of them Moroccans who have settled there in the past 25 years. Figures given in this book apply to Morocco proper, without the Western Sahara.

DEMOGRAPHIC SNAPSHOTS

There is no substitute for the vivid and lasting impression that is left with anyone who visits Morocco, and a personal account often can be far more informative than facts and figures on a page. Still, a few statistics may help to place Morocco in context.

Morocco in the World

With an area of 446,550 sq km (172,368 sq miles), Morocco is a country roughly the size of Sweden. By contrast, it has more than three times as many people as Sweden (approaching 30 million), who on average earn about 15 per cent of the annual income of Swedes. Morocco is indeed poor, but is actually better off than many countries it may be lumped together with. Virtually all Moroccans have easy access to potable water and adequate fuel for cooking and heating, and all but the remotest rural areas have electric power. There is no starvation, though malnutrition is an ongoing problem. There is little homelessness, nor any burden of refugees or displaced populations from other countries.

Morocco is also a young country: nearly half of its population is under the age of 19 and nearly a third are under ten. Its high population growth rate of 2.1 per cent annually means that its population will double in 33 years. To keep that figure in perspective, Morocco ranks 96th in the world community of 208 countries in terms of population growth, and it is growing much slower than many other African countries. Population density is not so different from that in much of Europe, at about 390 people per sq km.

Morocco in Regional Focus: The Maghrib

The three countries of north-west Africa—Morocco, Algeria and Tunisia—are often called collectively the Maghrib (meaning 'the West' or 'where the sun sets'), and it is instructive to look at Morocco compared with its neighbours, which share many features both current and historical. All three countries were colonised by France, all eventually gained independence, but all still retain close ties with their former master; French is still widely spoken all over the Maghrib. All three countries have indigenous Berber populations, though Morocco's is certainly the most prominent and numerous. Finally, all have been under the influence of Islam since the Muslim invasions beginning in the 8th century.

Of the countries of the Maghrib, Morocco has the lowest standard of social welfare as measured by some key statistics, although some differences are very slight. It has the lowest per capita annual earnings at US$ 3,260, compared with US$ 4,000 in Algeria and US$ 4,800 in Tunisia. It also has the lowest life expectancy by slight margins, at 66 for males and 70 for females. Morocco suffers the highest rate of infant mortality, at 53 per 1,000 live births (in Algeria and Tunisia, the numbers are 45 and 33 per 1,000 respectively), though it should be noted that the figure for Morocco is half of what it was 20 years ago. Tellingly, Morocco has only one doctor for every 2,923 people in the country, fewer than its neighbours enjoy.

By way of further contrast, the citizens of Spain, just across the Strait of Gibraltar, have average annual earnings of US$ 15,300, nearly five times those of the average Moroccan. Its men and women live longer, and its infant mortality rate is less than one third that of Morocco. Spain has a doctor for every 241 citizens. It comes as no surprise then that Spain is an attractive destination for economic migrants from Morocco who are hoping to make a short hop to European prosperity.

If demographic Morocco could be summed up in a few words (though anyone who has been there will say that's impossible), it could be called a fast-developing country, rich in resources both human and natural, that is doing a pretty good job keeping abreast of its growing population with economic and social progress.

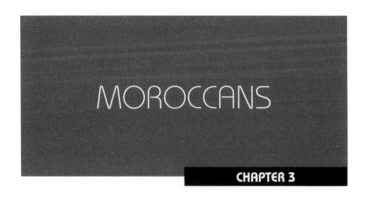

MOROCCANS

'We wanted something thoroughly and uncompromisingly foreign—foreign from top to bottom—foreign from centre to circumference—foreign inside and outside and all around—nothing anywhere about it to dilute its foreignness—nothing to remind us of any other people or any other land under the sun. And lo! In Tangiers we have found it.'
—Mark Twain, *The Innocents Abroad*

THE MOROCCAN WITHIN

The sharp contrasts visible in so much of the Moroccan demographic landscape—differences between old and young, Arab and Berber, Muslim and European—are in a sense the tip of the iceberg: the evidence of diversity above the surface, where everyone can see it. But there is a lot more happening underneath that is not so obvious. In this chapter, we will begin a deeper excavation to the parts that don't show at the top, to the inner landscape, in order to find out what makes Moroccans tick.

CULTURAL SMORGASBORD

It doesn't take very long in Morocco to notice that many of the natives are not only multilingual, but multicultural as well. When they switch from one language to another, the words aren't the only things that change. The tone of voice, the manner of speaking, the subjects covered, even gestures and personal mannerisms undergo a transformation when a Moroccan switches from Arabic to French, or from Berber to English. Which one is the real Moroccan? All of them are, and more importantly, none of them is fake. Moroccans, even in the remotest village, may grow up with exposure to two distinct cultural patterns—Arab and Berber—and young people are especially enamoured of Western culture. They take every opportunity to internalise it, or at least affect what they see.

The foreign observer may look upon this chameleon-like approach to cultural behaviour as hypocrisy, but the natives generally don't see it or feel it this way. Moroccans live with contrasts in every sphere of life, and they have a very high tolerance for dualities of all kinds. Consistency of behaviour is not necessarily regarded as a virtue, since behaviour is very much context-driven, and contexts change a lot in Morocco. Moroccans are thus quite masterful at adapting to different contexts, even those which are polar opposites. Hand in hand with this ability comes a talent for reconciling conflicts, for finding a happy medium between the diverse forces and ideas that influence them. In a culture as rich in contrast as Morocco's, this is not only an admirable trait, it is a survival skill.

Life at the Extremes

There are a few who do not find this balance in the midst of conflicting ideas and methods, and they represent the extremes of Moroccan cultural stereotypes. At one end is the Muslim fundamentalist, who rejects all things Western (especially French), non-Islamic, modern and new. At the other extreme is the completely Europeanised Moroccan, who rejects (at least privately) all things traditional, Islamic, Arabic and old, and embraces their opposites, especially all things French. But these types are small minorities, and most Moroccans do a comfortable juggling act with all of their diverse cultural heritage.

The rest of this chapter will explore the varied influences in Morocco's rich culture that express themselves in values. We begin with the great unifiers: Islam, family values and the concept of shame. About these, there is little dissent (at least outwardly), little sense of humour and massive conformity.

ISLAM

The influence of Islam is totally pervasive in Moroccan society, so it is helpful for the foreigner to have some understanding of its philosophy, in order to comprehend some potentially confusing phenomena. First, we look at the tenets of Islam, for these are the same throughout the Muslim world and constitute the primer that many people will expect you to be familiar with.

Muslims view Islam as the final and most perfect of the three revealed, monotheistic religions, the other two being Judaism and Christianity. Jews and Christians are recognised by Muslims as People of the Book, and many prophets of the Old and New Testaments are respectfully treated in the Koran, the sacred book of Islam. Thus Muslims are familiar with many biblical figures by their Arabic names, including Moses and Jesus, though they accord them no special distinction among the prophets. For them, the pre-eminent prophet is Mohammed, the founder and revealer of Islam. In conversation and writing, he is referred to as *n-nabi*, the Prophet, rather than by his name, and no other mortal religious figure compares with him.

Many cosmological and theological ideas familiar to Jews and Christians are also found in Islam, including heaven and hell, the existence of angels and Satan, the importance of faith and a day of judgment. However, Islam rejects the idea of a divine Christ, and of any intermediary between man and Allah. When Muslims refer to Allah, they mean the same God to whom Jews and Christians pray. Allah simply means 'The God', distinguishing him from *lah*, a god, which would be implicitly a false god.

A sincere Muslim observes the five pillars of Islam to the degree possible. Recitation of these is a kind of pop quiz that religious Moroccans put to foreigners, so if you don't know them, you'll very likely learn them soon enough:

- Making the profession of faith. A person converts to Islam (and you will be admonished, chided and encouraged frequently to do so) by sincerely uttering the profession of faith in Arabic, which translates, 'There is no god but Allah, and Mohammed is his prophet.' This should be done in the presence of two male Muslim witnesses.
- Praying five times a day. The five times are dawn, noon, afternoon, sunset and night. The exact times are determined by the position of the sun and thus change throughout the year. Each time has a particular name, and each is signalled by the *mueddin*, or prayer

announcer, chanting from the minaret of a mosque, usually over loudspeakers. Muslims pray in a mosque if it is convenient, but may pray in practically any clean, relatively secluded spot. Ritual ablutions (washing) are performed before praying. Women generally do not go to mosques, their presence being considered too distracting to the men, but hours are set aside for them to attend at some point in the week. Muslims face Mecca, to the east, when they pray. (Incidentally, you will find that Moroccans tend to orient themselves by locating east, rather than locating north as is more common in the English-speaking world.)

- Giving alms to those in need. This is done casually to those begging on the street and in more formal ways, through various charitable institutions. In Morocco, a governmental foundation called the *habous* oversees religious charity. The Koran stipulates that 2.5 per cent of one's income and 10 per cent of one's crops be given in alms, but few seem to observe these strictures. Further information on the treatment of beggars will be discussed at the end of the chapter.

- Fasting during the month of Ramadan. Muslims observe a very strict fast, believed to be spiritually cleansing and a sign of one's faith, between dawn and sunset for a whole month each year. More information about Ramadan can be found in Chapter Six: Food and Beverages on page 181.

- Making a pilgrimage to Mecca at least once in one's lifetime. Muslims from around the world converge on Saudi Arabia once a year to perform rituals associated with the pilgrimage to the holy sites of their religion. Those who have made the journey gain the title <u>H</u>ajj (for men) or <u>H</u>ajja (for women). The traditional time to go on the pilgrimage is in the 12th month of the Muslim calendar, *Du al-<u>h</u>ijja*.

Any visitor in Morocco will quickly observe that *not all Moroccans are doing these things*. And yet they call themselves Muslims. What gives? First, remember that Morocco is not considered a 'hard-line' Muslim country; life does not come

A mosque in Fez in standard Moroccan architectural style.

to a halt when prayers begin, eating during Ramadan is fairly common (though never public) and many Moroccans would much rather go to Disneyworld or Paris than make the pilgrimage to Mecca. There is also a prevalent idea, especially among the young, that practising religion is something to do when one is older, married and settled down. But don't think that on account of this apparent laxity in devotion that Moroccans are not serious about Islam. Their faith in it is such that they feel it embraces them, even without their practising it mindfully. It is the state religion, and you will meet Moroccans only rarely who do not profess a belief in Islam, whatever their outward behaviour may be.

THE MUSLIM WORLD VIEW
The following are some features of the inner Moroccan landscape that can be traced directly to Islam.

Fatalism

There is a very strong sense in Islam that all events are pre-ordained, and that one cannot escape one's destiny. The Arabic word *maktoub*, literally 'written', sums up the idea that everything is already decreed by Allah before it comes to pass. Moroccans say that you cannot escape what is *maktoub*, written for you.

The practical effects of this point of view are many. To the inexperienced foreigner, it manifests itself primarily as an unwillingness to get involved, a passive acceptance of all that happens without any volition to intervene or change the course of events, even when it appears that one could easily do so.

An American tourist once related how he was mugged at knifepoint in Tangier in broad daylight. It was a rather lengthy process, and by the time the muggers had finished, a small crowd had gathered to watch. The American was baffled that the onlookers didn't attempt to intervene or alert the police; they only stared.

Fatalism is also evident in Moroccans' acceptance of their position in life, and a seeming lack of ambition to improve their lot. Those born poor expect to stay poor; those born rich are perfectly at ease with the gulf that separates them from the less fortunate.

When events do not unfold as wished or as planned, Moroccans are generally quite ready to accept the new situation and let go of the past without a lot of remorse, regret or blame. They think it useless to rake over the past since events have transpired in the only way possible.

Finally, the future, from a fatalistic point of view, is highly conditional, contingent on the unknown. The Arabic phrase *in sha' allah*, 'If God wills', is a standard modifier of anything said of the future. It may often seem to the foreigner that the speaker is giving himself a way out of a commitment, and no doubt this is sometimes the case, but Moroccans feel they would be 'tempting fate' to speak of the future with great confidence and without reference to the will of God.

Views of Other Religions

For Muslims, a religion without God, or with many gods, would be blasphemous. Moreover, the lack of religious affiliation or a belief in God is not only incomprehensible, but contemptible to most Muslims. Since Muslims view Islam as the ultimate and perfect religion, the question of conversion to some other faith does not arise. By the same token, practitioners of other religions are encouraged to convert to Islam. Foreigners who do not adhere to one of the monotheistic religions, or who have no interest in exploring Islam, may find that the best course is to avoid religion as a topic of conversation. It can very quickly turn unpleasant if you have strongly held beliefs and views that are contrary to Islam.

Transmission of Islam

Children of Muslim men are considered Muslims from birth. Thus Muslim men may (though as a rule, do not) take non-Muslim wives, but a Muslim woman may only marry a Muslim man. A Moroccan family would certainly consider marrying one of their daughters to a foreigner, but not before he had sincerely converted to Islam. A Moroccan government-issued pamphlet states that, 'Except for a rather small Jewish community, all Moroccans are born Muslim.'

The Moroccan Slant

Not long after the death of Mohammed, questions arose concerning who the true inheritors of his teachings were. This dispute settled into an institutionalised split between the Sunni and Shi'a sects which continues to this day. Moroccans eventually embraced the Sunni teaching, the more orthodox and common form of the religion in the world today, which is practised by a majority of Muslims in all countries except Iran and Iraq.

Although Sunni Muslims everywhere share certain aspects of their beliefs, there are a few features peculiar to Moroccan Islam. Historians attribute them mostly to the meeting of Islam with pre-existing forms of Berber worship, and view them as a compromise between the two. Muslims elsewhere would view these beliefs and practices as unorthodox, but generally not heretical. The two chief features specific to Moroccan Islam are *baraka* and *Murabitin*, and the two are inextricably linked.

Baraka means blessing, grace or spiritual power; in some contexts, it may refer to a kind of supernatural power. The word exists in classical Arabic but has a special connotation in Morocco, and is indeed a household word. *Baraka* is believed to be bestowed upon individuals by Allah. It is also transferable in different ways, most commonly by direct male descent. The prophet Mohammed is viewed as the ultimate human possessor of *baraka*, and his male descendants are believed to possess it in varying degrees. *Baraka* is manifested in an individual's abilities, good fortune and putative spiritual power. It is thought advantageous to associate with anyone who has a lot of *baraka*, the idea being that some may rub off on you.

Numerous individuals in the course of Moroccan history are viewed as having possessed great *baraka*. Such men are called *Murabitin* (singular *Murabit*), a title somewhat analogous to the Christian 'saint'. When living, they are revered and looked to as authorities to settle all sorts of disputes. After the death of a *Murabit*, it is thought that his remains exude some of his spiritual power, and thus they are enshrined in a structure, also called a *Murabit* (in French *marabout*, which is also used in Moroccan Arabic). These *Murabitin* usually consist of a small domed, temple-like structure surrounded by a walled courtyard. Individuals make pilgrimages to these *Murabitin* in the belief that it is meritorious to do so, and also in the hope that favours or blessings will be conferred upon them. It is especially common for barren women to seek blessings from a *Murabit* in order to conceive a child.

Murabitin, and those who frequent them, are much more common in the countryside than in urban Morocco. Many *Murabitin* take on the status of quasi-official charitable institutions, collecting alms and dispensing them to needy pilgrims. Occasionally, however, a *Murabit* may fall into disrepair and lie in ruins. *Murabitin* are often maintained by the descendants of the departed 'saint', and these in turn live on the alms offered to the *Murabit*.

In truth, the Moroccan belief in *Murabitin* and the power of *baraka* conflict with Islam strictly defined, because they imply a tangible link or intermediary between God and

In the foreground lies the tomb of Moulay Idriss, in the village named for him. Many *Murabiṯin* attract pilgrims on their yearly feast day.

man, which the Koran denies. But these ideas are so widely practised and accepted in Morocco that they have become part of Moroccan orthodoxy.

Fundamentalism

Islamic fundamentalism, so prominent in world news from time to time, is less evident in Morocco than in many other Muslim countries, but it does exist. Morocco is among the most liberal countries in the Islamic world, but piety is nonetheless highly respected, so there is no stigma associated with the ardent and zealous practice of Islam—or at least, no stigma that would ever be openly expressed. The Muslim fundamentalist believes in strict adherence to the Koran. This means total, even rigid separation of the sexes, and perhaps complete seclusion of women. Fundamentalists are less inclined to welcome foreigners in Morocco, perceiving them generally as a corrupting influence.

Today there is a small but (to the government) worrying trend towards fundamentalism at Moroccan universities. Students are frustrated by the lack of opportunities available to them and by the growing divide between rich and poor, which they see as a result of Western and anti-Islamic influences. Proponents of these views may favour an Islamic revolution such as occurred in Iran. Greater employment opportunities for the young and educated would go a long way towards weakening this trend.

Fundamentalists are often referred to loosely as the *Ikhwan Muslimin*, the Muslim Brothers (or Brotherhood), but women are at least as likely to be among them. A fundamentalist man would very likely only take a like-minded wife, but a less ardently religious man would also consider a fundamentalist wife a good match, on the theory that she would be less inclined to be unfaithful.

A few points of etiquette should be observed by foreign men in relation to fundamentalist women, whether the women are married or not. First, they are not likely to shake hands, and it may be embarrassing for them if you were to initiate such a greeting. Certainly if a woman is gloved, whether in her home or on the street, do not offer a handshake. It may also be considered improper even to engage in conversation with such women, unless strictly in a professional capacity. In any case, it is unlikely that foreign men would even come into contact with a married fundamentalist woman in her home, as she would likely be segregated.

Folk Religion

A few aspects of belief in Morocco tread the line between religion and superstition, and deserve treatment here. Observance of and belief in all of these is much more common in the countryside, but certainly not unknown in cities, especially among the poor and uneducated. Those who practise or believe in them do not regard them as separate from Islam. Urban or educated Moroccans may denounce them as both backward and un-Islamic.

Fanatical Sects

A few departed saints have followers, usually within a limited geographical area, who observe the saint's feast day (death anniversary) with bizarre rituals, which may include frenzied dancing, chanting and self-mutilation. These sects are few but well known, and are as much a curiosity to most Moroccans as they are to foreigners.

Djinns

The English word jinni, or genie, comes directly from the Arabic *djinn*, denoting a spiritual being that may play some role in human affairs if called upon. Though properly a part of folk religion, belief in *djinns* is widespread in the Muslim world. In Morocco, they are believed to frequent places associated with water: public baths, drains, sinks, even pots and pans. A plumber working for foreigners in a small Moroccan town was once asked what had become of several taps and fixtures he had installed the previous day (and believed stolen in the night) and, with complete confidence, he attributed the mischief to *djinns*.

Aisha Qandisha

This mythical figure, a beautiful, seductive woman with the legs of a goat, is thought to live under the beds of rivers, in flames and in various other places. She is said to appear to men in dreams, or occasionally while awake. Well known to every Moroccan, children are often frightened of her.

Trance Dancing

Moroccans are very fond of making music, and very adept at different kinds of rhythmic patterns, often played on various drum- or tambourine-like instruments. There is a belief that many girls and women have an inner, ineffable connection to a particular beat, and when they hear it, they are compelled to dance to it. They may very quickly succumb to the rhythm and appear to go into a trance, in which they are not in control of their actions and seem to be possessed by the spirit of the music. This may culminate in fainting, or even a coma. It is not uncommon at gatherings that include dancing to see a young woman undergo this transformation.

Witchcraft and Occultism

In the countryside especially, *sehour*, or witchcraft, is practised by women (and rarely by men) to influence another person, usually of the opposite sex. It is almost always used for some dubious purpose, either to arouse love in one that appears disinclined, or to take revenge on one who has been unfaithful or adulterous. It is administered in curses and potions, the latter given surreptitiously in food or drink. At most country markets, one can find a *sehhira* (witch) who dispenses the peculiar ingredients of her trade and offers advice on their use.

As they direct the administration of curses, witches are also the source of antidotes and remedies for the afflicted. Victims or their families may also seek the aid of a *fquih*, a religious teacher connected with a mosque, to undo a spell.

Most towns, villages, and medina neighbourhoods have a resident fortune teller (*shuwwaf* for male, *shuwwafa* for female) who can, for a fee, reveal the unknown or the future, using cards and other prognostic devices. The reputation of fortune tellers varies with the accuracy of their visions, which can be startlingly on target.

Foreigners may take whatever view of these beliefs they wish,

Stories circulate everywhere about the horrible effects of those under spells. A well-known figure in many villages of the Middle Atlas in the 1980s was formerly a gendarme (provincial policeman) who was allegedly unfaithful to his wife. She is said to have placed a curse on him, and now he wanders the streets babbling and often naked.

but are best advised to have nothing to do with them. Moroccan women are very often strong believers in the power of witchcraft; men seem to vacillate between scoffing at its alleged powers and fearing that they will be treated with it.

FAMILY VALUES
No institution plays a greater role in forging the identity of nearly every Moroccan than the family does. Everything else revolves around family life and is secondary to it, including work, friendship, love and to some degree even marriage. Unless they go away to school or move away to find work, Moroccans usually live with their families until they marry. It is not unusual for a Moroccan man to bring his new wife home to live with his family, especially before they have children. Thus, when Moroccans ask you detailed questions about your family life, it is not out of nosiness but merely their way of placing you in the only context that ultimately matters for them.

If you are alone in Morocco, you will be called upon to explain early and often what in the world you are doing there without any member of your family or a spouse. If you live alone, no one will remark on this without adding *meskin*, meaning 'poor thing'.

Moroccans may feel that dire circumstances have driven you to come to their country all alone. The notion that you might enjoy living alone and spending time by yourself will take a lot of getting used to. A Moroccan professor once said that for him, the idea of sleeping alone in a room was like sleeping in a coffin!

Moroccans have separate kinship terms for maternal and paternal aunts and uncles, and other features of their language reflect the primacy of family relations; they use kinship terms—rather than names—for addressing one another. The words for mother, father, brother, sister, paternal uncle, maternal uncle and grandfather (*bba*, *mmu*, *akh*, *akht*, *âm*, *khal*, *jed*) are all very short, elemental monosyllables and normally carry a personal marker at the end, thus making them 'my father, my mother', and so on. Most of the worst

For young and old, life centres around the family. Here, a grandmother enjoys the sunshine with her granddaughter.

insults in Moroccan Arabic either call into question's one's parentage, or disparage one's mother.

The Pecking Order

Volumes of sociological literature notwithstanding, Moroccan families are not all 'standard', and thus do not conform to any hard and fast rules about their structure. Nevertheless, there is an indisputable hierarchy in the vast majority of homes. Put simply, age brings veneration, and the young are always beholden to their elders: children to parents, aunts, uncles, and grandparents and younger siblings to older siblings. The aged are revered and respected as long as they are able to exert active influence. Thereafter, they are cared for with devotion and dignity.

Whether the mother or the father is the 'boss' in the house depends largely on personalities and the configuration of the family. Note, however, that the mother or father who is head of the household may also be a grandparent and mother- or father-in-law to others in the home. A common view is that women orchestrate and supervise domestic affairs, but you will observe that this is not always true.

Among children, a sex-based hierarchy is inculcated early on. The message conveyed is that boys matter and girls don't. Girls begin to learn the ropes of domestic toil as soon as they are able. Rather than playing with dolls, they may well get to practice real-life surrogate mothering on a younger sibling by the time they are four or five. Boys, on the other hand, are not expected to work around the house and are indulged far more than girls, but they are at the beck and call of their parents and older siblings to run errands.

Marriage

The institution of marriage is highly esteemed and is viewed as the only normal state for an adult. Americans may say, 'There's no escaping death and taxes,' but the Moroccan proverb is, 'There's no escaping death and marriage.' Marriage and the subsequent raising of children are the natural aspiration of every man and, to some, the only aspiration—indeed, the only justification—for every woman. As another proverb puts it, 'A woman without a man is like a nest without a bird.'

Marriage is largely an economic and social contract in Morocco, and while not every marriage these days is strictly arranged, parents continue to play an active role in the choice of spouse for their children. Marriage agreements are negotiated much like commercial transactions. The bridegroom pays *sedaq*, or the bride price, to the family of the bride. In addition to her personal charms and virginity, a bride comes with a dowry, the contents of which are subject to scrutiny by the groom's family. A marriage to a first cousin is considered a very desirable match because it binds families closer together and also facilitates inheritance within the family. In other words, marriage

A woman who has reached her mid-20s without getting married begins to be called 'poor thing'—or worse, it is assumed that her virginity is no longer intact and that she is therefore not a suitable bride. Men are typically slightly older than their wives, but a majority marry before the age of 30.

doesn't always have much to do with love and romance (which seem mostly to be carried on outside of that institution). The expectations of prospective young brides and grooms are not necessarily of long-lasting conjugal bliss, but of a good working relationship that will enable them to protect and enhance the name of their families by producing children.

Divorce

Esteem value notwithstanding, not all Moroccan marriages are made in heaven, and an increasing number end in divorce. Young couples are the most likely to divorce, in the early years of a marriage and often before there are children. It is easier for a man to initiate divorce proceedings, but women can also sue for divorce on a reduced number of grounds. Men may also repudiate wives in circumstances where the marriage is deemed to be invalid. Both parties come off badly in cases of repudiation or divorce. All property of the household, and care of the children if any, usually go to the woman; but her chances of finding another husband are quite small, and if she has no education or qualifications, there are very few respectable or desirable ways for her to earn a living.

Polygamy

Under Islam, a man may take up to four wives—but he is obliged to treat all his wives equally, at least with regards to their material needs. In Morocco, this is an effective economic limit on maintaining multiple wives. You will occasionally meet or hear of men who have two wives, but rarely more. Sometimes the wives live together in the same house with all their children, sometimes separate households are maintained where children, if any, live in the house with their natural mother. There is no Arabic equivalent for stepmother and stepfather; the terms used translate as 'my father's wife' and 'my mother's husband' perhaps suggesting the weak link between stepparents and stepchildren.

HSHUMA

Pervasive in the Moroccan psyche, and closely related to identification with the family, is the concept of *hshuma*, or shame. One's personal honour and dignity, and by extension, the honour and dignity of one's family, are a Moroccan's most cherished possessions. Moroccans will go to any lengths to preserve them, and mount great defences if their honour or the honour of their family is ever threatened. Nothing can be worse than for *hshuma* to descend, raptor-like, and darken one's name.

It is important here to understand a fundamental difference between Moroccan *hshuma* and Western guilt. Guilt arises when one's conscience notes that one has done wrong. Shame arises with the awareness that others know one has done wrong. Guilt plays very little or no part in the conduct of Moroccan life; shame, on the other hand, is paramount. It is the censure of others that a Moroccan shrinks from, since his or her self-image is derived from others and is not cultivated internally.

What kinds of actions might evoke this shame and bring a person or family into disrepute? They fall into the general categories of behaviour that contravenes social norms, that breaks Islamic precepts or that abrogates personal obligations inside or outside the family. The shamed individual faces ostracism from society or even from family, and in the Moroccan context, no punishment could be worse. Misbehaviour by one member of the family impugns the reputation of all, so there is great pressure within the family to protect all its members.

You will probably become aware only gradually of *hshuma* operating in Moroccans' behaviour; reading about it and experiencing it are two very different things for someone coming from a Western guilt-oriented perspective. It is perhaps most important at the outset only to be aware of the significance of shame, and thus to adapt your behaviour accordingly. In this regard, the main points to remember are:

- If you feel it necessary to reprimand or criticise a Moroccan associate, never do so in public, and try to avoid direct criticism. It is more effective to relate your displeasure through an intermediary (a family member or colleague of the individual) or indicate through your actions that something has gone wrong. The loss of face that a Moroccan would suffer if criticised in front of peers would only threaten the harmony of your future relations.

- Be aware that what Moroccans say in public and what they confide to you privately may vary a great deal. Much may be said or done in the presence of others merely to make a good appearance, to avoid the loss of face or to prevent embarrassment and awkwardness.

- Offering profuse gratitude and thanks to your Moroccan friends for hospitality or favours is greatly appreciated, especially when you do it publicly—even though it may be turned away and diminished with various professions of humility and modesty. A Moroccan adage offers a useful rule of thumb: 'Praise your friend in public but reprimand him in private.'

THE LEGACY OF COLONIALISM

The French officially ruled Morocco for only 44 years, a short time in a region with such a long history. Nevertheless, partly because the colonial period was so recent, and partly because it was so different from everything previous to it, it still has a very profound effect on Moroccan thinking today.

The average Moroccan has a love-hate relationship with France. The average educated Moroccan has, in addition, a love-hate relationship with his own country. Despite years of intimate association, the French and the Moroccan ways of life are poles apart, and probably always will be. There are some things that are better done in one country, and some better in the other. Moroccans are fixated on these differences and dwell on them with great attachment.

A certain segment of the Moroccan population, typically those somewhat older and not very educated, may have a nostalgic view of the colonial period. Everything worked back then, and it may have been the last time they had a dependable job. Such people may portray the French as honest, upright and enterprising, and rue their departure.

Younger Moroccans are quite often torn between complete immersion in everything French—language, arts, media, consumer goods—and a studied resentment of the influence that these same things exert. They long to travel to France, but at the same time, they disparage it as a godless, corrupt and racist empire. They may behave towards French people with a fawning obsequiousness, seemingly the preferred manner in colonial times. Privately, however, they express hatred at what they see as typical French condescension towards them.

Moroccans who have actually travelled to or lived in France sometimes develop an inferiority complex about their native culture and develop the habit of criticising it, drawing constant comparisons between anything Moroccan and French, in which the Moroccan part always comes up short. Such Moroccans have a well-practised litany of the shortcomings of Morocco and Moroccans, and they may wish you to concur; you may find yourself occasionally in the odd position of defending Morocco to one of its own.

These descriptions are, of course, stereotypes. You may meet many people who fit them, but there are just as many who blend characteristics of several different types, or who adopt any number of different attitudes that seem mutually incompatible. In short, the relationship of the Moroccan to France is a complicated, often muddled one.

What has this got to do with you? Especially if you're not even French? First of all, if you are European or of European stock, you must come to expect that many Moroccans will respond to you initially as though you were French, with all the baggage that entails. Until there is more evidence to go on, a foreigner is considered French. By those who don't know you in Morocco, you will be addressed in French more often than any other language, and Moroccans may be surprised if you don't speak it. Even after many years of evidence to the contrary, there is a prevailing assumption that people of European appearance speak French.

As a foreigner, you must also be prepared, as far as you can be, to deal with the convoluted attitudes that Moroccans hold towards their former colonisers, until you can prove that it is inappropriate for them to pigeonhole you in that way. A good way to do this is to learn to communicate in Arabic. A bad way to do this is to speak only French.

FROM COLONY TO KINGDOM

We have seen already that Morocco's history includes a vast array of governments and rulers, with no structure lasting for very long and with chaos replacing order frequently. One constant, however, is that Morocco has never experienced democracy first-hand. The few have long ruled over the many, and even tribes that were relatively untouched by government rule in early times had a hierarchical authority structure.

What does this mean for you in matters of day-to-day relations with Moroccans? It means that a democratic way of doing things, which you may take for granted depending on where you come from, is completely foreign and incomprehensible to Moroccans in most contexts. The idea of a group decision made by a show of hands, for example, or of a teacher consulting students about what they would like to learn, would be surprising and mystifying. Such things may even be seen as a weakness in anyone who would propose them. In virtually any context, except for friendship among equals, Moroccans expect there to be a leader who makes decisions, and accepts responsibility for them.

TRADITION AND MODERNISATION

The dualities of Islam and the West, old and young, poor and rich—all are inherent in the contrast between tradition and modernity in Morocco. There is much that is old and venerable in Morocco, and only a Moroccan completely alienated from his roots could not have profound respect for the beauty and simplicity of the traditional way of life. But at the same time, it is difficult for any Moroccan not to appreciate the convenience, efficiency and sheer wonder of modern technology, and the Westerners' apparent freedom in personal behaviour and relationships. So in fact the two exist, old world and new, side by side. This coexistence can be found everywhere: on the modern four-lane superhighway that runs between Rabat and Casablanca, where cars whiz by at frightening speeds, bypassing the pedestrians and donkey carts that make slow progress on the shoulders; at the beach, where one may see veiled mothers side by side with girls in bathing suits; or on a village street where an old man in a dusty *jellaba* listens to a personal stereo.

Moroccans don't have a fixed attitude about the massive influx of new technology and behaviour arriving on their shores via foreign investment, aid programs, tourists or even from their own family members returning from abroad. Generally speaking, however, the young are likely to embrace the imports unquestioningly. Older Moroccans are more likely to require proof that something new is something better before they accept it. So the disparity between the traditional and modern roughly parallels a generation gap of staggering proportions. As in nearly every country, the youth of Morocco are often impatient with their old-fashioned parents and want to do everything the modern way.

The major obstacles to greater technical modernisation in Morocco are lack of education and poverty, but many older people would not view these as obstacles, when the old ways seem to work quite well and the new ways threaten stability. Younger people, on the other hand, may seem resentful and impatient of the lowly status and slow progress of their country, compared with European neighbours.

A great obstacle to wider acceptance of Western mores is Islam, though it is perhaps unfair to call it an obstacle, for—even though it entails contradiction—Moroccans old and young are deeply grateful for the values that their religion has bequeathed them, and they may see Western society as depraved and violent.

RICH AND POOR

The gulf between rich and poor in Morocco is very wide indeed, and only shows signs of growing wider. As everywhere else in the world, Moroccans typically reduce the rich and the poor to stereotypes, usually reserving their strongest characterisations for those at the opposite end of the spectrum from where they sit. There is, however, in Morocco a greater acceptance of the divide between rich and poor, owing to the comforting assurances of fatalism: it is all meant to be.

Still, the rich come in for a rather poor showing among those who aren't. One of the words for money in Moroccan Arabic is *wusakh ḏ-ḏunya*, dirt of the world, and the words can be quite menacingly spat from a poor man's mouth. A rich man with a big pot belly is called *kersh al-ḥarem*, stomach of sin, on the assumption that his size is due to overindulgence.

The poor go largely ignored and unnoticed by the rich on an immediate, personal level, but the Muslim precept of giving alms provides for a benevolent attitude towards beggars and the poor generally among all Moroccans. Pejorative notions about the poor, such as the idea that they are backward or largely responsible for their plight, are confined to only a tiny minority of wealthy, Europeanised Moroccans.

As a foreigner, you will automatically be perceived as a wealthy person, and by Moroccan standards, you probably are, whatever your status is in your own country. In Moroccan

slang, 'American' is sometimes used as a synonym for 'rich', and in truth, most foreigners who come to Morocco have enjoyed material wealth all their lives that is beyond the means of most Moroccans. It may be helpful to remember this when you feel taken advantage of because of your perceived wealth. Many times, you really are being taken advantage of, and there is probably nothing you can do about it. Chances are that you won't be fleeced too badly, and you will find it much easier in the long run to simply accept your status as a privileged person whose lifestyle costs a little more to maintain.

CITY AND COUNTRY

The contrasts between city life and country life are also quite sharp in Morocco. The split is a fairly predictable one that occurs in most countries of the world: cities are havens for everything modern, expensive, fast, exciting and changing—perhaps also for everything godless and dangerous. The countryside, on the other hand, is where you find everything old-fashioned and slow, but also cheap, dependable, safe and fresh. These are more or less the prevailing perspectives in Morocco, though admittedly vastly oversimplified.

The ancient divide between rural Berber and urban Arab persists to some degree today. All the parts of Morocco that can still be truly called Berber—where Berber is the language of the street, and most people identify themselves as Berbers—are in the countryside and in mountain villages. Moroccan cities, by contrast, are by and large the strongholds of Arabs. Here, too, stereotypes exist, in which each side is comfortable reducing the other to a caricature. Without getting into the ethnic divide, country people (*ârobiyen*, which means roughly 'bumpkin' or 'hick') are viewed as gullible and stupid in the city, whereas country dwellers contemptuously note that those living in the city are *fi shiki*, conceited or pompous.

If you live or work in rural Morocco, you will meet people who have never been as far as Rabat or Casablanca, and to whom the names of these cities conjure up fantasies. It may be comforting to know that a rural Moroccan can be just as perplexed and disoriented in the heart of Casablanca as you can!

Berber farmers cutting fodder in the countryside—a far cry from the bright lights of the city.

One of the most obvious differences between city and country is the relatively greater freedom allowed women in the city. Though one sees fully veiled women in cities, younger women are becoming more and more Europeanised, and even go to cafés now, something that was unheard of a generation ago. In Casablanca and Rabat, native women have even been seen smoking in cafés. Ten years ago, this behaviour would have marked them immediately as prostitutes—and in the countryside, it still would. But Moroccan cities are the vanguard of Europeanisation, home to most of the Moroccans who have lived and worked abroad, and the pace of change is therefore much faster.

PUBLIC AND PRIVATE

The contrast between public and private is not one that Moroccans struggle with; it's one that they are deeply familiar with, and its inflexible rules are so thoroughly ingrained in them that appropriate behaviour in each context is automatic. It is, however, a contrast that you will struggle with if you haven't spent time in the Arab world before. Here, it definitely pays to know the ropes before you start pulling on them.

Life on the Street

In Morocco, as in other Arab countries, public is very public, and private is very private. They are two separate worlds in which the rules of engagement are completely different and don't overlap. In rough terms, the contrasts look like this:

Public	Private
the street	the home
men's space	everyone's space
everything up for grabs	everything accounted for
every man for himself	defined relationships

Paradoxically, while Arabs are renowned for their hospitality, the streets of their cities offer some of the rudest and most inconsiderate behaviour found anywhere in the world. These phenomena are really flip sides of the same coin, one side being the public and the other the private world.

In Morocco, the street is the street. It belongs to no one and to everyone. If you're there, you are inviting any and every kind of attention. It is not considered rude or intrusive to stare at others or approach them on the street, whether you know them or not.

You will notice that eye contact is a kind of game that passers-by play with each other. Being on the street is a spectator sport, where one can be the audience or the attraction. Moroccan Arabic has a word, *joqa*, that means roughly 'crowd that forms to watch a spectacle', and Moroccans do love a spectacle. If you are the only foreigner in a tiny mountain village, the spectacle will be you.

Native women who want to avoid attention on the street cover themselves up, leaving nothing exposed but the hands and the eyes. This is because they know the rules: they are encroaching on men's space and they want to be as unobtrusive as possible. Women who appear on the street flamboyantly, revealing their hair and lots of skin, are in fact inviting attention, and they get it. Such women all too often are uninitiated foreigners who very quickly become

Life on the street: every man, woman and donkey for him—or herself.

bewildered at the aggressive attention they receive from men. Foreign women who dress modestly (it isn't necessary for them to cover up completely as traditional native women do) will not receive undue attention.

A minority of Moroccan girls and women are in the vanguard of liberating public places for women by going about in 'provocative' Western dress, with no gesture towards traditional restraints on their appearance. You will notice that such girls, whether alone or in groups, must brave catcalls and lewd remarks from men and boys they pass on the street. It is a public clash of values that has yet to be resolved.

The essence of street life in Morocco is profane. Without the matrix of family relationships, or those between guest and host that prevail in the home, there is virtually no protocol for the street. People fend for themselves. Moroccans feel no compunction about showing a temper in public, having fierce arguments with tradespeople or even strangers; these are not people one owes anything to, or has to impress. Shopkeepers and other people who work in public do not expect friendliness, nor do they often manifest it. Indeed, excessive friendliness or familiarity in public with strangers may be viewed as weakness or foolishness.

To the foreigner, much of what happens on the street may seem like a complete lack of what we call common courtesy. When a conflict of interest arises, even over very small matters, it probably won't be resolved by one party politely deferring to the other. More likely it will become a contest of wills, an argument for the sake of winning, whether by superior wit, stratagem or sheer forcefulness. This may all seem quite unnecessary, but remember, there is another side.

Private Lives

Private life, by contrast, is completely different, and often more private and secluded than Westerners are used to. If an Englishman's home is his castle, a Moroccan's home is his fortified inner sanctum. The very architecture reveals the sharp separation between street and home: windows are few, and always shuttered if they are at street level. In neighbourhoods that have the space, high walls surround the house to keep out inquiring eyes. The exteriors of houses are often completely nondescript, especially in the *medina*, suggesting nothing of the spaciousness or sumptuousness that may lie within.

Inside the Moroccan home, everyone has a defined relationship to everyone else. There is no turf to defend, nothing to prove to anyone, and both men and women can let their guard down. Here true gentleness and kindness can be expressed and shared, and everyone is relaxed. It is only at home that Moroccans are really at ease, because the street is no man's land. From this, it can be seen why Moroccans can really only entertain guests at home. While men may enjoy an outing in a café, it would be unthinkable to offer real hospitality outside the home; there is no public place in Morocco where one could rightly entertain guests.

It should also be noted that, because the home is so private, it is a place that you need to be invited to, until the time comes when you are on very intimate terms with the owner. Except with relatives, Moroccans do not operate a 'drop-in' society. If you do have occasion to call at a home where you have not been invited, the treatment you receive will likely be polite but distant. If you aren't left on the doorstep, you may be shown into a room on the periphery of the house and left there alone till someone can take care of you.

Right Hand, Left Hand

Another distinction roughly parallels the division between public and private. It may not be obvious to foreigners at first glance, but it is of great importance in most Arab countries. Not to put too fine a point on it, the general rule is that the right hand is the public hand, and the left hand the private one.

The right hand is used for shaking hands, for eating out of a common dish, for drinking if one draws water from a cistern, spring or well, for offering or handing over gifts, money or food and when necessary, for touching others.

Moroccan children who are born left-handed are deprogrammed to the extent possible. They may end up writing with the left hand, but they must learn all of the other functions noted above with their right.

The left hand is one's private business. It is used for personal hygiene, to clean oneself after using the toilet. It must never be used with common food (i.e., food that is available to others), and it is better not to use it for handing over objects or money to others.

MEN AND WOMEN

We save for last the topic that, of all contrasts in Morocco, strikes the foreigner more quickly, more forcefully and more continuously than any other—the differences between men and women, and the behaviours that define and limit them. At the outset, one caveat: trying to generalise about a topic so rife with feeling and under so many competing influences is a little like trying to pin down a wild animal. So you are advised to take in what you read here merely as raw data, to be evaluated on the basis of your particular experience.

The role of women in the home, in society and specifically in their relationship to men is detailed in the Koran in no uncertain terms: 'Men are in charge of women, because Allah hath made the one of them to excel the other, and because they spend of their property for the support of women. So good women are obedient. ... As for those from whom ye fear rebellion, admonish them and banish them to beds apart, and scourge them.' It must be noted, before the hackles of indignation arise, that the vast majority of Moroccan men and women are quite convinced of the truth of this formulation, and live contentedly with it. Contact with Western cultures has exposed Moroccans to other gender-based roles, but this contact has not had a great effect in changing behaviour or attitudes.

The separate roles and functions deemed appropriate for men and women penetrate to every area of life. As we have already seen, methods of child-rearing are quite sex-specific. The advantages boys have in the home carry over into education as well. Although school education is in principle free through the first university degree for all Moroccans, far fewer women get the benefit of education, and by the end of secondary school, more than three-quarters of enrolled students are boys.

The Battle of the Sexes
Underlying the strict division of the sexes in all social contexts is a corresponding view of the fixed roles suitable for men

Girls are in a minority by the beginning of secondary school, many having left to learn domestic skills.

and women in personal and sexual relations. By the time that boys and girls show any interest in the opposite sex, they are scrupulously segregated from each other in any situation in which they would have an opportunity to act on their passions. The only legitimate sexual relations between men and women are held to be those that take place in marriage. The Arabic word *bint* means girl, and is synonymous with virgin. The word *mar'a* means woman. A single event on her wedding night separates the girl from the woman, and if this event should happen at any time before her wedding, the girl becomes a woman without a future, burdened with an unshakable mantle of *ḥshuma*.

If the picture were only this simple, one could expect to find in Morocco paragons of domestic tranquillity and fidelity behind every shuttered window. But alas, other factors cloud the horizon. Marital fidelity aside, it is also assumed that men's sexual needs are natural, imperious and irresistible. Women, much more grudgingly and judgmentally, are held to have similar needs. So in Morocco, as the world over, much of the melodrama of life revolves around love and betrayal, and popular music is as full of love ballads and laments as the Top 40 anywhere in the world. There is a deeply seated and often expressed mistrust between men and women. Each imagines the other to possess a wildly uncontrollable sexuality that will express itself the moment a chink appears in the institutional armour of sexual segregation; each expects that the other will be unfaithful if given a chance; each characterises the other as the reason for so much difficulty in relationships.

Sex and the Single Moroccan

The societal expectation that there be no sex outside marriage is of course irreconcilable with the view that sexual impulses are irresistible—and so various institutions exist to relieve the tension that necessarily accompanies this conflict. Female prostitution, though not officially sanctioned, is widespread in Morocco. It is tolerated but derogated, as in most countries where it exists. Male homosexual prostitution is also commonplace, but happens mostly between foreigners and natives. Finally, homosexual relations among boys and young men are common, before they reach the age where they can be expected to visit female prostitutes.

In the Moroccan mind, sex can only take place between a male and a female, thus lesbianism is unheard of. By the same token, in male homosexual relations, one participant must play the woman's part, which is thought degrading and unmanly. The Moroccan term for homosexual, *zamel*, means 'mount' and is considered offensive. Thus there is no self-identified 'gay community' in Morocco, despite the prevalence of homosexuality.

Homosexual male prostitution is fairly common in cities on the tourist track, especially in Marrakech and Tangier. With the advent of AIDS, a certain degree of hostility has arisen towards foreign male homosexuals.

Prostitution

Female prostitution is widespread in Morocco, from village to city. Supply and demand for it seems to be about equally balanced. Women enter prostitution for a number of reasons, most of them economic. There are very few work opportunities for uneducated or unskilled women in Morocco (domestic service is a major exception) and women who are unmarried, either from divorce, widowhood or spinsterhood, may turn to prostitution to earn a living for lack of any other means of support.

While prostitutes are disparaged, it is not regarded as sinful or shameful for a man to visit a prostitute, unless he is married. Soldiers seem to provide the biggest customer base for prostitutes in Morocco, but single men, before they marry, also use their services. Prostitutes are rather freer in their public behaviour than other women, and indeed their behaviour is very often what identifies them. Women in bars are usually taken to be prostitutes, as well as women who smoke in public—though this is beginning to change in cities. Most towns and cities have a district known for the availability of prostitutes.

Where Does the Foreigner Fit into All This?

In regard to the separate and rather rigidly defined social roles of men and women, foreigners are in a special situation that overall is advantageous. Though foreign women in professional positions do find that they must fight for the recognition that men receive automatically, they are in no way expected to conform to the codes of behaviour for Moroccan women. Foreign men probably enjoy the best of both worlds, enjoying all the advantages that Moroccan society affords men, while at the same time being able to excuse themselves, as foreigners, from occupying male roles that don't suit them.

Great advantages will fall to those who sojourn in Morocco with a spouse. Having a husband or wife along enables Moroccans to place you in a context in which they can assume your personal needs are taken care of. No one will have any reason to inquire about them.

Those who spend time in Morocco alone, either because they are single or because their spouse is elsewhere, will find early on that it is advantageous to develop stock replies to the oft-repeated questions: Are you married? Why aren't you married? Why don't you get married? Why don't you get married to a Moroccan? And so forth. You should also be prepared for probing and detailed questions about your personal life from Moroccans of your own sex. Even among educated professional men, 'locker room' talk is fairly common, and Moroccan women also pull no punches in learning what they can of foreign women's experiences and outlook.

Foreign Women: Moroccan Stereotypes

Moroccans have had adequate exposure to other cultures to develop their own views about foreign sexual and social norms. At the same time, they value very highly the idea that a Moroccan girl is a virgin until her wedding night. In fact, the revelation of her breached virginity is a central feature of the wedding celebration, and the failure to produce it is considered adequate grounds for abandoning the would-be bride. So, in light of the implicit freedom women enjoy in Western films and television, it is not uncommon for Moroccans to view foreign women as 'loose', and also not uncommon for Moroccan men to try to take advantage of this alleged 'looseness'.

It is an erroneous but deeply held conviction of Moroccan men that Western women are a source of continuous and unfailing sensuous delight. So engrained is the stereotype that when a Moroccan male is rebuffed in his (very direct) advances to a Western woman, he is inclined to think that she is just having a bad day, that she is playing hard to get, or that she simply doesn't conform to type. It is unlikely to occur to him that his behaviour is deeply offensive and insulting.

What Western women view as sexual harassment in Morocco—catcalls, direct propositions, even lewd physical advances—are more likely to be viewed by Moroccan men as a barely conscious or controllable stimulus-response mechanism. Thus for any non-Muslim woman alone in Morocco, her relationship to men, especially in public, becomes a major personal issue.

If only two words of advice could be offered about this subject, they would be *Don't react*. Note how modern Moroccan women deal with this sort of behaviour in men: they do not even acknowledge it. Western women are often uncomfortable with the idea that they have to tone themselves down in public, that they can't be themselves. But you may very well find that the price of 'being yourself' in public in Morocco is continuous, unwanted, aggressive attention from men—and that it is much cheaper, more practical and less taxing to 'be someone else' in public, just as Moroccan women do.

SOCIALISING

CHAPTER 4

'There is no way of knowing, once one has left Tangier
behind, where the long trail over the Rif is going to land
one, in the sense understood by anyone accustomed to
European uncertainties. The air of the unforeseen blows on
one from the roadless passes of the Atlas.'
—Edith Wharton, *In Morocco*

THE MOROCCAN YOU KNOW

In the last chapter, we tried to look at Moroccans from the inside out, explaining how different values and traditions have shaped Moroccans' belief and behaviour. In this chapter, we'll start from the outside, taking a look at details of everyday life you may notice but initially not understand, and try to discern explanations. In some cases, we will touch on the same topics that we looked at in the last chapter, but we will try to see them now more from the perspective of 'where you're coming from', rather than from the Moroccan standpoint. Taken together, the two chapters will hopefully demystify much of what linkages between the apparent and hidden realities in Morocco, between daily life and the Moroccan world view.

NAMES, TITLES AND IDENTITIES

Until the advent of French administration, there wasn't a fixed method of recording a person's official name, but like the French, Moroccans carry national identity cards (indeed, they are obliged to) and the system of names they have adopted is also similar to the French. For official purposes, Moroccans take the family name of their father, followed by their personal given name. Women retain their family name when they marry and do not take their husband's family name. Moroccans have adopted the French practice of writing their family name first, often in capital letters, followed by their personal name, for example, GHARBAOUI Driss.

Moroccans, men especially, may go by either of their names. It is more familiar and personal to call someone by his or her personal name, but it is by no means impersonal or formal to use the family name alone. Particularly since some given names are so common—Mohammed, Ali and Hassan for men, Fatima, Aisha and Khadija for women— using a family name in conversation is often the only way to distinguish among individuals. Teachers usually address students with the family name alone.

Arabic and Berber Names

If you develop any knowledge of Arabic, you wil very soon get a feel for the differences between Arab and Berber names, and thus gain a clue to an individual's identity, or at least his or her paternity. The typical Moroccan Arabic family name is a derivation of a three consonant root, ending in 'i', as transliterated the French way, or in 'y' as transliterated the English way (in Morocco, only the French way is used). Thus you will find Wahami (Ouahami to the French), Ghazzouli, Sabri. Even without the terminal 'i', many Arabic surnames are related to three consonant roots. A few of them begin with Ben-, Bint- or Bou-, meaning son of, daughter of and father of respectively.

Berber names are less easily classifiable, but many begin or end in –ou (Barrou, Khallou, Oundir) or end with –an (Ittoban, Amezyan) and will sound different from Arabic names: fewer have a terminal 'i', and many have two or four rather than the three consonant sounds that are typical of Arabic names. A family name beginning with Aït (land of) is a Berber name.

Titles

For women, the only general title of respect is *Lalla*, which can be prefixed to a personal or family name for a woman older than yourself, or when referring to a woman of royalty. *Lalla* can be used alone to get the attention of a woman whose name you don't know, the way Ma'am or lady is sometimes used in English. A woman who has completed the pilgrimage to Mecca may have *Hajja* prefixed to her name.

Any woman or man who is *sherfa* (believed to be descended from Mohammed) has the title *Lalla*, *Sidi* or *Moulay* as a matter of course.

The general title of respect for men is *Sidi*, sometimes shortened in speech to *Si*. It is roughly comparable to the English Sir or Mr, and can be used in all of the same ways as *Lalla*: prefixed to any name, or alone. It is acceptable usage to call any man *Sidi* if you don't know his name and want to get his attention. Less respectful, but often used for waiters, shop keepers and servicemen, is to call any man Mohammed (or Si Mohammed) if you don't know his name.

More elevated than *Sidi* is *Moulay*. Most departed saints and sultans have *Moulay* prefixed to their names, and some living holy men may be addressed this way, though the combination 'Moulay Mohammed' could only refer to the prophet. Finally, men who have completed the pilgrimage to Mecca may take *Hajj* as a title.

Men's titles are used somewhat loosely and for certain individuals, they take on the status of nicknames. Thus it can't always be assumed that a Hajj So-and-So is a returned pilgrim—he may only be a respected or rich member of the community. Similarly, Sidi Mohammed seems to be a given name in its own right apart from Mohammed alone, and one meets the occasional *Moulay* who has no apparent claims to veneration.

ETHNIC AND TRIBAL IDENTIFICATION

Despite centuries of mixed marriages and the likelihood that a completely 'pure' Arab or Berber cannot be found in Morocco today, a majority of Moroccans do not identify themselves as one or the other. Berbers are further subdivided into the Rifi (origins in northern Morocco, in the Rif mountains), the Soussi (origins in southern Morocco, in the Anti-Atlas and the edge of the desert) and Amazigh (primarily Berbers of the Middle Atlas). In Arabic, the term *Shluḥ* usually means Berber in general and can designate any of them.

Berbers maintain a nominal tribal identification that is subordinate to the divisions given above; in the countryside this may still have some active influence in their lives, but for those living elsewhere, it usually doesn't. Arabs are also historically a tribal people, but their links with tribal identity in Morocco are quite tenuous, except in small Arab villages where they may still carry some importance.

DIVISIONS IN MOROCCAN SOCIETY: WHAT YOU SEE

In Moroccan society, the sociologists can find more divisions than they can shake a paradigm at. We will look here only at a handful of differences that present themselves to the foreign observer. In making these distinctions, it is not the intention to present facile stereotypes of different elements in Moroccan society, but rather to give you some cues similar to the ones that Moroccans use for distinguishable people. While there is a compulsion to conform in values and behaviour in Moroccan society, there is no corresponding uniformity in appearance, and indeed many groups that make up the mosaic of Moroccan culture are proud to distinguish themselves by their appearance.

Speech, occupation (or lack thereof) and dress all provide clues by which Moroccans discern the relative social status of their fellow countrymen, and you can use largely the same measure if the need arises. Moroccans' behaviour towards one another usually reflects their awareness of a difference in social status (see 'Cross-Class Traffic' later in this chapter). Your interactions with Moroccans will probably be more successful if you behave towards them in a way that they think reflects your social distance, if any, from them.

Speech

The politics and sociology of speech will be dealt with in more detail in Chapter Eight, but suffice to say here that French is the language of refinement in Morocco, followed by classical Arabic—which, however, is hardly used for ordinary conversation, and when it is, it observes the grammar and syntax of Modern Standard Arabic. Moroccan Arabic is the most common language on the street. The better a Moroccan speaks French, the better he or she can successfully create an aura of sophistication, which can serve as a springboard into higher circles under some circumstances. By the same token, an inability to speak French well indicates a lack of education, and education is generally valued and respected in Morocco.

Great fluency in classical Arabic is highly respectable, but wins no prizes in the social climbing contest. Speaking Berber is a worthy skill only among Berbers, and Arabs look down their noses at all the dialects of that language.

Earning a Living

A person's occupation is another clue to social status. The distinctions noted here are not statistically verified, but rather are based on popular observations of the Moroccan pecking order.

At the top are the idle rich, who don't work but also don't consort much with others in public, so you will probably have little contact with them. This group includes the 'jet-set' Moroccans who seem to spend as much time flitting around Europe as they spend at home. Also among the elite are members of what could be called the wealthy merchant class. These are not the corner shop owners, but more likely the wholesalers who supply them, and such people as factory owners, car dealership owners, magnates of expensive shops in the larger cities, importers and exporters.

Coming in behind the wealthy merchants is a group of Moroccans educated abroad, most of whom come from respectable families and work in professional positions for Moroccan and multinational concerns. Also at this level is a very large segment of educated Moroccans who are university teachers, higher civil servants, lawyers, doctors and other professionals; these two educated groups may be called a middle class. Primary and secondary school teachers, though not as highly regarded or as highly paid, figure in this group as well. Education in Morocco is one of the only avenues to upward social mobility, and many take advantage of it.

For most social purposes, working foreigners in Morocco fit in with the middle class and are treated as such, but with the acknowledged difference that they are outside the system, and are assumed to have much more money than any ordinary middle-class Moroccan.

From here on down, everyone is poor by the standard of any developed nation. This segment includes, in more or less descending order:

- Those who have skills acquired outside of formal schooling, such as those who work in traditional crafts, or as production workers in factories
- Those who have lowly jobs, such as unskilled farm workers, or servants
- The unemployed poor, who take casual work wherever they can find it, usually of the demeaning kind that no one else will do
- At the bottom of the Moroccan social pile, the beggars

Work in skilled but not necessarily literate trades, such as leather tanning, provides a meagre living.

Outside the occupational system but nevertheless worthy of mention are the Sherfa, those who claim descent from the prophet Mohammed. As this group includes the king and royal family, the Sherfa figure quite prominently in Moroccan society. It is thought unfitting for such people to work, so those who have no inherited wealth live humbly, but with great dignity, off the alms of others—contributions to the well-being of the Sherfa are thought to bring benefits to the donor as well. There are also, however, quite wealthy Sherfa in the rich merchant class, and they are not averse to working in order to maintain and increase their wealth.

Dress

Traditional as opposed to modern (i.e. European-style) clothing is not a class marker in itself, because all Moroccans may have occasion to wear clothes of either kind. However, the quality of clothing is a good clue to an individual's status. What one wears in public reflects on oneself and on one's family; looking less than one's best would invite _hshuma_.

Casual clothes that are obviously imported from Europe or North America carry great status with younger people, because they indicate either that one has been abroad or that one knows someone who has been. Such clothing is the overwhelming favourite among the young, especially young men.

Some differences in dress and decoration may also provide clues to ethnic identification. Berber women, especially in their villages, are much more colourful and liberal in public dress than Arab women. They may go about with their hair uncovered and their faces unveiled, and often wear bright polychrome scarves, wraps and skirts.

Perhaps ironically, those less well connected tend to be somewhat more formal and flashy in European dress, with dress shirts, sport coats and tailored slacks for everyday street wear. These are not expensive in Morocco, but again there is a wide range of quality. Among urban Moroccan men who can afford the accessories, flashy clothes are popularly worn with bits of gold jewellery here and there, the net effect being what some would call a 'lounge lizard look'.

At the other end of the clothes closet from the glitz, the quitessence of traditional Moroccan dress is the *jellaba*, the one-piece, unisex, hooded coverall garment that qualifies as the Moroccan national costume. *Jellaba* come in a wide range of fabrics and qualities; those that are the best fitting, of the richest fabrics and (most importantly) with the most ornate needlework lining the seams are of the highest quality, and of course the most expensive. The well-to-do would never buy an 'off-the-rack' *jellaba*, but would have one tailor-made, and you will see that tailors thrive everywhere in Morocco. In addition to the *jellaba*, there are many other coverall garments for both men and women. A sign of preference for tradition over modern influences, they are more indicative of conservative politics and values than of wealth or social standing.

Shoes are also a very good indication of status, for everything is available in Morocco, from throwaway plastic sandals to expensive Italian imports. Like Arabs generally, Moroccans tend not to wear shoes indoors and never wear them inside mosques, thus they prefer open-backed shoes that can be removed easily. Moroccan slippers, called *bilgha*, are very common and a trip through any *medina* will reveal that they are an industry to themselves. The classic for men is a bright yellow, pointy-toed model. Women's *bilgha* come in a rainbow of colours, some with gold brocade designs on them. As with clothing, quality tells all. The 'well-heeled' would never wear faded or worn shoes of any kind in public. Footwear that tourists find comfortable (sandals, for instance, or comfortable walking shoes) are regarded as rather déclassé by Moroccans. Sandals in particular are more or less shepherd-wear to the natives.

Personal Ornamentation

Cosmetics and jewellery are worn by Moroccans who can afford them. In jewellery, gold is the standard and is worn conspicuously by both men and women as a token of wealth. More exotic jewellery fashioned from silver filigree, amber beads and precious stones is popular with Berbers and tourists. Many women enhance their appearance by circling their eyes with a thin black line of *kohl* (antimony). Some women also use lipstick and fingernail polish. Those who do so openly are usually 'modern' Westernised women. Those who do so excessively may be advertising their (available) charms to men.

Henna, in the raw form of crushed leaves, is sold everywhere in Morocco and is used by most Moroccan women. It is applied to the hair on a regular basis, mixed with water and egg or any number of other substances thought to enhance the beauty of the hair. Women may also sport intricate patterns drawn on their hands with henna; this is *de rigeur* for brides and may be done on other special occasions. Henna is thought to have beneficial properties for both skin and hair.

Though the practice is becoming less common, many Berber women still have tattoos in geometric designs on their faces, sometimes covering much of the forehead, cheeks and neck. These are marks of tribal identification and date from a time when it was necessary to be able to spot women of one's tribe who had been carried off in raids.

Headgear

Moroccans often like to wear head coverings, and what they wear may give some clues as to who they are.

Among those who wear turbans (mostly rural men), Berbers' are often white, and Arabs' orange or gold.

Knit stocking caps are worn more in the countryside or by the urban poor. Such caps would never be worn by middle-class or upper-class men. Slightly more dressy or respectable is the crocheted skullcap, which may be white or have some coloured design. Sometimes, the design is associated with a particular religious brotherhood. These are often worn by men at the mosque.

Further upscale is the fez. It marks a man who is sure to have a few more dirhams in his pocket than the one in the skullcap. Fezzes carry an air of respectability, perhaps even a slightly religious connotation. You will note that many public portraits of the king and his late father show them wearing fezzes. Young men never wear them, thinking them old and stuffy, and the fez may by on his way out in Morocco, except as a ceremonial hat (worn, for example, by government officials to events on religious holidays).

Popular wisdom has it that Muslims only wear brimless hats since a brim would keep a man from touching his head to the ground when praying. A cursory glance at street life will reveal that the international craze for baseball caps has not bypassed Morocco, and many young men sport them. Others who work in the sun, notably water sellers and parking attendants, often wear wide-brimmed straw hats.

Most women (not girls, and we have already learned what the difference is) cover their heads in public, either with a scarf or with the hood of the *jellaba*. A girl who wears a scarf completely covering the hairline may come from a fundamentalist family, or she may dress conservatively in order not to attract the attention of men in public.

This covers just about everyone except those with towels wrapped around their heads. They have probably just come from the public baths (discussed in Chapter 7). The poular notion is that you should conserve all the heat you soaked up there, so as not to catch a cold upon leaving.

Men in Uniform

Soldiers are a regular feature of the street everywhere in Morocco, and they can be identified by hat colour to some degree. Soldiers of the ordinary army wear bright green

Men in uniform. Here, a policeman and a *makhazni* (member of the *makhzan*) talk to a young *mul l-garro* (seller of individual cigarettes).

berets, the royal guard (those who guard the king and his many palaces) wear red berets, the tan- or olive-coloured berets are worn by the *makhzan*, a kind of national guard force. All of these wear olive drab in winter (until 1st May), khaki in summer. Traffic-cop hats (round, flat top with a brim) mark policemen and *gendarmes* (rural police).

The rank-and-file of all military forces—and they are the ones seen most often in the street—are regarded as low-class by most people, and they have a reputation (perhaps undeserved) of being easily provoked. They tend to associate mostly with each other.

RELIGIOUS AFFILIATION

Dress and personal appearance can be a marker for religious affiliation. As noted above, a scarf covering the hairline, typically folded so that it has a little 'lip' projecting upwards from the forehead, is the preferred covering of the fundamentalist girl or woman. A *jellaba* in public for such women is obligatory, and if they have Western clothes underneath, you'll never know it.

Fundamentalist Muslim men, 'Muslim brothers' as they are popularly called, are more inclined to wear traditional Moroccan coverall clothes than a shirt and trousers, but this is not a fast rule. Muslim brothers also very often have beards. This is a common enough marker that a man who does not want to be identified as a 'brother' may refrain from growing a beard. Note that this does not apply to moustaches, sported by any fashionable man.

SKIN GAMES

We have seen already that Moroccans may identify themselves along ethnic lines, i.e. primarily as Arab or some variety of Berber. Moroccans also make distinctions among themselves based on skin colour and their language has many words to distinguish the shades between northern European white and sub-Saharan black. To some extent, colour differences correspond to class differences as well as ethnic ones. To understand this, we must return briefly to history to learn how 'black' blood entered the Moroccan gene pool.

Sub-Saharan Africans have been finding their way to Morocco since the earliest times when they travelled the trade routes across the desert, but a significant number came to Morocco unwillingly—as slaves, soldiers or concubines. Long before slave trading was finally halted officially with the establishment of the protectorate, there were large numbers of blacks living in Morocco as slaves, free men, harem wives and

This woman of sub-Saharan origins lives in the Middle Atlas and considers herself a Berber.

concubines. Sultans in the past had entire armies composed of blacks, some said to number more than 100,000. Today, the descendants of these blacks live everywhere in Morocco, and depending on their ancestry, blacks in Morocco may identify themselves as Arabs or Berbers.

There is a degree of discrimination towards blacks among some fairer-skinned Arabs and Berbers, but it is not of the intensity (or even violence) that exists in some Western countries. Some fairer-skinned Moroccans might view marriage into a black family as unacceptable.

At the other end of the colour spectrum, there are a number of very fair-skinned Berbers living in mountain areas who still manifest their Caucasian origins, having fair or reddish hair, and blue or green eyes. A popular myth exists in Morocco that the people of Fez are traditionally fair-skinned, but observation doesn't bear this out. Fair skin is regarded appreciatively by most Moroccans.

Moroccans are likely to use the same 'colour guide' on foreigners that they use among themselves. African-Americans in Morocco sometimes express frustration at the fact that many Moroccans refuse to believe that they are American at all. Foreigners who can 'pass' for Moroccan may find it advantageous in some situations (e.g. tourist areas, where they may be left undisturbed). It is unlikely that non-white foreigners will experience any professional or economic discrimination in Morocco; Moroccans are aware of the advantages that foreigners generally bring to Morocco, and are inclined to treat them with consideration and respect, whatever their skin colour.

Jews

Jews once comprised a significant bloc of the Moroccan population, and their presence in Morocco is well documented in historical and first-hand accounts. Beginning with the creation of Israel in 1948, an exodus began that has gradually reduced the Jewish population of Morocco to the tiny minority that it is today.

Jews of Moroccan descent constitute a considerable proportion of the Israeli population and a few of them are now

Morocco is second only to Egypt in the Arab world for encouraging moderation and friendly dialogue with Israel. At the end of 1993, a number of measures to improve relations between the two countries were announced by the king. They include the opening of direct air, telephone and postal links.

beginning to return to Morocco to re-establish their roots. They continue to maintain synagogues, schools and cemeteries in Moroccan cities.

Down from the more than 500,000 who once lived there, about 10,000 Jews live in Morocco today, mostly in cities, and especially Casablanca. Mostly prosperous, they suffer no obvious discrimination from the Muslim majority, and in terms of physical features, are indistinguishable from the wide range of other Moroccan types. They generally dress in Western clothes, and may be conspicuous only during Ramadan, when they may eat and drink (discreetly) in public with impunity.

Moroccan proverbs are peppered with derogatory references to Jews. The Arabic word for Jew, *yahudi*, is used as a general slur. Despite this, Moroccan Jews seem to fare very well. The king has referred to them as 'dynamic elements' in Moroccan society, and one cabinet minister is Jewish.

CROSS-CLASS TRAFFIC

In a traditionally hierarchical and fatalistic society such as Morocco, class divisions create little tension; individuals largely accept their own station, and those of others above and below them. Behaviour in situations in which different classes interact is geared towards keeping everyone happily in their place. Thus not too much friendliness or familiarity is shown to persons of other classes; for example, a handshake would be acceptable, but a kiss would not.

Two Moroccan sayings offer insight into the relationship. 'Play with the dog and he'll lick your face' is one of them. The other is, 'We played with dogs, and woke up being their cousins.' The respective ideas of the two are, roughly, 'indulge someone beneath you and he'll surely take advantage,' and, 'get familiar with someone beneath you and you become like him.' Thus, when persons of elevated rank show a

condescending or imperious attitude towards those below, this is generally neither resented nor objected to. However, it is also common for those of higher status to maintain a cordial, if distant, manner with those below. Where the gap is quite wide, those at the low end may show signs of servility, for instance by attempting to kiss the ring or hand of the higher person.

An important fact to note is that persons of the middle class or higher—basically, all those with an education or in the process of getting one—don't do physical labour. They have someone else do it for them, usually for a pittance. This includes even simple things, like working around the house. The do-it-yourself craze that prevails in the English-speaking world finds no purchase in Morocco, and you as a foreigner risk looking like you're slumming if you do physical work in the presence of Moroccans.

PERSONAL RELATIONSHIPS AND SOCIAL INTERACTION

Context plays a large role in how Moroccan interact—and how you will interact with Moroccans—so it is useful to examine some of these contexts, and how you fit in. Here, it is important to keep in mind the central distinction between public and private life, as discussed in the previous chapter.

The Family at Home

As we have seen, this private sphere is the most relaxed of all contexts. Everyone talks at once, and talking louder gets more attention. Moroccans love to talk and love to laugh. Within the family circle, joking and teasing are very common. What may appear as an argument to a foreigner is in fact quite normal banter among family members, even when voices are raised and gestures vehement.

Initially, your relationship to a Moroccan family, or even to an individual Moroccan when you are in his or her home, is that of guest to host: a mostly passive role in which your needs are attended to in every possible way. However, it is not unusual for foreigners to become adjunct members of Moroccan families and for role expectations to loosen up considerably. In time, and if you have the inclination, you may enjoy virtually the same freedom within the family that individual members enjoy. Moroccans are not people to place limits on familial intimacy, and there are probably more foreigners who find themselves resisting this kind of unofficial adoption than cultivating it.

Families differ in the degree to which segregation of the sexes is practised at home in the presence of guests. The determining factors are, first, how traditional the family is, and secondly, how familiar the guest is. In a modern home hosting well-known visitors, men and women mix freely. At the other extreme, a traditional family entertaining foreign guests for the first time, women might not appear at all except to bring in food and take away dishes.

Your connection to a Moroccan family, at the outset anyway, will probably be through an individual: friend, employer, employee or colleague. If this is a person of the same sex as you, the situation is uncomplicated and you will be accommodated with others of the same sex within the home.

If your Moroccan contact is of the opposite sex, the situation may be slightly tense in a traditional home, but conventions will usually dictate how you are to be treated so that propriety—or more importantly, the appearance of it—is maintained. Foreign men are unlikely to have the opportunity to develop terms of friendship with Moroccan women. A male relative of a Moroccan woman, such as a brother or cousin, is a necessary intermediary in any hospitality that would involve this kind of pairing.

Foreign women, on the other hand, have a bit more freedom to negotiate friendships with male colleagues, since they are regarded to some extent as being outside the system that applies to Moroccan women. A foreign woman may freely accept hospitality in the family homes of male colleagues, where it will be assumed that she is developing relationships with the women there. But a lone foreign woman who visits the home of a single man, without the presence of his family, would set tongues wagging in overdrive and cause many a withering glance. What, after all, could she be up to?

Where the Boys Are

Outside the family circle, socialising is generally segregated: men in one place, women in another. Men have the whole outdoors, the public world, in which to cultivate their relationships; women have only a few select spaces. Foreigners in the contexts participate more or less on equal terms with Moroccans.

Cafés are the traditional hangout of the Moroccan male. Many hours can be spent nursing single cups of coffee, while conversation flows and the passing parade of the street is monitored. A table in a café is a kind of intersection between the public and private world. Host/guest dynamics prevail to some extent, in that person nearly always picks up the tab, but it is understood that everyone is there on his own, and all may come and go at will. Card-playing is a fairly standard activity, and smoking is nearly epidemic. A packet of cigarettes on the table is assumed to be common property, and all take from it freely.

Bars, which are often joined to cafés, are also the province of men, and any native women seen in bars are assumed to be prostitutes. Except for the lounges of the best tourist hotels, all Moroccan bars have at least a slightly, and sometimes an overwhelmingly, seedy atmosphere. Islam officially prohibits drinking, thus drinking has a connotation of unwholesomeness about it, even among those who regularly imbibe, for there is an awareness of *hshuma*. Moroccans generally will not drink alcohol at outdoor café tables where it is available, even though foreigners often do so.

Some other points of etiquette about the café and bar scene, as well as information about the other main male gathering places in Morocco, the cinema and the public baths, are discussed in Chapter Seven: Culture and Travel on page 200.

For Women Only

In the countryside, women's use of public places such as busy main thoroughfares is strictly limited to transit; in the city, they enjoy much greater freedom of behaviour. A few places have the status of 'women's space' where no man would dare tread. These are the women's public baths (discussed in Chapter Seven), rooftops and cemeteries on Friday afternoons.

Most Moroccan homes are built with flat roofs that are used for any number of activities: washing and hanging out clothes, drying grain and other foods, airing rugs and linens, etc. It is also an outdoor space where women can enjoy the freedom that men enjoy on the street, and men respect this separate space.

When weather permits, there is also a tradition of women having graveyard klatsches on Friday afternoons, when men are (ostensibly) at the mosque. At the cemetery too, men would not intrude. This is one of the few places that women seem to be truly at leisure, for there is plenty of work to do on the rooftops and in the baths.

In the countryside, and especially in Berber villages, women's appearance in public may be slightly more relaxed. It is common to see groups of women sitting in the sun

Up on the roof—in addition to doing the laundry, women also gather here to socialise.

outside their houses on spring and autumn days, usually engaged in some sit-down domestic activity. In this case, the women's space that exists inside the home is merely moved outdoors for a short time to take advantage of the weather.

Foreign women can easily integrate themselves into the women's network of the public baths and the rooftops. The cemetery setting would be more difficult one for a non-Muslim to gain acceptance.

One on One

As fond as Moroccans are of company and group conversation, they also very much like spending time with a single friend. The Arabic word *anawiak* is a conglomeration of particles that means 'just me and you' and is used to convey the kind of intimacy that is only possible between two people of the same sex.

Same-sex friendships are very important for Moroccans all through their lives, and marriage does not necessarily disrupt such friendships, as it is sometimes felt to do in Western countries. Since Moroccans are more likely to marry out of a sense of duty and with the object of raising a family (rather than for love, as Westerners purport to do), they do not often look to their spouses to provide the kind of support that friendship gives. Both Moroccan men and women spend a good deal of 'quality time' with friends, away from their spouses, and they would find it strange not to do so—though women's time together is not necessarily leisure time, and is more likely to be a slight variation on the constant theme of domestic toil.

Behaviour between same-sex friends is more intimate than in Western countries. Man and women both hold hands while walking together. Kissing both cheeks on greeting is standard, and sometimes extends to multiple passes from one side to the other. Touching is frequent and natural, and sitting side by side, maintaining bodily contact, is also usual where seats permit it. In short, intimacy between friends is very close indeed and much more physical than many foreigners are used to, or comfortable with. The best course for the foreigner to follow in this regard is to simply get used to it and join in. Not doing so will maintain a permanent distance between you and your Moroccan friends.

Friendship

There are few limits to intimacy in same-sex friendships among Moroccans, or between Moroccans and foreigners. This is one of the great dilemmas for foreigners, because the terms of friendship and its implications are rather different here than they are in other countries, and the relationship between a Moroccan and a foreigner is too often an unequal one.

Friendship in Morocco has a much more pronounced element of practical utility and interdependency than it has in many Western countries. Outside the family circle, Moroccans look next to their friends for their psychological, social and even material sustenance. It is considered desirable, and a sign of deepening intimacy, to increase the level of interdependence in a friendship: the more you can do for your friends and they for you, the greater friends you are. Favours are the very currency of friendship in Morocco, and it is here that foreigners often find the greatest difficulty in striking a balance between feeling appreciated and feeling put upon. Stated simply, the foreigner is usually in a much better position to get for his Moroccan friends what they want and need than the other way around, since a Moroccan's needs are much more likely to be material, and easily obtainable by foreigners.

The situation is further complicated by the norms of what it is acceptable to do for one's friends in Morocco, norms that are often at odds with prevailing ideas in other countries. In Morocco, as across the Arab world, handing out jobs and other benefits that fall within one's demesne is standard practice. Actions that would provoke accusations of nepotism and favouritism elsewhere are simply the way things are done for Moroccans.

It is common for objects and money to be lent and borrowed among friends for indefinite periods. Indeed, doing so is seen as a desirable means of deepening one's connection with one's friends. Foreigners may be very uncomfortable with this seeming disappearance of their property and hard-earned cash.

How to find a way through these complications that will leave all parties feeling satisfied and supported? There is probably no easy way to find the right balance of commitment and independence in your friendships with Moroccans because you are each approaching the matter from very different directions, but it can be done, with time, patience and attention to detail.

WHERE THE GUEST IS KING

Generous, frequent and friendly hospitality is a hallmark of the Arab world and Morocco exemplifies the best of this tradition. Until you have been the guest of a family at home, you have experienced only a shadow of the real Morocco.

If you are in Morocco for any length of time at all, you will no doubt receive invitations to homes, and this is particularly true if you are there without your own family. Since the idea of living alone is so abhorrent to most Moroccans, it is likely that someone will feel frankly obligated to take you in. But before you start filling in your social calendar, be sure that the invitation you have received should be taken at face value.

Where Invitations Come From

Moroccans' obligation and love of hospitality may lead them to invite you to their home before they even learn your name. This doesn't oblige you to accept, and probably no offence will be taken if you decline or evade an invitation, even if it is extended repeatedly, from a casual acquaintance or even from a stranger. But when someone you know socially or professionally is trying to tie you down to a particular date

Befriending a Morrocan

- Be very careful in the beginning of your stay about whom you try to befriend, and who tries to befriend you. Remember that you are especially vulnerable at this point, being a stranger in a strange land, and perhaps a little lonely. If any individual very early on seems too demanding of your time or favours, don't be afraid to step back and create a distance. It is easier to do this in the beginning than later on when your association may have deepened and 'shaking off' someone may seem like a major project.

- At the same time, you should be aware that in the beginning of your stay, when you are relatively helpless and must call upon Moroccans to assist you in any number of ways, you are creating the context in which they will naturally ask you to reciprocate at some point. You mustn't be surprised when this happens, and if you refuse, you will cause misunderstandings and hurt feelings.

- If you are asked a favour that for whatever reason you feel you cannot grant, it is better to indicate your answer indirectly, by procrastination or inaction rather than by directly refusing. Saying no to friends may devalue your friendship in their eyes, and cause a breach far greater than you may think the circumstances warrant. Try especially not to directly refuse your friends anything in the presence and time, and if they have tried before without success, they probably really mean it. Accept graciously. Work out details of whether you are to merely show up or be picked up; the latter is more usual. Count on the invitation including a meal, even if nothing is said about one.

Having accepted an invitation to someone's home, only the most elaborate of excuses will save you from loss of face if you don't show up. Do your best to get there,

of others, as this would be very embarrassing for them. If you feel put on the spot, you can simply delay your answer, be noncommittal or appear to go along as much as you are able. 'Let them down easy' is the approach that works best if you have to refuse.

- If you are used to spending some time alone and you enjoy doing so, you will have to make this point repeatedly to your Moroccan friends. It is a foreign concept that they won't understand, but they will respect it if you make yourself clear.

- Remember that you are not trying to bend over backwards and become a completely different person. Just as you have a job to do in finding a balance with your Moroccan friends, they have a job to do as well in figuring out who you are.

- If you can cultivate an attitude of generosity and detachment concerning your possessions, you will be in the greatest harmony with Moroccans who are, in the end, not very materialistic. Foreigners often get the idea that there is a mercenary streak in the Moroccan nature. This results from a failure to understand that the exchange of possessions is a token of the strength of the connection with another person, and *this* is what Moroccans value most, not the objects exchanged.

and be reasonably on time (not more than half an hour after the time given). It isn't expected that you bring anything, or do anything in the way of helping once you're there: as a guest, you should *never* have to fend for yourself.

Meeting the Family

You may arrive at a Moroccan's home to find you are not the only guest; it is quite usual for Moroccans to entertain informally, especially on Fridays. Furthermore, members of the extended family, whether they live in the house or not, may be regulars at the dinner table. It is also possible that your hosts will be showing you, the foreigner, off to their other friends.

As in all other social situations, the first thing to do if you're brought into a roomful of people is to shake everyone's hand; names will come later for those you don't know. You may also take off your shoes, if there is a carpet and others have done so, even though you may be told not to bother. This isn't a strict obligation, but it is appreciated if you do. Having exchanged handshakes and greetings all around, sit where your host indicates and get comfortable. You're not leaving anytime soon.

Where you come from, it may be customary for the host to give a short tour of the house; this isn't done in Morocco. The only room you will likely see at the outset is the *bit ḏiyaf*, or guests' room. It is the most expensively furnished room in the house, and reserved for entertaining guests or for the man of the house. This is probably where you will stay for the whole visit, including the meal. If you are inclined to express admiration for some small object you see in the room, perhaps it is better to suppress it for now. Your host, in his desire to please, may well present you with the object as a gift.

In a very traditional or conservative household, there may not be any women present except for servants, or women of the household may only make cameo appearances. In any case, for purposes of entertaining, foreign women are usually awarded honorary status and seated with the men, even if the other women are out of sight.

Rooms facing the courtyard in a Moroccan house. Though they invite your curiosity, as a guest you are likely to see only one, the *bit ḏiyaf.*

Whatever the time of day, a good interval is likely to pass before food appears. This may be filled with conversation over tea or coffee. It is not impolite, after a respectable period, to make some (oblique) reference to food, the passing of time or your hunger. If you don't, chances are the host or a Moroccan guest will, and this will be the signal for the food service to begin. This custom serves the idea that guests get what they want when they want it, and need only ask for anything that is not forthcoming. For the same reason, you may note that during the meal, requests for anything not present are issued in short, peremptory grunts from host and Moroccan guests alike rather than polite inquiries; it is the host's duty to meet every possible need.

DINING, MOROCCAN STYLE

You'll know things are getting under way when someone appears with a basin and kettle for guests to wash their hands. Don't get up, it will come to you. When it does, hold your hands over the basin and they will be wetted. You can then use the soap provided, and hold out you hand again to be rinsed. A towel will appear for you to dry them on. This kind service may be offered by any member of the household or possibly a servant. If you wish, you may thank them, or say _hashak_.

Napkins or napkin-like cloths may be distributed before you start eating, but mind you, these are _not_ for wiping your hands on! They are to protect your lap from whatever crumbs may fall between the dish and your mouth. It is normal to get through the meal with sticky hands—you'll get to wash them again when it's over.

Except for _cous-cous_, covered in the following pages, Moroccan guest meals tend to follow a pattern, familiarity with which may help you to avoid completely stuffing yourself. It is a point of pride among Moroccans to serve their guests as fully and richly as they can; to them, it would be unthinkable for you to leave their house unsatisfied. Your job is to eat as much as you can, or at least give the appearance of doing so.

Moroccans usually eat at a knee-high, round table, out of a large common dish and without utensils. Food is taken with the fingers or scooped up with bread. The meal may begin with various salads and relishes (olives, pickles, etc.) set around the periphery of the table. Take from the ones nearest you, even if those at a distance look more enticing. Freshly baked bread also usually appears at this time; it is broken or cut into diner-friendly pieces, often by the host, and set in front of each guest.

After the salads, a main course will appear. This is typically a _tajin_, or stew, served in a round earthenware dish, consisting of meat and vegetables in a rich broth. Eat from the portion of the dish nearest you; do not reach over to claim an attractive morsel from the other side. Your host will probably select choice bites and place them in your section of the dish.

It is worth noting here that the concept of vegetarianism is foreign to Moroccans. Though they may occasionally have meatless meals themselves, they would never serve one when entertaining. So you'll have some explaining to do if you don't eat meat. Note also that no meat is wasted; poultry and fish are often cooked with the head still on, and marrow is sucked out of large bones. These are considered special treats and may be placed in front of you for your consumption. You will not cause deep or lasting offence by failing to eat something put before you; if you really can't eat it, make profuse apologies and never express revulsion.

A couple of pointers to keep host and guest happy:

- Pace yourself. The rule in Moroccan hospitality is 'More is Better.' Don't assume that what appears to be the main course is the only one. Two or even more main courses may appear. Though you will be gently prodded throughout the meal with cries of "*Kul! Kul!*" (Eat! Eat!) by your hosts, let good judgment be your guide. Stop as soon as someone else does, and make profuse apologies about your inability to take in more. You may be able to get an idea of how many courses will be served by discreetly counting the number of tablecloths on the table. Typically, one of these is whisked away—with all accumulated debris—at the end of every course, to reveal a fresh, clean one underneath.

- Don't put your left hand in a common dish. If you're left-handed, retrain yourself. Food is taken with the right hand. Once you touch it, it's yours and you can do with it as you wish, but it may be viewed as polluting to touch common food with your left hand. (See Chapter Three for a fuller explanation.)

- Food waste (bones, pits, peels, etc.) can be placed on the (usually plastic) table covering in front of you, and will be cleared away with the remains of the meal.

- A course of fresh fruit usually marks the end of the meal. Sugary Western desserts are not often served.

- At any time, and especially at the end of the meal, it is appropriate to praise the quality and quantity of the food, and to express one's satisfaction. *Shebâat*, 'I'm full,' is the usual phrase. Belching is also appropriate. The natives may say *besahatik*, 'to your health,' to which you may reply *Allah iyâtik s-sehah*, 'God give you health.'

- Also at the end of the meal, the hand-washing apparatus may circulate again. Moroccans may clean their mouths at this point, taking water into the mouth in a cupped right hand, and even reaching inside to dislodge food particles, then spitting into the basin.

Cous-cous

With a few exceptions, the etiquette and customs described above apply to *cous-cous*, what might be called the Moroccan national dish. This delicious granulated pasta dish is most typically served on Fridays, and if you're invited to dine on that day, you can be sure what's on the menu. In the countryside, *cous-cous* (called *ks-ksu* or *tâam*) is sometimes eaten with the fingers, but generally spoons are provided. It is also served in a common dish, and eaten with meat and vegetables. As with *tajin*, eat from the section of the dish in front of you. *Merqa*, or broth, may be added to the *cous-cous* from time to time to dampen it. It has a tendency to expand in the stomach,

Cous-cous, the national dish: meat and vegetables nestling on a mound of steamed semolina.

so if you eat your fill, you will feel like exploding an hour or so later. Bread is not served with *cous-cous*.

Will I Ever Get Out of Here?

Nothing is more pleasant to Moroccans than spending time with their friends. The concept of 'eat and run' will find no sympathy, so if you approach your visit to a Moroccan home as something likely to take a good chunk out of the day, you will enjoy it more. Often, people take a siesta after a big meal; guests may join in if they wish. After this, tea or coffee may be served, and conversation may continue at great length. Anytime you announce your imminent departure, you will be met with protests, but these will become perfunctory after a time and you can then depart with grace. The more often you repeat your intention to leave, the more likely your host will be to believe you.

You Scratch My Back...

Reciprocation is viewed as a reasonable, perhaps an obligatory response to generosity in Morocco, so you shouldn't be surprised if, after enjoying a lavish meal, the talk turns to some (enormous) favour asked of you, especially one that you are uniquely placed to grant. This is a cultural norm, not an attempt to take advantage of the foreigner. But don't hesitate to defer discussion to a later time if there would be some awkwardness in refusing or if you foresee complications. It is likely that any requests coming from your friends will be entirely reasonable and a pleasure for you to fulfil, and that any unreasonable requests will come from persons who were perhaps overly eager to entertain you in the first place.

Prolonged Visits

For whatever reason, you may be a guest in a Moroccan home for an extended period. In this case, it is appropriate to contribute to your keep, particularly if you know that you are stretching the resources of your host. But this must be done very delicately, to prevent _hshuma_ from taking a swipe at your host family: they would not want to be seen as offering you substandard hospitality, or as expecting you to pay your way.

The chances are that there is a member of the family better known to you than the others. Approach him or her privately, express your deep conviction that you need to contribute and ask what you might do. You can insist on their taking money from you (to buy food), but only if you are quite sure that it is needed. If it is not—that is, if your hosts are well-to-do—this would be quite insulting. If you are really unsure about whether you're doing the right thing in this regard, consult a Moroccan friend outside the family for his advice.

Unexpected Visits

You may find yourself a guest at short notice when one of your Moroccan friends takes you along to somewhere he or she has already been invited. Never doubt that you will be welcome. If arrangements need to be made to accommodate you, you can be assured that your intermediate host will make them seamlessly.

WHEN YOU ENTERTAIN

It would not be viewed as complimentary for you to invite your Moroccan friends to a restaurant meal, unless they are Europeanised, urban natives whom you know to frequent restaurants. There are some excellent restaurants in the large cities, but eating out is not viewed as an entertainment in Morocco. Rather, it is something to be endured by travellers who have no friends or relatives to dine with in the town where they find themselves. This is reflected in the paucity or complete lack of good restaurants in smaller towns and villages; those in cities often cater mostly to foreigners.

If you are entertaining Moroccans in your home, feel free to treat them to the food and customs of your country, but don't be offended if they eat little. So strong is their attachment to bread and *tajin* that they may not be able to make sense of a meal that doesn't include them. If you have native domestic help, you should find it no trouble to feed Moroccans in the way they're accustomed to. You needn't be concerned with providing separate facilities for men and women, unless this is something customary for you; Moroccans would not expect to find sexual segregation in the home of a foreigner.

There are a few 'don'ts' to keep in mind when entertaining Moroccans in your home:

- Whatever your menu, do not serve any pork or alcoholic drinks.
- Try not to mix guests of different social strata, and definitely don't seat them together (e.g., your maid with your landlord).
- Don't serve food or appetizers 'buffet style,' as the idea of having to serve yourself is contrary to the spirit of Moroccan hospitality.

LARGE GATHERINGS

Parties in Morocco centre around family rituals and are not given just for fun or for any personal, congratulatory reason. Four kinds of gatherings you may be invited to are discussed below, roughly in descending order of the likelihood that a foreigner might be included. All of these are occasions for feasting. If you are invited to any of these, you should dress well. A jacket and tie, though not essential, would not be out of place. Women should dress fashionably but conservatively (no short skirts or plunging necklines, long sleeves preferred).

Wedding (ârs)

These are large, noisy and lengthy affairs, often conducted in the summer months and lasting two or three days. The families of the bride and groom may hold separate parties. Food, drink, dancing and music are regular features. Reception rooms are usually sexually segregated, but among more modern Moroccans, there is considerable crossover, and co-ed dancing may even be permitted. There are two main rituals of the party: the presentation of the bride, who is carried on a table and is bedecked in fine clothes and no end of personal ornamentation, and the presentation of the bloodied sheets of the marriage bed, to indicate that the bride was indeed a virgin and therefore worth the bride price. Customs vary in different parts of the country and among people of different social and economic backgrounds, so if you have the chance, you might ask some other invited guest what an appropriate gift might be—but you can't go wrong by giving some useful household item.

Name-giving Party (sbouaâ)

Held on the seventh day after a child is born, this is the occasion on which the child is formally named. There will be plenty of food and a great number of relatives, particularly women. If the family can afford it, a sheep is slaughtered and consumed for the occasion. A gift for the baby, such as clothing, and a small gift for the mother may be offered. A *sbouaâ* for a boy is a much bigger deal than one for a girl.

Circumcision (khetana)

Islam dictates that males be circumcised and that no Muslim woman can have sexual relations with one who isn't. Moroccan boys usually undergo this ritual some time before the age of six, and most often at the age of three or four. A barber performs the deed at the boy's home. A large festive meal accompanies the proceedings. It is appropriate to give some small gift to the boy.

Memorial Meal (sadaqa)

Forty days after the death of an immediate family member, or on some anniversary thereafter, a meal may be offered at which special food is prepared. This may be followed or preceded by chanting from the Koran. Charity is the guiding principle of these occasions, and they may be used to feed those less fortunate than the bereaved. A *sadaqa* being primarily a religious affair, it is unlikely a non-Muslim foreigner would be specifically invited, other than one very close to the family. But the overriding spirit of the *sadaqa* is open, unqualified charity, and anyone appearing, whether invited or not, will be fed.

Many of the national religious holidays are also occasions for feasting, and it is quite likely that you will be invited to partake in these. They are discussed in Chapter Seven.

Except for picnics which families may enjoy together, any other activities that you are likely to enjoy at the invitation of your Moroccan friends will probably be with friends of the same sex. It is not a custom—yet—for Moroccan couples, married or otherwise, to 'go out' together. More normally, men spend time away from home with their men friends, and women spend time either at home or away with their women friends. Some activities that you might enjoy with your same sex Moroccan friends are also discussed in Chapter Seven.

THE ROYAL TREATMENT

At the extreme of Moroccan hospitality, the guest may find that he doesn't really want to be king. The host may show so much deference and respect to the invited guest that the two hardly see each other. This sort of treatment is uncommon, and will only take place when relations between host and guest are professional (perhaps even strained) rather than personal, or when the host does not presume to be the equal of the guest. Such treatment may seem neither cordial nor friendly, but it is probably not intended to offend; indeed, it is offered as the highest honour. (On the other hand, it may indicate that the host is showing hospitality out of a sense of duty, rather than personal desire.) Under this form of hospitality, guests are shown into the *bit diyaf* and may be left there unattended, except when exquisitely prepared food is brought in and out, and when the guests' needs are surveyed. Guests are expected to make their needs known if they are not anticipated by the imagination of the host.

If this sort of hospitality doesn't sit well with you, don't worry: chances are you won't be subjected to it more than once from the same host, who may consider it the honourable manner for a first visit. If it persists, it is a sign that your host doesn't feel that a friendlier relationship is developing. You may prefer the distance, but if you don't, it wouldn't go amiss to say that you would rather enjoy a meal with the family.

FUNERALS

An Arab and Islamic custom dictates that corpses be buried within 24 hours of death. This makes death and burial very much a no-nonsense affair in Morocco. With mortality rates considerably higher than those found in developed countries from infancy on up, Moroccans are no strangers to death, and it is a rare person who has not suffered the death of a near relative, even a sibling.

Bodies are prepared for burial at home, sometimes with the help of one who is skilled in caring for the dead. The washed corpse is carried to the cemetery on a simple bier, wrapped in a simple shroud, in which it is buried. Only men carry the corpse, and they chant the profession of faith as they march to the graveyard. In Morocco, Muslims are buried on their right side with the head to the south; thus they face Mecca and are well situated for their anticipated resurrection on Judgment Day.

White is the colour of mourning in Morocco. A woman bereft of her husband wears white for 40 days. During this time, she is not permitted to have sexual relations with any man.

It is the custom where a death has occurred for neighbours, friends and relatives to bring food to the home of the bereaved to feed them and those who come

Orderly arrangement of graves facilitates good viewing on Judgement Day, as at this cemetery in Salé.

to offer condolences. On the day or the day after a death, a dinner, called simply *l-âsha*, is served in the home of the bereaved, and passages from the Koran are read aloud. This is a strictly Muslim affair at which a non-Muslim foreigner would be out of place, but it is appropriate to make a short visit in the days following a death to offer condolences.

GIFT-GIVING

A gift may be given at any time in Morocco. Birthday gifts are not usual, since people are not generally aware of their birthdays, and so do not celebrate them. A typical response to a gift is a simple thank you. The gift is usually not opened in the presence of the giver, and it may indeed be put away out of sight as soon as it is given. It is possible that the gift won't be referred to or acknowledged again, at least not in a group of people where anyone but the family is present. All of these practices reflect the idea that showing great appreciation or enthusiasm for a gift received would imply one actually needed the thing, and thus *hshuma* would descend in its winged glory on the one whose needs were greater than self or family could provide.

Moroccans very much like to give gifts and you will probably receive casual gifts from your Moroccan friends from time to time. Gift-giving is part of the system of personal inter-dependency that is so valued by Moroccans, and by giving you a gift, they are deepening their connection with you—in a sense, bringing you into the family. The deeper their connection with you, the more comfortable they will feel in calling upon you to help them when they perceive that you are able to. This is just the way the system works, among Moroccans themselves, and between Moroccans and foreigners. So you mustn't be surprised if a request for a favour follows in the wake of a gift, nor are you far off the mark in associating the one with the other. But the intention is to strengthen the relationship with you, and thus the gift should be perceived as an honour, an expression of a person's wish to be closer to you.

It is not suitable to offer the remainder of something that you have used or eaten as a 'gift' to someone else. This would be seen as an insult, not as a gift. If you wish to share what you have with others, you must offer from it while, or even better, before you partake of it, not after you have finished with it.

PUNCTUALITY

In common with other Arab cultures, Moroccans do not regard punctuality as a virtue—indeed, they are hardly aware of it as a concept. Some things do run on a schedule out of practical necessity—schools, for instance, that have regular classroom periods punctuated by bells. For other things supposedly run on a schedule, the schedule is regarded as a contingent things, and no one is very surprised by anything that is running late: people, trains, buses, starting times for films in cinemas, sporting events, public ceremonies and the like. This general looseness about observing agreed upon times extends to engagements and appointments as well. Westerners may regard something late that has missed its appointed time by five minutes; Moroccans would not be very concerned until an hour has passed.

There is everything to be gained for your mental health by adopting as much as possible the Moroccan attitude towards time. Everything happens in its time, the saying goes. So if something isn't happening, it mustn't be time for it, and there's nothing to be gained by getting anxious about it.

QUEUING

The practice of lining up in an orderly way so that each person can be served in turn doesn't always hold in Morocco. Writers on cultural differences attribute this to a number of things; for example, some distinguish between monochronic and polychronic cultures. In the former, typical of many Western cultures, there is an emphasis on doing only one thing at a time; in polychronic cultures, of which Morocco is one, many activities are carried on simultaneously. At the bank, this means that the teller is dealing with five people at once, not just you because you think you're at the top of the line.

Another contributing factor to the pandemonium that often prevails in Morocco where otherwise you might expect queuing is the general aggressiveness that characterises public behaviour—every man for himself. Still another element that may contribute to this behaviour in Morocco is the scarcity of some goods or services and the feeling that if you don't go for it assertively, you won't get it. Whatever the reasons, they will all be academic to you when you are in the midst of a swarming crowd that you think should be a queue. Here, your only saving grace is to remember that this is normal, and not something to get angry or excited about.

NUDITY

Moroccans are quite modest about revealing their skin in public, although this is changing. Men either bare-chested or wearing short pants are seldom seen in public places, the beach being the one exception. The general rule for women in public is, the more covered up, the better. Women at the beach in swimwear are either foreigners, or offspring of the Europeanised urban bourgeoisie. Even in same-sex public baths, one never exposes one's genitals. Foreigners from countries where such modesty does not exist should be aware of the affront they may cause by not respecting Moroccans' customs in this regard. Dressing in comfortable clothing that covers all but the head and hands is most appreciated by Moroccans. Skin-tight leggings for women will attract as much (unwanted) attention as if the legs weren't covered at all.

Breastfeeding

Moroccan women breastfeed their babies wherever they wish, with little or no shielding from public view. Moroccan Arabic has a separate word for a 'lactating' breast, as if to de-eroticise it. Public breastfeeding is quite normal and unremarkable, and you should never stare at a woman breastfeeding her child.

CRIME

For anyone coming from a Western country, Morocco will seem quite peaceful and safe. Guns in private ownership are nearly unheard of, and weapons of any kind used in fighting are quite rare. Conflicts occasionally erupt into physical violence, but it is far more common for dire words and horrifying threats to take the place of actual fighting.

Theft and robbery are rather common in Morocco. The haves are very often the victims of the have-nots. Unfortunately, tourists and other obvious foreigners are singled out in disproportionate numbers; therefore, you should always guard your valuables carefully when in public places, especially in crowds, and don't leave things of obvious value lying around at home if anyone has access to your house when you are not there, including domestic help.

Burglaries by forced entry are also becoming more common in Morocco, as more unemployed rural people migrate to cities. If you live in a city, you should survey security risks at your house and minimise them in any way possible. Low-tech means are the most reliable way of doing this, and often the only means available. One Moroccan professional says that his 24-hour security system is his live-in maid. If your house is empty during the day or at other times, lock it up tight, and cultivate good relations with neighbours who can keep an eye out for you.

DRUGS

Hard drugs such as cocaine and heroin, and abusable pharmaceuticals such as amphetamines and barbiturates are practically unheard of in Morocco. However, hashish and *kif* (marijuana) are both quite common, despite being illegal.

Until recently, a more lenient attitude existed towards those who used this drugs in Morocco. It was fairly ordinary for males, from their mid-teens upward, to be in possession of a small piece of hash which they softened over a flame, crumbled, rolled into a cigarette with tobacco and smoked. This concoction is called a *jwan*. Smoking these in public or semi-public places (cafés, for example) still goes on without drawing much attention, but those who indulge must be ever vigilant, for if they are caught by the police, they will be arrested. Possession of hashish is illegal.

> Many foreigners languish in Moroccan or Spanish prisons following their attempts to smuggle out hashish or *kif*. The drug trade in Morocco is treacherous and fraught with uncertainty and danger, as well as being illegal, and no one but a fool would attempt to get involved in it.

Kif is more often associated with those who are addicted to it, and who smoke it throughout the day. It is cut up very fine, sometimes with a small admixture of tobacco, and smoked in a long stemmed, small-bowled pipe called a *sabsi*. These are sold everywhere in Morocco. *Kif* addicts are a sizeable minority of the older adult population in Morocco, more in the countryside than in cities. *Kif* addiction is by no means respectable; it is viewed rather in the same way that alcoholism is viewed in the West.

Foreigners should avoid using and buying these drugs. The same rules do not apply to you as to Moroccans, and the seeming impunity that Moroccans enjoy using *kif* and hashish will not be extended to you, whether you are in their company or not. Chemical dependency of any kind—whether on alcohol, prescription or illicit drugs—is a dicey business in Morocco, because supplies may be very undependable. Avoiding all of these to the extent possible will enhance your well-being.

SMOKING

Moroccan men are avid smokers generally, and the Western sentiment against smoking in public places has penetrated very little in Morocco. This means that smoking is quite usual in taxis, buses, cinemas, cafés, restaurants and the like. Strong smelling 'black tobacco', as it is called, is more popular in Morocco than 'blond tobacco', and its pungent odour is never very far away. It is difficult for those who wish to avoid cigarette smoke to find a way of doing so in Morocco. You can ban smoking in your home, but be aware that this may be thought inhospitable by Moroccan guests.

It is an irritating habit of some Moroccan males to smoke anywhere in a train carriage, whether in the designated smoking area or not. Don't hesitate to remind someone politely that he is smoking in a non-smoking area. He will usually oblige you, perhaps by standing up and stomping away indignantly, but at least the smoke will go away.

GREEN ISSUES

In general, Morocco's natural resources are under- rather than over-exploited, and it does not suffer from some of the industrial and environmental problems found in other parts of the world, both developed and underdeveloped. One notable exception is overgrazing, trying to support too many ruminants on land that cannot, as a result, renew itself properly. Awareness of environmental issues in Morocco is rather faint, but it is growing.

If you are quite well versed in problems of the environment, you may well experience alarm or concern about many things that Moroccans take for granted. Air quality in the big cities, for example, is often quite poor owing to the lack of regulations concerning automobile emissions. Litter is a problem everywhere in the country, but in most places, it is more unsightly than actually harmful: very little is wasted and the average family probably produces about a bucketful of rubbish a week. Only what can't be burned as fuel, composted, recycled, reused or fed to animals will end up on a rubbish heap, which often seems to consist of no more than plastic bags.

PETS

The kind of affection that people in many cultures lavish on domestic animals isn't much found in Morocco; rather pets are viewed for their utilitarian aspect. This reflects the very strict division in the Moroccan mind between humans and animals, a division that tends to get blurred in cultures where children are raised with cartoon animals that speak and act like people. Dogs are kept outside and are expected to ward off strangers and would-be intruders. Many Moroccans have a real fear of dogs and shrink from approaching them, perhaps because the dogs themselves are conditioned to bark and growl at, or even attack strangers. Cats also usually live outside, and there are many feral cats everywhere in Morocco, especially in *medinas* in the vicinity of butchers' shops.

Prepared pet foods are available at French-style supermarchés in cities, but nowhere else. Moroccans who keep dogs and cats feed them table scraps.

Birds such as canaries and parakeets are the only animals kept as pets merely for the owners' enjoyment.

SETTLING IN

CHAPTER 5

'Though I did not go a second time to see the
Frenchman's house and instructed Idrees the *simsar*
to return the key to Monsieur D with a polite message,
the result of all these abortive visits is that I am now
determined to find some place to rent. I want my own
front door. Until I acquire one I shall not belong in this city,
and I have need of even synthetic roots.'
—Peter Mayne, *A Year in Marrakesh*

Your first days in Morocco may be spent with friends, colleagues or in hotels. Whatever the degree of comfort available to you, chances are that it won't go very far towards compensating the fact that you're not in a place you can call home. Having a place that feels like your own and where you are comfortable is one of the most important steps towards your successful adjustment, so do what you have to do to get there as soon as you can. If your housing isn't arranged for you, there are several fronts on which you can proceed.

FINDING A HOUSE

If you are responsible for finding your own accommodation in Morocco, start as early as possible, even before you get there if you can send word ahead. The best leads may be provided by your employer, colleagues, your fellow expatriates and the domestic help of all of these. Get as many people working on the project as possible. Moroccans and foreigners with experience in Morocco will be your best sources of tips.

If all these fail, you may wish to engage the services of a professional—the Moroccan equivalent of a rental agent, called a *simsar*. This step is not recommended, unless the *simsar* himself comes highly recommended to you by someone you know and trust. *Simsars* collect a fee from you, usually the equivalent of a month's rent (but it may be more), and they collect from the landlord—often a percentage of the rent. In other words, they have no interest in seeing that the rent is kept low, and as a foreigner, you can already expect that you will be paying something of a premium. One fact you should simply resign yourself to: unless you have a trusted Moroccan friend doing some hard negotiating for you, it is unlikely that a landlord can be persuaded that you deserve a break on the rent.

Which Four Walls?

In Moroccan cities, where most foreigners look for housing, there is a great variety of styles with different standards of quality, available services and costs. The basic types, along with descriptions of the areas you are likely to find them in, are discussed here.

Medina Houses—Inside the Walled City

Typical of all Moroccan cities is the divide between old and new. The old parts of cities are usually enclosed by ancient walls more than 1 m thick and 5 or 6 m high, sometimes with ramparts along the top. These enclosed areas are called *medinas*, though some have other names, especially in cities that have more than one walled-off section. They may contain houses that are literally centuries old, but some newer homes are there as well, and you will find a whole range of quality, from one-room hovels with no water to multi-room, multi-storey palaces. Likewise, water, electricity, sewer services and the range of goods available are usually a complete hodgepodge of the old and the new, with the accent on the former.

There is a curious uniformity to the eclectic architecture in *medinas* all over Morocco, as the basic building philosophy is, add another room, wall, or storey when you can afford to, wherever you can find a place. The only obvious distinguishing characteristic of *medinas* is colour; cities in the north of Morocco are whitewashed. In the south, they 'redwash': walls and houses tend towards a ruddy colour that matches the soil.

Tourism is heavy in *medinas*, as will be obvious to you when you take a walk through one and find yourself invited to view the goods in every shop. Foreigners generally don't

Horseshoe arches and crenellated walls—the hallmark of Moroccan walled cities. This is Bab Mansour (Mansour Gate) in Meknes.

seek accommodation in *medinas*, but there is no reason you shouldn't live there, and rents tend to be cheaper than in the French-built parts of town.

Villas in the Ville Nouvelle

The parts of town dating from the colonial period, normally adjacent to the *medinas*, are typically laid out in French fashion, with grand tree-lined boulevards and radiating cross streets leading past many fine examples of Nouveau and Art Deco architecture. Goods, services and facilities, including modern plumbing, are much more Europeanised (and generally more expensive) than in the *medinas*. Every city has a French style *marché* (market) where fresh food is available daily, and this is always located in the *ville nouvelle*.

In residential parts of the new areas, villas built during the colonial period or after that time by wealthy Moroccans are the rule. A typical villa is a detached house with thick stuccoed walls, a tiled roof, large shuttered windows and terrazzo floors, with a yard or garden enclosed by a high wall. Inside are rooms with names and uses you're familiar with: kitchen, bathroom with Western fixtures and other rooms for use as bedrooms, sitting rooms and so forth. Houses such as these are of course the most expensive, and favoured by relocated multinational executives and diplomats. Demand exceeds supply. If this is the market you're in, you may wish to engage the services of a proper real estate agent (*agence immobilière*) who specialises in such houses. Rents are in the range of DH 40,000–DH 75,000 per month [the currency of Morocco is the dirham (DH)] in the Atlantic coastal cities, considerably cheaper elsewhere.

Townhouses in New Subdivisions

Morocco appears to be a country very much 'under construction', as new homes are constantly being built everywhere to accommodate the growing population. New subdivisions of existing towns and cities are generally similar, with three- and four-storey blocks of houses going up along new roads, usually still without the benefit of sidewalks and paving, but with water, electricity and street lighting provided. Shops, cafés and other services for these newer areas tend to spring up as soon as there is a need for them.

The townhouses in these areas are attached back to back and side to side, with only corner houses having two exposed facades. The only windows are on the front of the house, but most have either a large skylight or an accessible roof. Construction is of cinderblock or brick, coated with stucco and painted. Beautiful tiles are a thriving

Modern townhouses. The ground floor is for garages, shops or storage. Upper storeys have one or two residences on each floor.

industry in Morocco, and in the newer houses, they cover the floor and extend part way up the walls. Toilets may be Western or Moroccan, usually the latter (explained in the following pages). Rooms are usually arranged around a central courtyard, which may be open to the sky or covered with glass brick. Rents may range from DH 5,000 to DH 10,000 in the Atlantic coastal cities, somewhat cheaper inland.

Old Townhouses

In style and construction, these are like their newer counterparts, but a little less flashy and probably not ship-shape, as there is an unfortunate tendency in Morocco to overlook proper maintenance. Still, many old traditional houses are quite livable. Rents are slightly cheaper than those for new townhouses.

Regional Variations

Different parts of Morocco may have very specialised kinds of houses, depending on climate and tradition. In villages north of Fez, the style is thick mud walls with thatched roofs. In Marrakech, there is hardly a house without a courtyard open to the sky. The village of Ifrane in the Middle Atlas, the 'Switzerland of Morocco', does indeed look like a Swiss village with steep pitched roofs for the heavy snowfalls to slide off.

Small mud houses cling to the hillside at Imlil, south of Marrakech.

House Particulars

You must rely on your own experience of house-hunting to know whether the place you're looking at is a place where you could live, but there are a few things you may want to check out or ask specifically about:

- If the house has a common entrance, who else uses it? Who has keys? Your front door should lock with a unique key.
- Does the house seem to get enough light? Winters can be cool and dark in Morocco.
- If you are in an area that requires heat in the winter, are there any stoves in the house, or chimneys where you can connect woodstoves? Will the landlord permit this?
- Traditional houses, even some newer ones, have on average one electrical outlet per room. Have a look around. Are there enough for you?
- Is the water supply to the neighbourhood dependable? You may have to ask the neighbours this. If it is not, how far do you have to go to fill up your bottles and buckets?
- Is there a mosque nearby? If so, will you get used to being blasted out of bed by the early morning and night-time calls to prayer?
- Finally, if you're living in a city, consider a house in terms of security. Are neighbours around at all times? Would a break-in be easy to carry off without anyone noticing?

You may find some things in a Moroccan house unfamiliar, and you may also be used to some domestic fixtures that are hard to come by in Morocco. This table names a few, in no particular order.

What Most Moroccan Houses Have

- a Turkish toilet
- shuttered casement windows
- tiled or terrazzo floors
- high ceilings
- plaster walls
- 220V electricity
- a flat, usable roof
- few electrical outlets

What Few Moroccan Houses Have

- a bathtub
- a sit-down toilet
- running hot water
- central heating
- wiring for a telephone
- built-in appliances
- closets
- a private yard or garden

What we call in this book a Turkish toilet or a Moroccan toilet is a standard plumbing fixture in Morocco. It is a porcelain or concrete basin set in the floor with two raised platforms for the feet, and a hole leading to a sewer to carry away waste. There is also a cold water tap at about knee level, used for cleaning both the toilet and the user. The toilet can be used in a standing (for men) or squatting position, but there is nothing to sit on; thus by contrast, we call a Western toilet a 'sit-down' toilet. These too can be found in Morocco, but they are not standard. You are most likely to come upon them in better hotels and colonial houses. Even here, they may be missing features you expect, such as the seat or the lid.

Striking the Deal

If you have the time, you should look at several places before you make up your mind. Or even look at the same place several times, if circumstances permit, and at several different times of day. But don't appear overly enthusiastic about any particular place, even if it's love at first sight. On the other hand, if you know what's wrong with a place and why you don't want it, say so: you may have objections that a Moroccan wouldn't even think about, and if they know what you don't want, perhaps they can help you avoid it.

If you are used to a great deal of personal privacy, you may have to compromise somewhat in Morocco. Except in the villas, people live thick as thieves with each other, and are generally quite happy doing so. Moroccans are baffled by the amount—indeed, the very concept—of 'personal space' that Westerners take for granted.

Once you have settled on a house, be sure you understand how much the rent is, when and to whom it is to be paid and what it includes. If you are asked to pay a deposit (common in cities, less so elsewhere), make sure you get a proper receipt for it that you can read. If there is any question in your mind about any of these things, have them clarified and written down if necessary. If you are living in a city, you will probably sign an actual lease. In towns and villages, there may not be a written agreement. In this case, be sure that you understand completely what you've agreed to. If you have a pretty good idea of how long you wish to stay, be sure this gets into your agreement too: a few months down the road, you won't want to have to move just because of your landlord's whim.

UTILITIES

Once you've rented a place, make it your next priority to see about the utilities, namely electricity and water. There is no piped gas in Morocco. It is possible, even likely, that the house you rent will already have both electricity and water connected, but you must determine whose names the accounts are in, who is responsible for paying them and whether a single bill for water or electricity (more likely for the former) covers more than one household. If you are responsible for paying the water and electricity bills, be sure there is no balance outstanding on the accounts when you move in. Failing to do this may result in your being presented with a hefty bill later on.

To get the accounts for water and electricity in your name you must present yourself at the local office of the RED (*Regie Autonome de la Distribution de l'eau et l'Electricité*)—find out where it is from your neighbours or landlord. The procedure for establishing your accounts may be more formalised in a city, requiring you to produce proof of

If you live in a flat, or part of a house that receives a common water or electricity supply with other households, determine at the outset what your share is to be. This could spare you a spirited shouting match with your neighbours when the bill comes, if they think your share should be more than you think it should be.

your residency and a copy of your lease. In the countryside, you may simply fill in a form.

If your house doesn't have water or electricity working, go to the office of the RED to establish new service in your own name. For electricity, you may have to schedule an appointment when you will be home. This shouldn't be necessary for water.

Voltages and Plugs

Older buildings in Morocco are normally served with 120 volts (or thereabouts) of alternating current. Newer buildings use 220 volts. In either case, a European-style plug with two round pins is standard. You can buy a *prise americaine* in Morocco that converts a standard American two-bar plug into a two-pin plug. These are available wherever electrical gadgetry is sold. If you're coming from Britain, you will be better off to leave your plugs at home, and thereby knock several pounds off the weight of your luggage to boot!

Butagaz

Bottled propane or butane goes by the name of Butagaz and is used in Morocco for a number of appliances: kitchen ovens, ranges and ring burners, hot water heaters and space heaters. You will need either a separate bottle for each appliance, or in the case of appliances that are used next to each other, a branching hose from a single bottle. A full bottle can be obtained for a deposit and the price of the gas from any of various merchants. Thereafter, you return your empty bottle and pick up a full one for the price of the gas.

Be warned that the use of bottled gas can be extremely dangerous. There are hazards you should be aware of. Failure to be heedful of the dangers claims many lives in Morocco each year, and foreigners' lives are probably claimed in disproportionate numbers because they are unfamiliar with using bottled gas. Be very careful about all of the following:

- Bottled gas is artificially scented, like most natural gas, to alert users to the possibility of a leak. As you would do if you smelled natural gas, do not light a match or turn on an electric light. Immediately ventilate the area

where you smelled the gas, determine the source of the
leak and remove it.

- When you are not using your gas bottle, turn it off firmly
  using the knob on the top of the bottle. If you buy a
  bottle that has a persistent odour, return it for another
  one. Always be very suspicious of any gas odour that you
  can't account for. Prolonged inhalation of gas fumes can
  be deadly, not to mention the fact that a room filled with
  gas will explode on contact with so much as a spark.

- Bottled gas draws its oxygen from the room in which
  it is burning. It will continue to burn until its supply
  of oxygen is exhausted. If you are operating a bottled
  gas appliance in an unventilated room, you are at
  risk of being asphyxiated. *Never* operate a bottled gas
  appliance in a room without an open door or window.
  Ventilation from the outside is preferable. If you are
  cooking in the kitchen, showering or warming yourself
  in front of a gas heater, take no comfort unless you know
  you have adequately ventilated the room.

TELEPHONES AND INTERNET

If you are moving into a house recently vacated by foreign
professionals, it may already have a telephone service that

you can simply take over. If there is no telephone service in your house, you can get it installed at a cost of about DH 1500, provided there are already existing telephone lines nearby. If there are none, it will take an unpredictable amount of time to get a telephone. In either case, you start by applying to your local office of the ONPT (*Office National de Postes et Télécommunications*; see http://www.onpt.net. ma). Most foreigners in Morocca take the easier option of getting a mobile phone; if you are city-based, you will find vendors everywhere.

Internet services in Morocca is constantly expanding, both in bandwidth and in numbers of providers. All cities now have cybercafés, where you can check web-based email accounts. For a list of Internet Service Providers (ISPs), have a look at http://www.maroc.net. Most of these are French-language based; if you're not able to negotiate a new account in French or Arabic, send them an email in English and see what comes back.

Home telephones are certainly not taken for granted in Morocco, and the majority of Moroccans do not have one. If you don't get a mobile telephone and don't expect you'll need a telephone regularly, you can probably rely on public phones at the PTT, or on a telephone where you work. There are public telephones on the street in cities. Pay telephones are increasingly used in Morocco, to supplement the general operator-assisted telephone service available at PTTs. Banks of pay phones are usually located inside and outside PTTs, as well as at various locations in cities.

Pay phones are of two kinds, coin-operated and card-operated. Coin phones are in notoriously bad repair and you can't always tell that a phone is not going to work till you've lost your money in it. Card phones are more reliable. Cards for them, in denominations of 50 units upwards, can be purchased in the phone section of the PTT.

When the message 'COMPOSER' flashes in the LCD display of a pay phone, dial your number. You will not hear tones as you would on a touch-tone phone.

There is a good way to communicate with people who don't own a telephone within Morocco at short notice: send a telegram. They are inexpensive, can be sent from any post office and are hand-delivered the day or the day after they are sent. Telegrams in French are more likely to get through error-free than those in English, but these can be deciphered with just a bit of guesswork.

FILLING THE ROOMS

There is very little furnished rental accommodation in Morocco. You may be the lucky recipient of hand-me-down furnishings from someone leaving Morocco at the time you are coming, but if not, don't despair. Furniture is easily purchased, and if you keep it simple, it won't set you back much. There are two approaches to take: furnishing Western style, which is rather costly, or furnishing in the Moroccan style, which is more reasonable. If you're living in a Moroccan-style house, the latter is the only option that makes sense, as rooms tend to be standard sizes, to accommodate furnishings that are also standardised.

Very good quality handmade furniture in both Moroccan and Western styles is widely available. Every city has woodcarvers, who specialise in making cabinets and furniture. They are easy to find as their wares are often displayed on the street outside their shops. The stock of ready-made furnishings is sometimes rather small, since these craftsmen tend to work on specific orders. If you are content with fairly basic furnishings, you will find them ready-made, but if you want something more specific or ornate, you will probably have to order it.

Following is a checklist of the bare essentials for settling into a three-room house; that is, the kitchen, bedroom and sitting room.

Kitchen

In case you hadn't figured it out, this is the room with the sink and running water in it, but probably nothing else. You will need a gas bottle, for which the deposit will be DH 200 or more. Make sure you get a receipt for your deposit (and one that you can read) if you ever want to see the money again.

You will also want to buy a three-ring cooker, standard in most Moroccan kitchens. It attaches to the gas bottle via a

A three-ring cooker is standard equipment in Moroccan kitchens. Here a chicken is prepared for plucking in a quick boiling water bath.

rubber hose, usually supplied. *Voilà!* You have something to cook on. But if you are a more adventurous cook, you can buy a full kitchen range that includes an oven. These also attach directly to a gas bottle. (See Chapter Six about using the *furan*, or public oven.)

There is probably a built-in counter top in your kitchen, but if not, you will need a work table. If there are no built-in shelves, you may want to buy some wooden or bamboo shelves. Wooden ones are more expensive and harder to find. All other kitchen equipment is best acquired on an as-needed basis. *Souqs* and *medina* shops are the best sources for all sorts of cutlery, dishes and gadgets.

Sitting Room

Moroccans sit and sleep on banquettes, long, narrow couches with no back. The base is a wooden frame; on top of it sits a cushion of foam rubber or a sack filled with uncarded wool. These are upholstered, or simply covered up, with brightly-coloured chintz (cheap) or brocade (expensive) fabric. The Moroccan style is to line the walls with them, supplying matching pillows for people to rest against. Rooms in Moroccan houses are built to standard banquette size such that they will fit all the way around leaving no gaps. But you may want to start more modestly, perhaps lining only a wall or a wall and a half, unless you expect to fill the room with people all the way around soon. You will also want one or more round tables, which are used for eating, and at non-meal times as you would use coffee tables. If there is no overhead light, you may want lamps, but first make sure there are places to plug them in. All of these items can be purchased in *medina* or town shops, or at *souqs*.

Bedroom

This is a concession to foreigners, since Moroccans don't usually designate a room as a bedroom. Rather, they sleep in any of the rooms of the house that have banquettes in them. If you don't want to sleep on a banquette, you can buy a twin or double-sized mattress and bedsprings. You may have to look around for the latter as they are not standard issue in Morocco, but they can be found. Chances are your house will have no closets or cupboards built in, so you'll want to scout around for a chest of drawers or a wardrobe. The most common ones are of bamboo. Wooden ones are harder to come by, but can be found, often deep in the recesses of the *medina*, where the cast-off trappings of the colonial period are sold and resold at knockdown prices. Or you may purchase a new one made to order or ready-made.

What You Can't Get Here

Your compatriots in Morocco, if you know any, are probably the best source of information about what material things you may want to bring from home, as we each have our own special attachment to small objects from our own countries. Here is a list of a few widely used items which are either hard to find, expensive or of poor quality in Morocco.

Bedsheets tend to be expensive (if imported) or shabby (if not), so you may want to bring your own; but blankets are widely available. A good fingernail clipper will save you from using one of the local variety, which are dull and tend to rip off rather than cut your nails. Can openers (crank variety) are also better brought with you if you expect to be eating canned foods, and you shouldn't pass up the tuna and sardines. Teapots in Morocco are the small metallic kind used for making mint tea, and are not so good for ordinary black tea. If you're strongly attached to particular spices, bring them along, as they may not be available.

You will probably be able to use small, low-voltage electrical appliances, preferably with a variable voltage switch.

SHOPPING AND BARGAINING

Even if the big things such as furniture are taken care of for you, there will be no end of small things you may want to buy for your house, so here is as good a place as any for some vital lessons in Moroccan shopping. We start where all shopping starts, with money.

Flous

The Moroccan word for money is *flous*, a lovely, simple word that sounds like just what it is. If only life were this simple! In fact, the words that Moroccans use to talk about amounts of money are legion. The dirham (abbrev. DH) is the actual unit of currency and the one appearing on all paper currency, but there are two or three different systems of counting and each uses different units. The one used for any particular occasion depends on what you're buying, where you're buying it and what language you're speaking. If that sounds hopelessly confusing, here are a few general guidelines:

- If you are shopping in a *ville nouvelle* (non-*medina* part of a city) frequented by foreigners, this is the easiest of all. Merchants are accustomed to quoting prices in dirhams and centimes, so 5 dirhams 60 means just what you think: 5 dirhams and 60 centimes. Any prices marked with tags are likely to be in dirhams and centimes, sometimes with a comma separating them, e.g. 5,60.

- If you're anywhere else in town and speaking in French, prices will most likely be given to you in francs. But mind you, this does not mean French francs (which are slightly more valuable than dirhams), it means centimes—that is, a hundredth of a dirham. So get this down if you're using French: franc = centime, and 100 francs = 1 dirham.

- If you're using Arabic, the most common unit of currency is the riyal. A riyal is 5 centimes. Oddly enough, the word riyal doesn't appear on any Moroccan currency, but everyone uses it to count. This is a little like the old English system of counting in shillings, or the French one of counting in sous. For an American or other dollar-based person, it would be like counting in nickels (units of 5 cents).

- Finally, if you're using English, you are probably shopping only for souvenirs in tourist shops, as these are about the only places you'll find shopkeepers proficient in English. They will deal with you in dirhams, which makes your part easy since you can at least tell the amount by reading the money.

How to make sense of this business? The first bit of advice is to settle on a shopping language and stick to it—then you have only one system to master, not several. Once you have done that, develop a quick mental table of equivalents for the various denominations of paper currency and coins under the system you have chosen, so that if in your innermost mind, you are still thinking in dirhams and centimes (most foreigners do, even if they won't admit it!), you can quickly translate into a meaningful unit. The table below gives the currency units in English (the way you think of them) and their equivalents under the riyal (Arabic) and franc (French) systems. In the Arabic column, the number is written in Arabic for pronunciation, and given as a numeral in parentheses.

Unit	Arabic equivalent	French equivalent
Coins:		
5 centimes	*riyal wahad (1)*	*cinq francs*
10 centimes	*jouj d'riyal (2)*	*dix francs*
20 centimes	*ârba d'riyal (4)*	*vingt francs*
50 centimes	*âshera d'riyal (10)*	*cinquante francs*

1 dirham	*âshrin d'riyal (20)*	*cent francs*
5 dirhams	*miat d'riyal (100)*	*cinq cent francs*
Notes:		
10 dirhams	*miatain d'riyal (200)*	*mille francs*
50 dirhams	*alf riyal (1000)*	*cinq mille francs*
100 dirhams	*alfain riyal (2000)*	*dix mille francs*
200 dirhams	*ârba alf riyal (4000)*	*vingt mille francs*

Got that? Good! The only way to internalise one or the other of these systems is to use it. Practice makes perfect, but on your way to perfect, expect to stumble around a bit.

Where the Buys Are

As with shopping for food, Morocco offers several different shopping venues to cover your general household needs. *Souqs* are the cheapest place to buy everything, shops in the *medina* are more expensive and finally, shops in the new part of town are the most expensive. Again, the countryside is cheaper than the city, but offers poorer quality and selection.

So much for where you shop. More important is how you shop, and that means haggling. You'll see the natives do it as a matter of course, and you'll do it too if you don't want to make every purchase an opportunity for extortion.

Haggling, or bargaining, if you wish, is a little like learning a language. At first, your performance is slow and halting, with frequent mistakes and constant reference to mental notes. After some practice, you get better; it starts to feel more natural and before long, you know what you're doing without thinking about it very much.

As a primer, familiarise yourself with what is bargained for and what is not in Morocco. You should find these lists dependable:

Usually Bargained For

Any article of clothing; any household or kitchen utensil, appliance, or furniture; any handicraft item, such as carpets, jewellery, leather goods, brassware, pottery and the like; house rental; grand taxi fares on unscheduled runs; anything bought in a *souq*, except price-controlled items noted below;

anything bought from a roving street vendor; petit taxi fares
if the meter isn't working; anything second-hand; domestic
help and services (i.e., maid, plumber, electrician, etc.).

Seldom or Never Bargained For

Grand taxi fares on regular runs; everyday purchases such as
mint, bread, parsley and coriander; gas bottle refills; cigarettes
and alcohol; meals and beverages in restaurants; bus fares
between scheduled stops; price-controlled staple foods (flour,
butter, sugar, oil, tea, milk, etc.); pharmacy purchases; food,
when the price is posted; goods from shops with *prix fixe*
signs posted. Such shops may well sell goods that would be
bargained for if you were buying them elsewhere.

Guidelines and Tactics

You may read rules about bargaining in guidebooks.
Respectfully disregard them all till you know what you're
doing. For example, you may be told to offer 50 per cent
of the asking price of a product, but that could be way too
much or too little, depending on where the seller has chosen
to start. If you don't know the value or usual selling price of

the thing you're after, you won't know what to make of the seller's initial ploy. So begin by knowing what you think a thing is worth. Use your intuitive evaluation (what you think a thing is worth), or ask a trusted Moroccan friend what the going price for a thing is.

Both buyer and seller have a host of stratagems for getting their way in a sale. You may wish to use some of the common repertory given below, and even if you don't, be aware of what the seller may be trying on you.

Buyer's Tactics	Seller's Tactics
Not showing too much enthusiasm	Not showing too much enthusiasm
Walking away when seller has named his 'lowest' price	Turning away when buyer has named his 'highest' price
Pointing out flaws in the product	Noting the superior quality of the product
Quoting a lower price for the same item that you saw elsewhere	Insisting that the lower-priced item was of inferior quality
Claiming not to have enough money to meet seller's 'lowest' price	Claiming that buyer's 'highest' price would force him to take a loss
Praise and flattery for seller's shop, goods, children, piety, etc.	Praise and flattery for buyer's homeland, knowledge, expertise etc.
Acting insulted by seller's price	Acting insulted by buyer's offer
Pulling out money as if your offer was accepted	Wrapping up the product as if his price was agreed

From this, you see that buyer and seller have the same weapons to fight with. Superior handling makes all the difference.

There are a few things you can avoid in order to save money. Don't show too much interest in a particular item (although merchants are expert at perceiving the point when you've made up your mind, even if you're trying to conceal it), don't carry lots of money and look like a tourist, don't be in a hurry and never buy with a guide in tow—he gets a commission.

If you're not sure you want to buy something, you can begin haggling in a casual way, 'testing the waters' to see how much leeway there might be in a price—merchants are used to this, and don't view it as a commitment on your part. On the other hand, if you try to back out when the seller has agreed to your price, especially after protracted bargaining, you will cause offence; this is against the rules.

Finally, it may be useful as well to note that a successful purchase is not always one in which everyone is happy at the end. The Western model, wherein buyer and seller are all smiles, handshakes and thankyous at the conclusion of a purchase does not prevail in Morocco. If at the conclusion of a long haggle, you feel a mild sense of relief, combined with guilt for having been so ruthless, and the seller looks black and miserable, you've probably done very well. If he's smiling and asking you to come back again soon, and you're thinking 'Gosh, that was easy!' you've probably been fleeced.

Can You Take It With You?

Anything that you may wish to buy for personal use while in Morocco can in all likelihood be taken with you when you leave the country. There is no restriction on taking goods out of Morocco and the government encourages the stimulation to the economy that exportation of handicraft and manufactured goods provides. The only restriction on exportation concerns antiques, which are roughly defined as artifacts over 100 years old. These, if they are to be exported at all, require an export licence from the Ministry of Cultural Affairs.

SHOPPING FOR FOOD

There are several choices available to you for food shopping. One or the other of them will probably supply everything you need, but what they sell varies a great deal in selection and price. We begin with the cheapest.

- *souq*: Weekly travelling *souqs* (markets) thrive all over rural Morocco. They are the best and cheapest supplier of fresh produce, as well as spices, dried fruits, staple groceries and household needs.
- *souwiqa*: This means 'little *souq*', and is the part of a village where vendors sell from knockdown stalls; or in cities, the part of the *medina* where food is sold. Not as cheap as the weekly *souq*, but open every day. Good mostly for produce.
- *hanut*: This means 'shop', usually a little neighbourhood shop, where you can buy whatever it is you just ran out of. More expensive than either of the foregoing, you pay for the convenience. If a *hanut* is large and has a wide selection, it achieves the status of *epicerie*.
- *marché*: Cities and good-sized towns have a French-style market that includes greengrocers, staple vendors, butchers, fishmongers and even florists. It is the best one-stop shopping if you live in a city. Not surprisingly, it is more expensive than the *souq* in the countryside, but also offers a wider variety of goods.

Stack em' high and sell em' cheap seems to be the philosophy of these olive merchants at the *marché* in Meknes.

An open-air market in Morocco provides the people with a variety of affordable vegetables and fruits.

- *supermarché*: Cities have indoor supermarkets that have mostly imported foods, or local imitations. They are expensive and cater largely to foreigners, but they may be the only places that carry the thing you're hankering for from back home.
- Other vendors: Butchers are usually stand-alone shops, typically set up in a street full of butcher shops. All meat in Morocco is *halal*, i.e., slaughtered according to Islamic dictates. In practical terms, this means quite freshly killed, usually on the same day you buy it. Animals are not usually cut up until sold. When you order some beef, lamb or goat (pork is not available), the butcher will lob off the next convenient piece from the carcass hanging in his shop. If you require a particular cut or part, it is probably easier to get it in a *marché*, where the whims of foreigners are better appreciated, or to have your maid do the shopping for you, making sure she understands your instructions.

Chicken and other fowl (turkey, pigeon, guinea fowl) and rabbits may be bought dressed or still alive. In the latter case, the one you pick out is killed on the spot. City *marchés* have the most alarming plucking machines that make a harrowing noise—but the alternative is plucking the bird yourself.

If you find meat processing in Morocco a little below your standards of hygiene, eggs are a good alternative source of protein. You can buy them in *ḥanuts* or *marchés*, and from women who sell them on the street. In the countryside, delicious duck eggs and turkey eggs can be had as well as chicken eggs. If you inquire whether the eggs are fresh, you will certainly be told that they are. Those purchased from women on the street are likely the freshest, as they go to market as soon as they are laid.

Bakeries are also stand-alone shops, and may double as pastry shops. They are the best places to get fresh, hot Moroccan or French bread, though many other places sell bread, including the corner *ḥanut*.

TAKING GOOD MEASURE

If you come from a developed country, many things that you are used to buying prepackaged in a jar or box are sold

Mounds of spices for sale in a _hanut_. Prices given are dirhams per kilo.

differently in Morocco—that is, weighed according to the amount you order and wrapped in a temporary package, often paper, to last just until you can get it home. This includes produce, meat, butter, olives, spices and dried fruits and nuts. Morocco uses the metric system. Here are some convenient measures for ordering different foods, with approximate imperial equivalents:

Amount	French	Arabic	Equivalent
For spices:			
20 grams	_vingt grammes_	_âshrin gram_	¾ ounce
50 grams	_cinquante g_	_khamsin gram_	1 ¾ ounce
For cheese, butter, olives, rice, pasta, cous-cous, meat in small quantities:			
200 grams	_deux cent g_	_miatain gram_	7 ounces
500 grams	_cinq cent g_	_khamsemiat g_	just over a pound
For fruits, vegetables and meat:			
¼ kilo	_deux cent/ cinquante g_	_lârba kilo_	half a pound
½ kilo	_un demi kilo_	_nou<u>s</u> kilo_	just over a pound

Amount	French	Arabic	Equivalent
1 kilo	*un kilo*	*kilo*	just over 2 pounds
1 ½ kilos	*un kilo et demi*	*kilo (ou) nous*	3 ¼ pounds
2 kilos	*deux kilos*	*jouj kilo*	4 ⅓ pounds

Finally, if you know how much you want by looking at what's on the scale but don't know the weight, you can say 'a little more' (French *ajoutez un peu*, Arabic *zid shwia*) or 'a little less' (*enlevez un peu*, *nqs shwia*).

REGISTERING WITH THE POLICE

So, you've found your house, filled it up with pleasant objects, got the electricity and water flowing and now you're ready to kick off those yellow slippers, put your feet up on the round dining table and relax with that cup of mint tea. Not quite yet! As a foreigner in Morocco, you are required to carry an identification document called a *carte de séjour*, or residence card. You must take care of this by the end of your first three months in Morocco, but the sooner you do it, the better.

If you live in a city, the central police station (*Sûreté National*) normally accepts applications. If in the country or a village, go to the gendarmerie. You will need to take:

- 8 ID-sized photos
- A DH 60 tax stamp
- Your passport
- Your *attestation de travail*
- Some proof of your residence, such as a copy of your lease or a utility bill with your name on it
- The completed application forms

An *attestation de travail* is a government ministry-issued document stating that you have an official job in Morocco. Your employer should supply this to you. More information on tax stamps is found later in this chapter. Precise requirements for the *carte de séjour* may change from time to time, or may even vary in different parts of the country if officials are not properly informed or up-to-date about what is required. So you will do best by making two trips to the police station, the first to obtain the forms and find out everything that you'll need, and the second to turn in the application. Once submitted, it takes two to three months to obtain the *carte de séjour*. During that time, your passport, combined with the receipt for your application, serve as your identity. Therefore, it is essential that you request and get a receipt when you put in your application.

The Homebody

If you are in Morocco primarily in your capacity as the spouse of a working husband or wife and don't expect to work outside the home, you will be able to get a *carte de séjour* in that capacity, but you should wait until your working spouse has gone through the formalities and then apply for yours. You will need to show proof of your relationship to the working spouse (a marriage licence) and also satisfy the authorities that the working spouse has obtained the proper residency documentation.

Unofficial Residency

An alternative exists to this formal registration process that is not recommended, but that has been known to work for years on end. It is to simply leave and re-enter Morocco every three months, thus being (officially) a perpetual tourist, while in fact living in Morocco. Those who pursue this lifestyle usually make quarterly trips to Ceuta or Melilla, the Spanish enclaves on the Mediterranean coast, in order to satisfy the requirements of leaving the country. Upon re-entering a day or so later, their passports are re-stamped with a new tourist visa, valid for three more months.

The major disadvantage to this arrangement is that immigration officials may refuse to let you re-enter Morocco at any time, if they note your pattern of repeated comings and goings. You will also find administrative tasks more difficult to pull off, such as banking and licensing procedures, and you will not enjoy discounts at some hotels and museums that are available to official foreign residents.

Visa de Retour

Another item you may require is a stamp in your passport called a *visa de retour*. This enables you, once you have residency in Morocco, to enter and leave at will, without having your passport stamped as a tourist on your re-entry. If you intend to leave Morocco for business or a holiday and then return, you must have a *visa de retour*. The visa is good for one year, but must be used within three months of issue, so you must give some thought to the timing of your application.

As with your residency card, the exact requirements for a *visa de retour* may vary, but are likely to include at least the following:

- 4 ID-sized photos
- Your passport
- A DH 100 tax stamp (amount subject to change)
- A copy of your *attestation de travail*
- A copy of your *carte de séjour*, or the receipt for its application if you haven't received it yet
- Completed application forms

There are two ways to get a *visa de retour*. Read about them and choose the one you prefer:

- Surrender your passport and the requisite photos and forms to your local police station or gendarmerie when you apply for the visa. Wait several months. Notice that nothing happens, and no one knows what has happened to your application. Spend several days on its trail, touring bureaucratic offices of the provincial capitals all the way to Rabat—to no avail. Book yourself into a nice hotel room and have a panic attack.
- Collect the requisite forms and information from your local police station as if to make an application for the visa de retour. Then make a trip to Rabat and visit the Direction Generale de la Sûreté National; it's right behind the main PTT and is known as the 'Comissariat'. Indicate very politely and respectfully, but firmly, that you are in town for only a short time, leaving the country very soon, and therefore must get your *visa de retour* quickly. Using this method, you can usually get the visa in two or three days.

If you should have to leave Morocco at very short notice and are unable to get a *visa de retour* before you leave, you may be able to get one from a Moroccan embassy abroad, provided you have the requisite documentation. This will enable you to return to Morocco as a resident.

EMERGENCIES

You and your household should agree on a procedure to follow in the event of any particular emergency. Services that exist to deal with these in your country may be undeveloped or nonexistent in Morocco. It is better to have a plan of action in mind for certain contingencies, so that if they arise, you will not have to figure out everything while 'in the line of fire', as it were. Possible emergencies include:

- An automobile accident
- The need for first aid or critical life support
- Fire
- The need to evacuate the country, or the part of it where you are residing

There is no standard procedure for any of these, and how you handle each one depends on where you are. The important thing is to agree on a plan in each case so that you, or others in your absence, will be able to act appropriately. Consult with your compatriots or your consulate if necessary to assure yourself that you will know what to do in any critical situation.

HEALTH, HEALTH CARE AND PHARMACIES

After an initial adjustment that may well include traveller's diarrhoea, most foreigners find that it is easy to maintain good health in Morocco. This doesn't mean that you can relax your vigilance about what you eat, and the following pages will go into more detail about this.

You may also find that in Morocco, at the outset at least, you are more prone to nuisance illnesses such as colds and flu than you were at home. This may be from exposure to new strains of viruses, from stress, or both. After an initial period, chances are that you will experience no more of these in Morocco than you did at home.

There are some other infectious diseases present in Morocco that you need to be aware of. Following is a rundown of what lurks about, and what you can do to avoid infection.

Typhoid Fever

Though the risk is minimal in Morocco, cases are occasionally reported in places well off the beaten path. If you will be spending long periods of time in villages or rural areas, you may want to consider vaccination, which in any case is only 70 per cent to 90 per cent effective. Typhoid fever is a bacterial infection spread through food and water, and observing the usual precautions for ingesting these is really the best prevention. The disease is treatable with antibiotics.

Cholera

Outbreaks of cholera are rare in Morocco and word of them spreads very fast. It is probably not worthwhile getting vaccinated as a routine precaution, unless you already have stomach ulcers or use antacids frequently. If you should hear of a cholera-infested area, avoid it at all costs. Again, taking standard precautions in what you eat and drink goes a long way towards minimising or eliminating your risk.

Hepatitis A (infectious hepatitis)

This strain of hepatitis, spread through contact with contaminated food and water, is relatively common in Morocco, and non-urban residents are advised to protect themselves against it by taking the usual food and water precautions, and if possible, receiving injections of immunoglobulin (also called Immune globulin, IG, or GG for gamma globulin) every five months.

Immune globulin prepared by the Cohn-Oncley procedure (standard in the US) is certified to be free from infectious agents such as hepatitis B and HIV. Immune globulin manufactured in some other countries may not meet this standard.

Hepatitis B (serum hepatitis)

This variety of hepatitis is spread primarily by sexual contact and other interpersonal contact that results in the exchange of bodily fluids. It is common enough to put at risk anyone who has intimate contact with Moroccans. For those without immunity, conferred by previous infection and development of antibodies, a vaccine is available and recommended for health-care workers, year-round, non-urban residents and anyone likely to have sexual contact, or seek medical treatment in Morocco. The vaccine is administered in injections over a period of six months, which ideally should be completed before entry into Morocco. But it is still worthwhile getting the vaccine even if you will not be able to get the last shot until after you are already in Morocco.

HIV and AIDS

There is little dependable information about rates of infection for HIV and AIDS in Morocco, but the virus is present and spreading. Documented cases of AIDS (called by its French name SIDA) in Morocco are in the mid-hundreds (1997), but international health authorities suspect that actual cases of HIV and AIDS may be as much as ten times higher. There is very little intravenous drug use, but unsafe sex is rampant in Morocco and the main source of infection for HIV. You should always follow safe sex guidelines scrupulously if you have any sexual contact, especially homosexual contact, with Moroccans.

Rabies

This disease is reported sporadically in Morocco, spread by the bite of infected animals. A vaccination, which in the event of infection makes treatment a little less traumatic, is available but recommended only to those who will be working directly with animals. The main precaution against rabies is to avoid direct contact with animals.

Intestinal Parasites

The following pages will give some indications of the risks of parasitic infection through food and water, and how they can be minimised. Nearly all parasitic infections result in diarrhoea. Some may also induce blood and mucus in stools, or cause fevers, cramps and nausea. The most common infections are shigella, giardia and various other nonspecific amoebas. All should be attended to as soon as they appear. All can be treated allopathically with various specific drugs and antibiotics, the recommended method in severe cases. For milder cases, you may wish to try altering your diet, homeopathic remedies or mere patience.

Professional Health Care

Most foreigners in Morocco depend on doctors and medical professionals of their own nationality, or in the absence of these, on private, foreign doctors both for regular health care and for immunisations and vaccinations. Most embassies have referral lists. Morocco's health care system is not of a standard to inspire confidence in anyone who comes from a developed country; there is only one doctor for every 2,900 people. You should consult with your compatriots about what health care facilities and provisions are available and make the best use of them. There are a number of foreign doctors practising in Morocco, as well as Western-trained Moroccans. As you would do in your own country, seek the recommendation of someone familiar with a particular doctor before you engage his or her services.

If you have an identified medical condition that doctors or people around you need to know about, try to get documentation for it in French, and also learn to talk about it, or at least to name the condition, in French and Arabic. If you are dependent on a prescription drug such as insulin, investigate with your embassy what options are available for maintaining a dependable supply.

The best health care you will find in Morocco is that which you provide yourself. Making a conscious effort to maintain a healthy diet and to get enough sleep will go a long way towards keeping you in the pink. You will also find it worth your while to note early symptoms of stress as you make your adjustment to Morocco, track down their sources and treat them as well as you can.

Berrechid

South of Casablanca is the town of Berrechid, site of Morocco's main residential psychiatric hospital. The name of the town is synonymous with the hospital, and thus Berrechid is referred to as a destination for anyone thought certifiably mad, in both humorous and serious contexts.

If you need or anticipate any major dental work, it is better to have it done before you get to Morocco. There is one dentist for every 80,000 residents. The standard treatment for toothache in Morocco is to extract the tooth. At country *souqs*, you will see specialists in this art, identified by their set of pliers and the small carpets littered with bloody molars.

Childbearing

Most Moroccan women have their children at home, with the delivery being a joint effort of other women in the family, friends, and most importantly, a midwife. More modern-style births (i.e., in hospitals and clinics) are becoming available and fashionable in cities, particularly on the Atlantic coast, but in most of Morocco, having children at home is still the norm. If you and your spouse anticipate having a child in Morocco, you should seek the advice of your compatriots and your consulate about what options are available, and plan accordingly. It should not be necessary to leave Morocco in order to deliver a baby in whatever way suits you.

Contraception

Interfering with conception and pregnancy is not forbidden under Islam, but the idea of it goes against the generally held value that being fruitful and multiplying is a good thing. Increasingly, however, Moroccan couples are taking to the idea of family planning, and having only two children (hoping that at least one will be a boy!). The pill is available in Morocco, as are condoms. Foreigners may find that facilities exist for getting these through their embassy. Abortion is not easily available in Morocco.

Pharmacies

Prescription drugs are a thriving business in Morocco, and it is a rare village that doesn't have a pharmacy of some kind, identified by a green cross or crescent and the French name *pharmacie*. As well as prescription drugs, pharmacies sell various non-prescription remedies and health care products such as toothpaste, hydrogen peroxide, cold and flu remedies and the like. Control of so-called prescription drugs is rather lax, and if you know the French generic or proprietary name of a drug, you can probably buy it over the counter in most pharmacies in Morocco. Like the French, doctors in Morocco tend towards drug bombardment therapies, prescribing several drugs at once for the treatment of a condition. Also following the French, there is a predilection for drugs in suppository rather than capsule form in Morocco. Homeopathic remedies, though not widely available in Morocco, can be obtained from some city pharmacies, and provide a good alternative to Western drug therapy for many minor and chronic ailments.

PARASITES HAVE TO EAT TOO

It is usually food that causes the most illness among foreigners, so it is wise to be forewarned of the hazards in order to avoid them.

Morocco has an extensive and exotic range of endemic intestinal flora, as well as standards of hygiene that most foreigners will find somewhat lacking, and a few will find downright appalling. The upshot of this is that these little bugs will find their way into your system at some point. Depending on your constitution, you may suffer no ill effects whatever, or you may be stricken by occasional, even frequent bouts of diarrhoea, nausea, fever or other symptoms associated with parasitic infection.

Chances are you will know very early on in Morocco how careful you will have to be about what you eat and drink. Necessary precautions vary quite widely from one person to another, and you really must adapt yourself to the way your system responds. To minimise the distress of getting used to the Moroccan microbe scene, and to ensure that you stay healthy, follow these sensible guidelines at all times:

- Drink bottled water to begin with. You may want to try the tap water where you live after some time, but when travelling in parts of Morocco away from where you live, it makes sense to stick with bottled water.
- Observe proper personal hygiene. If you are used to toilet paper (*papier hygenique, warqat l-merḥaḍ*), be sure you have a dependable supply; it isn't available everywhere in Morocco. If you adopt the Moroccan system of hygiene (left hand and water), it is paramount that you wash your hands thoroughly with soap after using the toilet, and refrain from taking food with your left hand. It is also sensible to keep your fingernails neatly trimmed. The so-called 'oral-faecal' route is the primary means of infection for most intestinal diseases, and the hands are very often the courier between the two.
- Don't eat street food that isn't freshly cooked, or thoroughly heated.
- Don't use ice if you're unsure where the water came from; it could be other than tap water. Ice cream in cities is dependable, but in the countryside, it may well have contaminated ingredients.

Beyond these precautions, there are several grades of circumspection that can be observed in your eating and personal habits to avoid parasitic infection. Choose the one that keeps you healthy and happy as much of the time as possible.

Iron Stomach
If you seem to have no trouble with food or drink in Morocco, perhaps after an initial breaking-in period, chances are that you can eat and drink more or less what you want with impunity.

That Queasy Feeling
If diarrhoea or nausea bother you more often than you're comfortable with, investigate your food sources. Is someone else cooking for you? Are you regularly eating in the same place that may be causing or exacerbating infection? In addition, you must be scrupulous about the general guidelines noted above.

Losing Weight and Turning Mighty Pale

If you seem to go from one bout of infection to another, it's time to face these bugs head on. If someone is cooking for you, see that they are treated for parasites. Avoid uncooked dishes such as salads. Turn down invitations if necessary to avoid eating where you haven't eaten before. Try to cut down on fatty and high-protein components of your diet, which generally cause parasites to thrive.

State of Siege

Have you forgotten what normal digestion and regularity are like? Eat only food that you have cooked yourself. Drink only bottled water and manufactured drinks. Peel all fruits and vegetables, or soak them in water in which iodine tablets have been dissolved. Be sure that meats are thoroughly cooked, or better, avoid them altogether.

These precautions may sound dire, but it should be emphasised that if you are prudent about what and where you eat, you will probably not have any appreciable difficulty with food and digestion in Morocco.

GETTING DOMESTIC HELP

It is assumed throughout this book that you will take advantage of hired domestic help while living in Morocco. There is no good reason not to do so, and every reason that you should. First, there is a large class of women, mostly unmarried, widowed or divorced, who depend on finding domestic work as the most respectable form of livelihood available to them. Second, getting things done in a technologically underdeveloped country such as Morocco is a very time- and labour-intensive business, and it is unlikely that you will have time to do everything for yourself or for your family, even if you are not working outside the home. Third, domestic help can provide an entrée into Moroccan society and be an invaluable source of information about the country for you. Fourth, all this is possible for very little money compared to what it is worth to you.

Most foreigners in Morocco have a maid who may come anywhere from once to several times a week to clean, do laundry and perhaps to cook. This is the only help that a majority of foreigners take on, but if you have a large household or a big house, you may want to have both a cook and a maid (both usually women) and even a gardener, errand boy, handyman or chauffeur (always men).

The easy availability of helpers might suggest that there are no difficulties associated with the business of employing them, but alas, all is not so simple. The reason for complications, however, lies very often not in the people foreigners hire, but in the relationships that foreigners develop with them. The following remarks, therefore, are intended to help you get the kind of help you need and to keep all of you happy.

Settling on the Right Person

For the purposes of this discussion, we will look at the business of getting a maid, but the principles apply to any domestic help that you may wish to hire. Once you are set up in your house and are ready for the services of a maid, inquire first of people you know whether they know of a woman who might be available. It is quite common for two or more foreign households to share the services of a single maid.

A woman who provides good service in one household and comes recommended to you is certainly worth talking to. Consider, however, that a maid may come to know you and your household quite intimately, and anything she knows she may reveal to others. In short, a maid who works for both you and others known to you may well compromise your privacy, and if this is a concern to you, you will want to hire someone who works for no one else you know.

There also exists what might be called the 'spoilt maid' syndrome, wherein a woman who works, or has worked, for too many people of the same nationality learns to exploit their weaknesses rather expertly. If your observations of a particular maid suggest that this may be the case, look elsewhere.

You may well be approached by someone looking for work, or by someone in the family of someone looking for work, before you even set about to look for someone yourself. It is worth keeping in mind that a common confusion exists in Moroccan English between the words 'maid' and 'housewife', so if you are approached by someone asking if you want or need a housewife, they mean a maid!

Don't dismiss such petitions out of hand. It's possible that a good maid or other worker may come to you unbidden in this way, but if you do decide to take on someone completely unknown to you, ask for references and check them out. Don't hesitate to conduct a very thorough interview, with the help of an interpreter if necessary, to get all the information you want about a prospective maid before you hire one.

Hiring Help

When you are sure that you've found a person you feel comfortable with, engage her for a trial period—say for one month. Settle on a price per week, or a price per visit—the latter is recommended. You may ask your maid how much she wants and it's possible that she'll tell you, but more likely she'll ask you to make an offer, and you should be prepared to do so. What you pay varies between city (more expensive) and country, and may also vary according to what you actually want the maid to do. If you have friends who employ a woman in a similar capacity, ask them what they pay. As a rough guideline, DH 150 is quite reasonable for a woman who comes once a week to thoroughly clean your house and do your laundry. Thoroughly clean means dusting every room, sweeping and mopping all the floors, cleaning the kitchen and toilet, changing the linens and occasionally washing the windows.

Be very specific about what you want the maid to do, both before she visits and when she actually comes to work. Use gesture and pantomime if you are not conversant in a language that she speaks.

Chances are that your maid will want to use bleach (called *javel*), and a washboard for your clothes—Moroccans are somewhat fanatical about the cleanliness of fabrics. Their standard washing techniques will wreak havoc on your clothes and wear them out in no time. Try to persuade your maid to get along with only soap powder and water, except for white things of course.

The Foreigner-Maid Relationship

The majority of problems that arise between foreigners and their domestic help are due to relations becoming too intimate and informal. The domestics lose their perspective on their place in the household, and soon start to take advantage. This interpretation is not in any way intended as a slur on Moroccan domestic servants. It is a cross-cultural pitfall that arises out of very understandable but hard-to-avoid circumstances.

Remember that Moroccan society is stratified and that everyone is more or less resigned to, if not content with his or her place. Behaviour between people of different levels in every way reinforces the distance that is already established between them. Moroccans treat their domestic servants in a way that many foreigners think curt, unsympathetic or even rude. Chances are that the servants do not perceive their treatment in this way, or even if they do, they don't question it or resent it.

Foreigners, especially North Americans, are inclined to treat their servants with kindness, friendliness and a spirit of equality. This sounds the death knell for a successful relationship with domestic helpers in Morocco. They will think you are a pushover and find ways to increase their share of your real or perceived largesse.

How can you prevent this, without completely stifling the friendliness and goodwill that may come naturally to you? Remember that your domestic help, whatever their many virtues may be, are related to you as employees. When they are in your house, their business is to tend to their work. If they show interest in other areas of your life, or more importantly, if by your behaviour you invite them to look at other areas, you are letting an element into your relationship that could well spoil it. You will find that an attitude towards your help that is professional, detached, courteous and limited to your defined relationship to them will work best for both of you.

Socialising with the Help

A heading such as this may seem anathema after the foregoing lecture, but the fact is that the people you hire may actively seek to draw you into their family circle, especially if you live alone. They are not trying to con you; chances are that they simply feel sorry for you living on your own and see it as their duty to give you a room full of people to feel comfortable in. Remember that Moroccans are innately hospitable, and very open to friendships with foreigners.

There is no reason you should turn down invitations to your maid's or other servant's home simply because you fear becoming too close to them. Just remember this: when you are in their home, you are the guest and you should act like one. *Don't* act like your maid's boss. Don't talk about what she does at your house. Cultivate other interests and topics of conversation and just be a guest. When your maid comes to work for you again, *then* it is time to resume your role as boss.

Firing Help

If after your trial period of employing a maid or other helper, you think that things are not working out, you have several choices:

- Suffer in silence. This is not recommended. Surely there are enough things in Morocco that may cause you stress without creating new ones.
- Give your helper another, preferably shorter trial period with very specific instructions about what's not being done right and how it must be rectified.
- Dismiss your helper. If this is at the end of the trial period you established initially, there need be no difficulty. Thank them for the work done, pay for it and say that their services are no longer required.
- If you can't face a showdown with your domestic help, use a trusted Moroccan intermediary, such as a friend of yours, to set things straight.

If you wish to dismiss help at a later time, well after a trial period has ended, you should give your reasons for doing so

dispassionately, and simply dismiss them, with appropriate pay and thanks. Repeat this as many times as it takes to sink in, and speak unequivocally. If you are not firm, you may witness a shocking display of grovelling and pleading that results in your reinstating the person you had firmly resolved to dismiss.

As a final word of caution, don't employ two people of the same family. Should a conflict of interest ever arise, their loyalty to one another will be greater than their loyalty to you. There is also the danger that opening your door to a second family member will be perceived as a general welcoming for others to follow and share in your generosity.

SCHOOLS AND EDUCATION

If you have school-age children living with you in Morocco, you will want to arrange for their attendance in a school. The only schools offering English-language primary and secondary education in Morocco are the American Schools. They are located in Rabat, Casablanca and Tangier. At present, all offer programs leading to an American high school diploma, but none have an International Baccalaureate program; thus graduates are prepared for US higher education, but not for universities in other countries.

Private schools in which French is the medium of instruction are found in every city. These have programs leading to a French Baccalaureate or an International Baccalaureate. The Moroccan public school system is not suitable for children who do not intend to spend the rest of their lives in Morocco or in the Arab world. The medium of instruction is Arabic, and the system of education, modelled on the French one but with inferior pedagogy and inadequate resources, will not prepare youngsters for higher education or livelihood outside of Morocco.

All primary and secondary schools follow the standard North American and European school year, with classes beginning in September, ending in June and providing two longish breaks, one around the new year and the other in spring.

MOROCCAN MONEY, FOREIGN MONEY AND YOUR MONEY

At present, Moroccan dirhams are not hard currency and do not trade officially on any foreign currency exchange. Residents of Morocco are allowed to carry a token amount of dirhams in and out of the country, but their exportation is otherwise forbidden. Nevertheless, reputable currency exchanges in countries around the world often have a supply of dirhams that they are quite happy to deal in.

The exchange rate of the dirham against various foreign currencies is set by the Bank of Morocco. When changing money in Morocco, the rate generally does not vary from bank to bank. But it may vary quite considerably outside of Morocco. Moneychangers in border towns (Tangier, Oujda, Ceuta, Melilla, Algeciras, Gibraltar) often offer a slightly better deal than banks, whether you're buying or selling Moroccan currency, but it is not advisable to change large amounts of money this way, just as it is not advisable to carry large amounts of Moroccan currency across a Moroccan border. Either activity could lead to a considerable lightening of your pockets. Street moneychangers may well be con artists, and Moroccan customs officials may seize money being carried illegally.

Transferring Funds from Abroad

Whether or not you're starting your own business in Morocco, you may have need from time to time to get money into the

The familiar face of Moroccan currency: His Majesty King Hassan II.

country. Besides physically carrying it in, there are several methods of receiving money from abroad. In all cases, foreign currency is sent, and converted to dirhams in Morocco.

- International wire transfer. This will require that you have a bank account in Morocco, but even with this, the receipt of funds can be considerably delayed, sometimes up to six weeks before they are available to you.

- International money order. Money can be sent to and from Morocco via a *mandat*, or postal money order. These travel via air mail or telegraph and must be cashed at the PTT that delivers them. Not all countries have the facility to send funds to Morocco.

- Automated Teller Machines. An increasing number of ATMs in Morocco accept ATM and credit cards: Visa, Mastercard and the Plus and Cirrus networks are all represented. A given card will not necessarily work in a machine carrying a symbol that suggests it will. If you have a variety of cards, it is best to bring them all to Morocco, thus increasing the chances of having one that will work dependably. Using your credit card is effectively getting a cash advance on it, and entails all applicable surcharges.

Credit Cards

A minority of Moroccan business establishments accept internationally known credit cards. Those that do accept them are largely on the tourist track: four- and five-star hotels, better restaurants, expensive souvenir shops and dealers in large Moroccan handicrafts, such as carpets.

Banking

The Moroccan system of banking is based on the French system, but it is slower and not as sophisticated. The Bank of Morocco is the government-controlled central bank; it is also the only issuer of currency. Like the French system, there is no clearly defined distinction between commercial banks and merchant banks. There are 15 to 20 commercial banks in Morocco; the biggest three have more than half of the business.

As a resident foreigner (i.e., one who holds a valid *carte de séjour*), you can open a personal banking account. To encourage foreign investment, a number of other types of accounts can now be opened in Moroccan banks by resident and non-resident foreigners alike. These include foreign currency accounts, foreign accounts convertible in dirhams and convertible time deposit accounts.

Some foreign and joint Moroccan-foreign banks are beginning to operate in Morocco. They do not yet offer the same range of services that the Moroccan banks do, but they can facilitate financial relations with the foreign country they represent, in some cases better than the Moroccan banks can.

Various documents are required to open a bank account in Morocco. As many laws governing banking are relatively recent and banking personnel are not always familiar with all details, it is difficult to come up with a definitive list. You should start by making an appointment with the branch manager of the bank where you want to open your account, ask him or her what is needed, and then bring all required materials to the meeting.

If you are running a business, you will want to open a separate business account. If you require particular services for your business, you should shop around before settling on a bank. From bank to bank, the willingness and ability to accommodate your needs will vary, and may even vary from branch to branch within a single bank. Consult the experience of other foreigners in Morocco for the best information about business and personal banking.

Aside from very ordinary banking transactions such as making deposits, you will have to do most of your banking at the branch where you open your account. Telecommunications and data communications between branches of the same bank are not always very well developed in Morocco.

TRANSPORTATION IN MOROCCO

Morocco has an excellent system of roads, including a scenic toll motorway that runs along the Atlantic coast between Tangier and Casablanca, and good two-lane roads connecting all major towns and cities. Even remote villages are often served by paved roads or dirt roads good enough for passenger cars. This network makes it possible to get nearly everywhere without undue difficulty. There is nearly always more than one way of getting somewhere, and often there are three or four ways.

Driving in Morocco

If you have a car at your disposal, it will take you wherever you want to go. You may have your own or a work-related car to drive in Morocco, or you may rent a car. Car rental is expensive, comparable to rental prices in European countries, which for Morocco is expensive indeed. Gas (petrol) is also about the same price as in much of Europe, making it quite expensive compared to Moroccan living costs generally. Leaded, unleaded and diesel fuel are all available.

You can easily take your car to Morocco from Europe, using the ferry crossings from Algeciras or Gibraltar. Make sure that your insurance covers you for driving in Morocco. Also, if you mean to cross at peak travel times (summer, and just before or after major Moroccan holidays), you should book in advance. See your travel agent about this.

You can drive your car in Morocco for up to six months without registering it. Thereafter, you must register it with the Ministry of Transport. International and foreign driver's licences are valid in Morocco, but if you are resident in Morocco and driving there, you are advised to get a Moroccan licence, also issued by the Ministry of Transport.

It is necessary to drive defensively and with great caution on Moroccan roads. Driver education and safety are not of a high standard, and accidents with casualties are frequent. Never assume that you have or will get the right of way when you and another driver are on the same course. Like much else that passes between strangers in Morocco, driving can be a battle of wills and courtesy does not often prevail.

If you haven't got a car, fear not, for Morocco's other means of transportation are quite extensive and good.

Trains

The first railroads in Morocco were built by the French and are well maintained today. There is a major east-west line from

Oujda at the Algerian border in the east, through Fez, Meknes, Rabat, and thence south to Casablanca; a north-south line that links Tangier to the east-west line at Sidi Kacem; and a line that runs south from Casablanca to Marrakech. New lines have been built that link Safi, El-Jadida, Oued Zem and Bouârfa (near Figuig) to the existing network. Plans are now in hand to build a train line south into the 'Saharan Provinces' as far as Dakhla, that will serve Agadir, Tan Tan and Laâyoune along the way. These cities are served at present by bus service that is coordinated with the train schedules.

There are first- and second-class carriages on all trains, and third-class on some, but it is being phased out. First-class is inexpensive and recommended, as you will always be able to get a seat in a compartment for six people. Most people travel second-class, eight to a compartment, but you can usually get a seat if you board near the beginning of a train's journey or at a major stop. Third-class also nearly always offers a seat, and is used mostly by soldiers and the rural poor. It is an adventure not recommended for foreigners, who would be quite a curiosity in a third-class carriage. A more expensive high speed train runs hourly between Rabat and Casablanca, making the trip in less than an hour. A new train line links Mohammed V Airport with regular service to Casablanca and semi-regular service to Rabat.

Note that the electronic monitors in urban train stations are on a fixed program that displays details of the ideal schedule, but not what is actually happening on the platforms on any particular day. Consult station personnel for actual platform numbers and arrival and departure times.

Buses

Buses travel to every corner, nook and cranny of Morocco. There are three major classes of buses: the state-run intercity bus line C.T.M., private bus lines, which compete with C.T.M. and also travel to many even smaller localities, and city buses, which operate in all principal cities and larger towns where there is market for them.

C.T.M.

The state-run buses, called *say-tay-em* in both Arabic and French, run only between major cities and large towns. Their schedules are posted in their terminals, which are often separate from the private bus stations, and they usually run on time. They are slightly more expensive than private bus lines and not necessarily faster, but the buses are a little more comfortable, offering marginally more leg room.

Private Buses

A large number of private bus lines operate all over Morocco on loosely scheduled, established routes. The collective name for these is *kar*. In principle, the buses have fixed departure times, but in practice, they tend to leave when they fill up, whether this is before or after the scheduled time. Private buses are normally quite ready to drop people off along the way to a destination, and also to pick up those standing by the roadside, if there are seats (or sometimes, even standing room) available. Despite this, private buses tend to make better time than C.T.M. buses, perhaps because they have fewer scheduled stops.

In cities and towns, private buses of various lines stop to load and unload at the bus stations, and these places will appear quite chaotic to you at first. Some of them are just a wide spot in the road where people are milling about and shouting. Others are actually purpose-built enclosed structures where people are milling about and shouting. Here's how to negotiate your way:

- Ask *anyone*, but preferably a man in a blue coat who has money in his hand and is shouting, where you can get a bus to, say, Rabat: "*Kaien she kar l-Rabat?*"
- Alternatively, listen for the name of your destination. Typically ticket-sellers stand by the bus shouting the name of the city it is going to, in an attempt to fill it up.
- 'Cut' (buy) your ticket. This will probably be from the person standing next to the bus, but in larger cities with newer stations, you may be directed to a ticket window. You may say, for example, "*Bghit nqeţâ l-warqa l-Oujda.*"

("I want to cut a ticket to Oujda.") If you've got this far, the price will probably be rattled off to you in riyals or francs. If you don't understand, ask for it in dirhams ("*b-she*ḥ*al b-dirham*?")

- If you have luggage you don't want to hold on your lap, give it to the man in the blue coat to put on top of the bus; there is little room under the seats or in overhead racks inside. Tip the man a dirham or so, and when you reach your destination, likewise tip the man who gets your bag down for you. If they try to shake you down for more, which is quite common, you can either argue or pay.

City Buses

Ṭobis, a corruption of the French *autobus*, operate over fixed routes, on more or less fixed schedules. During rush hours (to and from work in the morning and evening, before and after lunch, and after school), they are extremely crowded, and the mob at the bus stop presses forward to board as soon as the doors open. If you come from a country of polite queuing, you'll have to change your ways for this. No one is deferred to and if you want to get on the bus, you'll have to push and shove like everyone else. Entry to the buses may be at the front or at the rear. Inside, you may find a person in a glass cage (for good reason) who sells tickets, or a roving conductor may collect fares. State your destination to learn what it costs to get there.

Taxis

Two kinds of taxis operate in Morocco: 'big taxis', which run on fixed routes between towns and cities or between distant points within an urban area, and 'little taxis', which operate within cities and go where you ask them to.

Big Taxis

Called *grand taxi* or *taxi kebir*, these are nearly all Mercedes-Benzes of recent or respectable vintage that have a red circular medallion on the front. They are largely owner-operated and licensed. Except for your own private car, they are the fastest (and most expensive) transportation between cities. They congregate in designated areas of towns and cities and operate on various fixed routes, for fixed fares. Each carries six passengers, two in the front and four in the back. They leave as soon as they fill up. There may be a central dispatcher for each destination, who directs passengers and takes money, or the driver himself may collect the fares.

You should be sure that you are at the proper taxi staging area that serves your destination. This will ensure that the taxi fills up and that you are paying the proper fare, not a special 'soak the ignorant tourists' fare.

On the other hand, if you are in a hurry to get where you're going, or if you want to travel in relatively more comfort, you can pay for the empty places in a taxi; in other words, any number of people fewer than six can pay the equivalent of six fares and charter the taxi. Taking a big taxi all alone is called *koursa* and is viewed as an ostentatious and wasteful indulgence. On the other hand, if people didn't sometimes do it, there wouldn't be a word for it!

If you wish to take a taxi to a place not on a fixed route, or to a destination that is not served by the taxi stand where you are, this is considered a *koursa* journey. The taxi driver must obtain permission from the police. This is usually routine and involves only a stop at the nearest station along the way, but you may be asked to show some identification, such as your passport. Negotiate the price for such a journey with the driver or dispatcher, and be prepared to bargain hard; foreigners are seen as having deep pockets for this kind of trip.

To find a big taxi to your destination, or to see if there is one, ask, "*Kaien she taxi l-Azrou,*" for example. If you are travelling between cities that don't lie on the same highway, you may have to change taxis in a major town along the way.

To find out the fare of a big taxi trip, you may ask "*b-shehal al-blasa l-Azrou?*" ("How much is a place to Azrou?") If you suspect you're being gouged, ask other passengers how much they paid.

Your luggage will be carried in the trunk at no charge, unless you have an inordinate amount of it. You needn't tip the driver for shifting it about, unless he carries it some distance for you, and if you have no luggage, you needn't tip the driver at all.

Little Taxis

Called *petit taxi* or *taxi seghir*, these operate within cities. They are usually European subcompacts, carrying a maximum of three passengers, though four can squeeze in. Each city's taxis are 'colour coded' and labelled so they are quite easy to spot on the street. They have taxi meters but the meters don't always work, when they work they are not always used, and when they are used they are not always consulted. So it is a good idea to settle on the fare before you proceed, not after you're in the cab. If the meter is not running, it is customary to haggle, or at least try to. In Casablanca and Marrakech, it is mandatory to haggle unless you want to be taken to the cleaners en route to your destination. It is customary to tip little taxi drivers, some small amount over the fare, unless you feel that they've already soaked you.

Little taxis routinely pick up and carry passengers to more than one destination on the same trip, so don't be surprised if the one you are in stops to pick up another passenger who seems to be going in the same general direction. By the same token, you can flag a taxi that already has a passenger in it, if you don't mind sharing. Figuring out how to split the fare on such trips is the fine art of the driver; the basic rule is that a person pays at his or her destination. Haggle if the fare asked seems inequitable.

Other Ways of Getting Around

All of the foregoing fills in the middle range of long-distance travel within Morocco, neither extremely expensive nor extremely fast. At the high end, Royal Air Maroc operates domestic flights between major cities and resorts; 15 airports are served altogether. Flights are at least once daily between Casablanca and all cities. There are several flights daily on

Petit taxis take you where you want to go in town.

popular runs, including Tangier, Agadir and Laâyoune. Cities in the Sahara are well-served, being relatively inaccessible otherwise. Fares are cheaper than European air travel over comparable distances; there is some seasonal variation, and occasional bargain fares are available.

That leaves the low end of getting around, which is hitchhiking. It is generally safe and quite common for men to hitchhike in Morocco, but women should not hitchhike alone. Hitchhiking is a business proposition: you should always offer money to whoever picks you up, whether you get a ride in the front seat of a BMW or the back of a pickup truck. An amount in the neighbourhood of the usual bus or taxi fare is acceptable. Wealthy Moroccans who offer you a ride may refuse payment, but for others, it is a way for them to defray the cost of their journey.

For short distances, the best choices are walking, a bicycle or a moped. Mopeds are legion in cities, and you will see entire armies of them parked or at traffic lights. They are fuel-efficient and good transportation for one or two persons. Bicycles are becoming more common, and most places in Morocco, you can ride them the year round. Be sure to get a good lock.

Walking is hands-down the national favourite mode of transportation, and people often walk great distances without giving it a thought. Be cautioned that pedestrians are pretty far down the list of moving things in terms of right-of-way. As with driving, you must always watch out for the other guy. The unofficial rule in Morocco seems to be that the person or object which is moving faster or with the greater force has the right of way. So don't ever put yourself in the path of something bigger or faster than you are, whether it be a bicycle, horse, donkey cart, car or bus.

Transportation Outside of Morocco

For more serious getaways, Europe is the most popular destination for foreigners in Morocco. There are flights from Casablanca and other larger Moroccan airports to several European countries (especially France) and to many places around the world.

You can take the train from anywhere in Morocco to Tangier, ferry to Algeciras in Spain, and connect there with the European rail system. Typically, you will travel from there at least as far as Madrid or even Paris before making other connections. Tickets for the entire journey from Morocco to your European rail destination can be purchased in Morocco, at a travel agent or railway station.

Though the railroad also connects with Algeria in the East, and thence to Tunisia, relations between Morocco and Algeria are rather on-again-off-again, and the political climate in Algeria is not always welcoming to foreigners. This is not a recommended exit from Morocco for non-Arabs and non-Muslims.

The PTT

Every city, town and larger village has a main post office, called the 'pay-tay-tay' in both French and Arabic, or occasionally *al-bosta* in Arabic. These are post offices in the

French and English sense, where many kinds of business other than the mailing of letters are conducted.

PTTs are the central distribution point for mail, and most of them have post office boxes to rent. They also vend stamps and handle anything that needs to be mailed, except parcels at post offices that have a Colis Postaux (see following pages). In addition, you can go to the PTT to

- Buy or cash a postal money order (*mandat*).
- Send telegrams.
- Buy tax stamps when it is required from various documents.
- Make telephone calls to anywhere in the world from booths provided. In towns and villages, these are not usually dial telephones; rather, you give the number you wish to call to the duty clerk who makes the call and then indicates the number of the booth you should enter.

There is normally a queue (or rather, a cluster) in front of the single, all-purpose clerk in a small post office, or separate mobs for separate windows in large post offices. In these, be sure you are standing in line for a window that provides the service you're after. These are usually identified in Arabic and French on signs above the windows. Ask someone if you are unsure where to go; there is normally only one window that sells postage stamps.

Tax Stamps

A thriving government money spinner in Morocco is the vending of tax stamps. They come in several denominations, from the very cheap (a few dirhams) to the very expensive (hundreds of dirhams). They are required for certain documents, and when you are turning in or using a document that requires one, you will probably be told what sort of tax stamp it needs to make it official and viable.

Cheap tax stamps are often affixed to small notices, written recommendations, little 'for sale' signs and the like, to give them an air of officialdom. In these cases, the tax stamp confers no real value or meaning, except to support the popular idea that the stamps somehow validate any written document.

Tax stamps are sold in post offices and at Tabacs—shops that sell cigarettes. If you mistakenly buy a tax stamp in the wrong denomination, the Tabac where you bought it is obligated to exchange it for full value. You must affix the proper tax stamp to a document. You cannot make up its value by using stamps of smaller denominations; thus two 50 dirham tax stamps will not substitute for a 100 dirham tax stamp.

Colis Postaux

Attached to the PTT in cities and larger towns is a small office called the Colis Postaux, or parcel post office. If you have a box to mail, take it here, not to the stamp window of the regular post office. If you are sending the box out of Morocco, do not seal it up at home—you will only have to open it again for customs inspection at the Colis Postaux. Inside the Colis Postaux, you will find one or more professional packagers who, for a small (negotiable) fee, will expertly seal up your parcel, once the customs people are satisfied about the contents. If you don't want to engage the professional packers, you can take your own tape and string and do the sealing up yourself. But you will have to brave frowns and grumbles from the packagers.

BEGGARS

Beggars come in every age, shape and size in Morocco. They are part and parcel of Islamic societies, in which giving alms is a religious duty. Mothers without husbands seem to make up the biggest lot of beggars in Morocco, the blind and deformed are another major group. Most Moroccans give to beggars at different times, but they don't give to every beggar they see, and when they do give it is usually only the very smallest coins, those in denominations of less than a dirham. Moroccans offer money to beggars in what may seem to be an impersonal and condescending way, often without even making eye contact, but this is in fact what beggars expect, and Westerners who give friendlier or more personal treatment may find that they become the favourite of one or another beggar, to the point that the beggar harasses them. So you will probably find it better in the long run to use the Moroccan approach when you offer money.

It is offensive and socially unacceptable to rudely turn away a beggar. They are best dismissed with any of a few stock religious phrases, such as *allah iâounik* (God help you) or *allah isehhal* (God make things easy for you).

You should distinguish, however, between genuine beggars and those who make a living or sport out of asking foreigners for money. This is a very unfortunate habit among young boys and young men. Their numbers are such that you may become wary of any native stranger who approaches; you can easily get the idea that the average Moroccan on the street envisions his encounter with you as one that will end with a transfer of funds from your pocket to his. These opportunists differ from beggars in several respects. They approach you rather than waiting for you to walk past them; they use French and even English, rather than Arabic; some get right to the point of naming the amount they want and others preface the request with a hard luck story. None deserves encouragement.

PEDDLERS

Itinerant peddlers are everywhere in Morocco. Their favourite circuits are residential neighbourhoods, where they call out their wares from the street, and cafés, where they hawk their merchandise from table to table. Any purchase made from one of them is strictly without warranty, so examine carefully before you buy. Haggling is mandatory, and the price should be considerably lower than you would pay in a shop. If you know you are not interested in something coming around, don't even make eye contact with the seller, as any sign of attention will be taken as interest.

SHOESHINE BOYS (AND MEN)

Those who would shine your shoes for you are ubiquitous in Morocco. It is a job for men and boys, never for women and girls, but women may well be approached by shoeshiners if they are wearing shinable shoes.

If you want your shoes to be shined, by all means engage one of these itinerant polishers. It's a good idea to agree on a price first. You can haggle if you wish; you shouldn't have to pay more than five dirhams, and Moroccan men often simply give what they think the job is worth afterwards without getting into a dispute about it.

If you don't feel that you need a shoeshine, which will very often be the case, dismiss the shiner politely, and repeatedly if necessary. The best way to avoid being approached by shoeshiners is to wear sandals or tennis shoes.

FOOD AND BEVERAGES

'Four things are necessary before a nation can develop a great cuisine. The first is an abundance of fine ingredients—a rich land. The second is a variety of cultural influences. Third, a great civilisation—if a country has not had its day in the sun, its cuisine will probably not be great. Last, the existence of a refined palace life—without the demands of a cultivated court the imaginations of a nation's cooks will not be challenged. Morocco, fortunately, is blessed with all four.'
—Paula Wolfert, *Couscous and Other Foods of Morocco*

MOROCCANS ENJOY A FABLED CUISINE, unique and rich in variety. The best traditional cooking tends to be quite labour-intensive, taking for granted the availability of women for work in the kitchen. Fortunately, however, many dishes can also be prepared quite easily.

The variety and complexity of dishes notwithstanding, raw materials for Moroccan cooking tend to be fairly standardised and available in all parts of the country. This doesn't mean there is no escape from Moroccan cuisine for foreigners who long for a taste of home. All cities have a French-style *marché* where imported foods, or local imitations of them, are available. But if you live in a village or the countryside, you may have to adapt your diet to some degree; some items such as cheese, good quality rice, wet fish and black tea, for example, are not generally available in rural Morocco.

As for cooking, you can do it yourself or let your maid do it, if you have one; female domestic helpers are nearly always dependable cooks. If you're a man living alone, your neighbours may think it quite strange for you to do your own cooking. A Moroccan man who lives alone very often has an arrangement with neighbours to do his cooking for him, in exchange for the cost of the food and some nominal fee or other compensation.

EATING IN MOROCCO: WHAT AND WHEN

Moroccans generally follow a standard three-meals-a-day plan. Following is a look at the general pattern, within which there are infinite variations.

Breakfast (l-ftour)

A light meal usually starts the day. Served with coffee or mint tea (more about this in the following pages), the bare minimum for breakfast is bread, with condiments of olive oil or butter, and apricot preserves, all of which are produced in abundance in Morocco. Other kinds of bread that may turn up on the breakfast table are *sfenj*, deliciously fried, yeast-raised doughnuts; *baghrir*, very thin, porous, crumpet-like pancakes; *milwi*, rather oily, thick, heavy pancakes; *rziza*, a long, spun-out version of *milwi*, made with spaghetti-like threads of dough shaped into flat cakes; and *harsha*, an unleavened, semolina-based oily bread. A city café breakfast may include French-style croissant, *petit pain*, or *pain chocolat*, all of which are just as good as the ones you buy in Paris, but a whole lot cheaper.

Hot or cold cereals don't figure much in Moroccan breakfasts, aside from *sikuk*, a mixture of *cous-cous* and buttermilk. A more substantial breakfast may include eggs cooked in olive oil and cumin.

As you would expect, breakfast is eaten shortly after getting up in the morning.

Lunch (la-ghda)

Lunch is the main meal of the day, and the heaviest. The minimum 'lunch hour' is in fact two hours long, and most businesses shut for three or even four hours in the middle of the day, to allow time for lunch and a nice siesta. Schools let out from noon to two o'clock; businesses shut from around noon until three or four in the afternoon. Nearly everyone goes home for lunch, or goes to someone's house, so there are in effect four 'rush hours' in cities: in the morning, evening, and two in midday.

The most typical lunch dishes, *tajin* and *cous-cous*, were discussed in Chapter Four: Socialising on page 96..

The preparation of *cous-cous* tends to be fairly standard everywhere, with seasonal vegetables and red meat or fowl. *Tajins* offer more variety but there are a handful of delicious classics that you will probably be served from time to time, and may want to learn to cook yourself. These include:

- chicken with preserved lemon and olives
- lamb with prunes, quince or artichoke hearts
- *kefta* (spiced ground meat) and egg

On very special occasions, a Moroccan specialty dish called *pastilla* (pronounced bas-TI-a) may be served. It is a multi-layered, flaky pastry, usually filled with pigeon, scrambled egg and ground nuts, topped with cinnamon and powdered sugar.

Another dish for grand occasions is *meshwi*, or roasted meat. Lambs or calves are roasted whole, or in very large pieces, often stuffed with *cous-cous* or other fillings.

Supper (l-âsha)

This is a light meal and may be served anytime from 6:00 pm onwards, often not until quite late, even just before bedtime. At the minimum, it consists of *harira*, a rich stew-like soup whose ingredients vary depending on what's available, served with bread. For stronger appetites, lunch leftovers may be served, or if guests are present at an evening meal, a lunch-type menu may be substituted.

Snacks

People who eat a late supper often take a snack break in the afternoon, perhaps around 4:00 or 5:00 pm, that includes coffee or tea, and some breakfast breads, such as *milwi* or *baghrir*.

BEVERAGES

Morocco is hot for long periods of the year, and happily, it offers a wide variety of liquid refreshments to suit nearly every taste. We start with the simplest and work our way up.

Water

Tap water, jokingly called 'Sidi Robinet' (*robinet* is French for tap) is drinkable in most parts of the country, and quite good in mountain towns. However, you will be doing your system a favour by slowly introducing Moroccan microbes to it. Start out your stay with bottled water, which is cheap and widely available. Sidi Harazem is the leading brand, but tastes quite flat and minerally, which Moroccans think is quite healthful. Sidi Ali is also popular, and tastes just like you probably want water to taste, i.e. like nothing at all.

Gerrab, the water sellers, are a common sight in Morocco, especially in crowded public places such as *souqs* and bus terminals. Typically, they dress in outlandishly colourful garb and wide-brimmed hats. They carry water in hide bags or large earthenware jars and sell by the cup, which may be of brass or pitch-lined clay (the pitch gives a slight flavour to the water which some find desirable). Sometimes, they advertise their water as having come from a particular spring, which you can believe or not, as you wish. Their most common cry is "*a-ma baird!*" (cold water). When nothing else is available, it hits the spot, provided you don't mind drinking from a common cup. The price is minimal, a few riyals.

Morocco also bottles its own brand of naturally carbonated water, Oulmes (pronounced WOL-mess), which is widely available and quite delicious.

Soft Drinks

All major international brands of carbonated drinks are available, as well as some Moroccan ones. These are popular in cafés, and are also often served at home when entertaining. There are, however, no diet drinks available. It is a favourite pastime of Moroccan men to order a soft drink in a café, feel the bottle when it arrives at the table, and reject it for not being cold enough. Note that Coke is called Coka.

Morocco bottles its own grape, orange and grapefruit juice, under the Sun Sous brand. All are quite concentrated and sweet.

Hard Drinks

Islam forbids the drinking of alcoholic beverages, but they are nonetheless widely available in Morocco. There are numerous bars in French-built parts of cities, but almost all are dives. Villages usually have a shop or two that sell beer and wine, often surreptitiously, since one who openly displays a liking for drink invites *hshuma*. Hours of opening at such shops are entirely unpredictable and undependable, but shops that sell beer and wine in cities keep regular hours. Hard liquor is all imported, very expensive and confined mostly to foreigners' commissaries and the haunts of the urban bourgeoisie.

Morocco limits the importation of beer and wine, so if you have a taste for these, you will want to sample the local varieties. There are a handful of bottled beers, all indistinguishable and tasting like a slightly weak American beer. Viniculture is widespread in Morocco, particularly in the Middle Atlas region, and a number of wines are produced for local consumption and export.

Moroccan vintners have yet to capture the praise or even the notice of international oenophiles, but they are trying, and have recently introduced a limited number of vintage labels. Moroccan wine can vary greatly from year to year and even from bottle to bottle, but a few varieties have distinguished themselves as standards. Vieux Papes (red) is the best known standard table wine. Guerouane, in red, rosé and gris, from the region of Meknes, is dependably good. Valpiere is an acceptable white wine. Toulal, one of the new varieties also from the Meknes area, has received favourable reviews from locals. Finally there is Doumi (red)—some of the cheapest, vilest rotgot you are ever likely to taste, and sold, tellingly, in plastic bottles.

Hot Drinks
Coffee
Morocco has excellent coffee. Very good quality espresso is served in nearly all cafés, even those in the smallest villages. Cities have coffee shops where several varieties of imported beans are available and ground on the spot. Coffee served at home is also quite good, and is often flavoured with cinnamon, cardamom, black pepper, ginger and other spices.

Being such avid coffee drinkers, Moroccans recognise several gradations in the degree to which coffee is diluted with milk. The names of these, which you will find convenient to know when ordering in cafés, are as follows.

Description	French Name	Arabic Name
black	*café noir* *café express*	*qahua kahela*
with a spot of milk	*café cassé*	*qahua mhersa*
half coffee, half milk	—	*nus-nus*
standard coffee with milk	*café au lait* *café crème*	*qahua ou halib*
mostly milk with a little coffee	—	*halib mhers*
steamed milk	*lait chaud*	*halib skhoun*

Moroccans always sweeten their coffee, and are repulsed by the idea of drinking it without sugar. Hot sweetened milk is also a popular beverage.

Tea

Moroccans drink green tea, flavoured with mint and heavily sweetened. This drink, which the locals call simply *atai* (the general word for tea), is the national beverage. It is the very minimum offered to a guest, whether in a home or a shop (where it may be offered in the interest of getting you to spend more time and/or money there), and Moroccans tend to drink it all day long, at every opportunity they get. It is in fact quite refreshing, and also temporarily calms the appetite. Foreigners often find it too sweet for their taste, but efforts to persuade a host to lay off the sugar are usually unavailing. In cafés, tea is sometimes served with sugar on the side, so you can decide for yourself how sweet to make it.

The green tea that is the basis of this drink is sold in several grades, marked from one to five stars, five being the best and most expensive. Except among the very poor, three star is used at home for everyday use. This five-star rating system tends to spill over into areas of life, and anything described as *khamsa njoum* (five stars) is the very best.

The common variety mint used in tea is grown all over Morocco. Here too, Moroccans recognise subtle distinctions in quality and flavour associated with different areas of the country that are probably lost on the foreigner. Mint is always sold fresh, and small stands selling fragrant mint, parsley and coriander are a familiar site in every corner of the country.

Two other herb teas are seasonally available in Morocco: *shiba* (absinthe), which is preferred in cold weather, and *louiza* (verbena). These are also made by adding the fresh leaves of the plant to sweetened green tea.

Black tea, usually Lipton, is available in city marchés and some cafés. It goes by the name *thé noir*, or *atai keḥal*.

Speciality Drinks

Cafés and occasionally street vendors sell some other drinks that you may want to try. These include:

- *ḥalib b-lluz*: Milk, almonds and sugar, puréed in a blender.
- fresh squeezed orange juice: available in many cafés and from street vendors, though the latter have very primitive facilities for washing used glasses. Moroccans often add sugar.
- *lben*: This is genuine buttermilk, curdled by shaking in a container made from a cow's or sheep's stomach. It is delicious, but has been known to wreak havoc in

foreigners' intestines, so don't drink it unless you know the milk it comes from is quite fresh.

FOODS TO BEFRIEND

Morocco offers a well-stocked pantry of delicious food. You'll find a lot of things there that you're already familiar with, but also a lot that's new. The following will help put you in the know about the Moroccan food scene.

Fruits and Nuts

Everything is available in its season. In spring, you'll find apricots, medlars, cherries, strawberries, kiwis and peaches; melons in summer; figs, pomegranates and grapes in late summer and autumn; and in winter, oranges and mandarins. Bananas and nuts (almonds, walnuts, peanuts) are available the year round. There is very little produce imported into Morocco, so what is out of season may be unavailable.

Vegetables

Potatoes, tomatoes and onions are good the year round. In midwinter, there is sometimes a lack of variety in vegetables, with only rooty things available. At other times of year, there is an abundance of everything: squashes, pumpkins, fava and green beans, quinces, eggplants, peppers, artichokes (cheap enough in summer to eat only the hearts) and more.

Olives and Oils

Olives are cured in several uniquely Moroccan varieties, and are one of the principal passions of foodies in Morocco. Moroccan olive oil is so rich and fragrant you can eat it plain with bread. Argan oil comes from the fruit of the argan tree that grows only in an area west of Marrakech. It has a unique flavour, somewhat reminiscent of olive or walnut oil, and is good in salad dressing.

Spices and Herbs

Standard Moroccan spices are cumin, ground coriander seed, ginger (sold in whole, dried roots), cinnamon, paprika, hot red pepper, turmeric, anise seed, sesame and black pepper.

Genuine *zafran ḥurr* (saffron) is available, but Moroccans also use a cheap yellow food colourant that they also call saffron. A mixture of spices called *ras-al-ḥanut* is what gives many dishes their 'Moroccan' taste. It is available in *souqs* and *ḥanuts*. Parsley and coriander leaf (sometimes called cilantro in the United States) are used in almost every dish, and are sold fresh everywhere. *Zâṭer* is a herb in the thyme/oregano family, slightly reminiscent of both.

Dairy Products
Dairy products don't figure in large quantities in the Moroccan diet. However, butter and *smen*, which is butter preserved with herbs and spices, often made from ewe's milk, are both used commonly. Fruit-flavoured yogurt in serving-sized containers is locally produced under the Danone label. Fresh milk is sold in half-litre paper and plastic cartons. In villages, raw (unpasteurized) milk can usually be bought from a roving milkman, with no guarantee that it is germ-free. *Lben* is also a specialty of the village and countryside.

STREET FOOD
As elsewhere in the world, food is a favourite accompaniment to life on the street and is available in ready-to-eat form almost everywhere you go in Morocco. A few paragraphs can't do justice to the rich variety of street food in Morocco; rather, the following represents those things that should not be missed.

Nuts, Grains, Beans
Children are the most frequent consumers of these treats, sold cheaply in paper cones made from recycled notebook pages. Roasted almonds, chickpeas, peanuts, squash and sunflower seeds are the most common. These are also sold in city cafés by itinerant vendors who offer you a free sample, hoping you'll buy a few dirhams' worth.

Pastries
Perhaps the least disparaged vestige of the colonial period is the rich variety of pastry shops and cafés, whose windows

showcase exquisite confections that could easily stand up to the competition in Paris. These are much more a feature of cities than villages and are somewhat expensive by Moroccan standards, but the price usually does not deter the sweet-toothed foreigner. There are also a number of native Moroccan sweets, similar to biscuits, that are served in homes for special occasions, or for afternoon snacks.

Mâqoda

These are spicy, yellow, fried potato dumplings and are completely addictive. You find them more in the countryside than the city. Ordered by the piece and served with bread.

Brochettes

Grilled meats, cooked over charcoal, are served at sidewalk braziers throughout Morocco. Varieties are steak-like bits of meat, *kefta* (spiced ground meat) and offal interspersed with pieces of suet. These are usually served unskewered and with a chunk of bread and some hot sauce, along with salt and cumin, the standard Moroccan table condiments. Ordered by the skewer.

RESTAURANTS

There are two kinds of restaurants in Morocco: the familiar kind, where a waiter takes your order from a menu; and a simpler variety, where only a handful of dishes are available, often only at lunchtime, and sitting down is tantamount to saying that you want some of whatever is on offer. The former are found only in cities and large towns; the latter are found everywhere, often near the bus stop or the *souq*, for they cater mostly to those who aren't near enough home to eat there.

The larger cities have a variety of restaurants specialising in various international cuisines. They are patronised heavily by foreigners, but also by urban Moroccans, especially the wealthy. They are reasonably priced by Western standards but expensive for the average Moroccan. French cuisine is probably the most readily available, even more common than traditional Moroccan, but you will also find Chinese and

Middle Eastern restaurants. International fast food chains are now appearing in Rabat and Casablanca.

The simpler village restaurants, though often quite primitive in decor and amenities, serve delicious, authentic Moroccan food, and are quite economical. They are less often patronised by foreigners, and you may find yourself the object of considerable curiosity if you visit one, but don't let this deter you from sampling the local fare.

RAMADAN (RAMEDAN)

Ramadan is the month in the Islamic calendar during which true believers past the age of puberty fast from dawn to dusk, abstaining also from smoking and sex. Owing to the shorter lunar year which is the basis of the Islamic calendar, the month recedes through the solar year. In 2000, it coincided roughly with the month of December, and starts about 11 days earlier each year thereafter. A complete cycle takes about 33 years.

To the non-Muslim foreigner in Morocco, Ramadan will appear most readily as a complete upheaval in the normal daily routine, especially as regards meals and meal times, hence its treatment in this chapter. Foreigners are not expected to observe the fast, but it is impossible not to make concessions to it, since the whole country is run on a different timetable during Ramadan. Many restaurants do not open at all, markets open late and cafés are shut throughout the day.

Moroccans seen eating or drinking during daylight hours in Ramadan are subject to arrest. Each year, there are a handful of exemplary diners of this kind whose cases are publicised to remind the populace of the consequences. In reality, surreptitious eating and smoking are rampant during Ramadan, especially among young men. As a foreigner, your home may provide the cover for such clandestine munching and puffing, if you are amenable. If the perpetrators are your friends, there is no danger in letting them eat with you; being an accessory to such activity is not a crime.

It is difficult to say whether Ramadan is a greater ordeal in the summer, when Moroccans spend the day parched and dreaming of a glass of water, or in the winter, when empty stomachs make it impossible to ever feel very warm. Whatever time of year it falls, it is an ordeal to be endured. In the daytime, tempers flare at the least provocation, arguments erupt over trivia (even more so than during normal times) and 'infidel' foreigners may be particularly singled out for abuse. Indeed, many foreigners make arrangements to be away from Morocco during Ramadan. No seasoned expatriate who employs Moroccans expects to accomplish very much during this time.

In the evening and at night, however, Ramadan is a completely different experience. There is a festive, holiday atmosphere. Moroccans who live abroad often come home during Ramadan just in order to be with family at this time, and hospitality is at its peak. People pour into the streets after the first evening meal (called, appropriately enough, breakfast) and promenade, greeting their friends and enjoying the effects of a satisfied appetite.

Meals

All activities restricted during Ramadan are allowed to commence the moment the sun goes down. This is signalled by the firing of a cannon or the sounding of a siren in every hamlet, village, town and city in the country. Television also advertises the times of sunrise and sunset, and gives the signal to chow down.

Breakfast (*l-ftour*, as in ordinary times) normally consists of *harira*, a delicious, tomato-based soup served with lemon wedges, dates, milk and a sickly-sweet pastry called *shebbakia*. Some time later, another meal is served, called *l-âsha*, the usual name for supper. Finally, the last meal of the Ramadan day is *s-sehour*, sometimes served quite late at night. Either *l-âsha* or *s-sehour* may be the main meal of the day, a lunch-type affair with several dishes and courses, though even more lavish than normal, with many expensive dishes that are traditionally prepared only during Ramadan.

In between these meals, there is general socialising, both at home and in public. Cafés do big business, and the streets are thick with promenaders.

After *l-âsha*, people may nap for some time. Late in the night, a herald passes through the streets sounding a trumpet, reminding people it is time to eat yet again, before everyone finally goes to bed.

The fast begins again the next day, when there is enough daylight to distinguish a black thread from a white thread in the hand. Few are actually about to make the test, as the rule is to sleep as late as possible, thus shortening the time until breakfast in the evening.

The month of fasting is considered the holiest time of year to Muslims, marking the occasion when the archangel Gabriel transmitted the Koran from Allah to Mohammed. For believers, there are activities in the mosque every night of Ramadan, and on the 27th night of Ramadan, called *lilt l-qader*, the entire Koran is recited in the mosque. One who dies on this night is said to catch a glimpse of the open doors of Paradise and go right in.

All those who are ill or travelling, as well as women who are pregnant, lactating or menstruating are not required to observe the fast during Ramadan. However, they must make up the days they missed before Ramadan falls again by fasting on days of their choosing.

CULTURE AND TRAVEL

CHAPTER 7

'When the soap is used up, the washerwoman rejoices.'
'If you want happiness, keep from idle talk and just rest.'
—Moroccan Proverbs

TIME TO RELAX

This chapter looks at features of life in Morocco that have mostly to do with your leisure time. For that very reason, it is one of the most important chapters in the book. A successful life in Morocco is one that enables you to release tensions in a way that doesn't insult or completely deny the Moroccan social environment. Besides that, it is mostly in your spare time that you will develop sustaining and fulfilling relationships with Moroccans, and this activity will make or break your success in Morocco. So if you're not getting everything from your work that you expected to get, or if it's not going as well as you want it to, that may not be an indication that you have to work harder; very often it's an indication that you have to back off a little and gain a new perspective.

A common feature of foreigners' lives in Morocco is what we might call 'fishbowlitis': the tendency to feel that you are unable to escape from a small, enclosed world where you are always being stared at, talked about or even followed. This is no imaginary phenomenon. You may hear of countries where foreigners are left to fend for themselves, but Morocco is not one of them. Moroccans are quite curious by nature, and hospitable and welcoming of foreigners to a degree you may never have experienced before. They are not going to leave you alone, and even if you don't cultivate close relationships with them, they are still very curious about you. If you live in a town or village where there are few or no foreigners present, the curiosity will be even greater. You may find that you are a spectacle every time you walk down the main street—for it is not considered rude to stare at something or someone curious in Morocco, it is considered normal.

Therefore, as our first task on the road to relaxation, we look at how to get away from it all, and that can often mean no more than taking a day or weekend trip away from where you live to a place where no one knows you and you're just another foreigner in the crowd. To do that, you need to know how to get there.

DESTINATIONS

Foreigners in Morocco, unless they are working on development projects in rural areas, tend to live in cities, and those who don't often pay regular visits for rest, recreation and goodies not available in their villages. Among the many options for a getaway, maybe you'll want to visit a new city in another part of the country, or perhaps even the desert, for a change of pace, or to escape from the 'fishbowl' existence foreigners may face. But where do you want to go?

To help with the decision, here are thumbnail sketches of some of the largest Moroccan cities. Morocco has two cities with populations of over a million, and ten other cities with more than 100,000 inhabitants. About one third of Moroccans live in these dozen cities. In cases where the Arabic name of the city is either different or differently pronounced than the English name, it is given in parentheses.

Casablanca (Dar l-Bida)

With three million plus inhabitants, 'Caza' (as the locals call it) is by far Morocco's biggest city. Until the protectorate, it was a fishing village, but the French built a harbour there and developed it—thus it has none of the charms of Morocco's ancient walled cities. It is a far cry from the 1940s film which made it famous, and those hopeful of finding romantic adventure here would be well advised to avoid it. It is home to some of Morocco's richest and poorest; its massive sprawl daily attracts migrants from the countryside seeking their fortune. They often end up in one of the many *bidonvilles* (shanty towns) that dot the city. Morocco's main international airport is outside Casablanca. Its other quite recent claim to fame is a gigantic Islamic cultural centre and mosque, the largest in the world outside of those in Saudi Arabia that host pilgrims. It was built with contributions from all Moroccans, even those living abroad, who were tracked down and asked to cough up. But today, Moroccans are proud to point to the Mosquée Hassan II as one of the Islamic world's great monuments.

Rabat-Salé

Rabat is a world away from most of Morocco's cities. It enjoys a very pleasant, Mediterranean climate, and as the national capital, it is something of a showpiece; its streets are kept incomparably cleaner than those in other Moroccan cities, and no riffraff is allowed to roam the streets, as the king is often in residence. It is probably the most Europeanised city in Morocco; its *medina* is small and unexceptional, though it is a main centre for the carpet trade. Moroccans in Rabat are almost totally inured to the presence of foreigners, and thus foreigners often feel most at home here; they are little stared at or accosted by guides. There are also dozens of very good restaurants here, catering to all tastes, and reasonably priced hotels are plentiful.

Across the river from Rabat and reachable by car, bus or ferry is Salé (*Sla*), which shares local government with Rabat but is in every other way a different city. It is older, slower and more traditional; its medina is larger and more exotic than Rabat's, and mostly ignored by tourists, making it an interesting shopping place for those who know about it. Foreigners are less common here, but not unwelcome. Salé is one of Morocco's three centres for the manufacture of pottery.

Fez (Fas)

Located in a valley between the Rif and Middle Atlas mountains, Fez is regarded as the intellectual capital of Morocco, and *Fassin*, natives of Fez, enjoy a sort of mystique,

The Hassan II Mosque, one of the largest and most spectacular religious monuments in the world.

being regarded as the highest rung of Moroccan society. Entering the *medina* in Fez is as close as one can come to time travel. Its narrow, winding passageways are too narrow for cars, and goods are carried in and out on pack animals as they have been for centuries. The Qairouin mosque and university, in the heart of Fas I-Bali, the oldest and biggest of Fez's *medinas*, was founded in the eighth century. It has been an active centre for Islamic studies since then, and is a splendid example of ancient Islamic architecture.

Fez is also home to many of Morocco's finest traditional craftsmen: carpets, leather goods, woodcarving, pottery and brass goods are all made here, and a walk through the *medina* will take you by many artisans, young and old, contentedly at their work. Unless your appearance is such that you can pass for a Moroccan, you will not be able to enjoy any of this alone, as the 'guide' problem in Fez is nearly epidemic. Many of the guides are students who can be engaged quite reasonably, and are excellent sources of information about the town.

Marrakech (Merraksh)

Marrakech shares with Fez the distinction of being one of the most exotic cities in Morocco, indeed, among the most exotic places in the world. It is in the 'red zone', with all walls, houses and public surfaces painted a uniform reddish brown. Marrakech was built up by the Almoravids, one of the Berber dynasties of Moorish times, and it is still very much a Berber city. It is also quite definitely on the beaten tourist track, and except for midsummer, when the beastly heat keeps some of them away, it is always packed with Europeans. If you live in Marrakech, you will become known and the 'guides' will leave you alone; if you are a casual visitor, you will either have to shake them off regularly, or simply engage one.

Oujda

The last outpost before the Algerian border, Oujda is the main metropolitan centre of eastern Morocco. It is unexceptional historically and architecturally, except for a small *medina*. Moneychangers on the street here are ready to change any currency into any other, usually at a rate that compares very favourably with the ones offered in banks. Saidia, north of Oujda on the Mediterranean coast, attracts sun and surf worshippers to its beaches and is an aspiring resort town.

Kenitra (Qnitra)

North-east of Rabat, Kenitra is also an unexceptional city whose main claim to fame was a US military base that closed down many years ago. Now it is expanding as part of Morocco's 'western seaboard' of cities, extending from Casablanca northwards, and is served by commuter trains. A fishing and shipping port provides some jobs.

Tetouan (Tetwan)

In the north of the country on the Mediterranean coast, Tetouan is in the part of Morocco that was under Spanish influence during the colonial period, and thus has a slightly different flavour from the cities further south. Spanish is on a par with French as a second language here, though Rifi Berber is also very commonly heard. Tetouan is mildly notorious as a distribution centre for hashish. If you value your personal security and happiness, you are advised never to engage in any drug dealings in Morocco, as dire consequences of all kinds can easily follow from even expressing interest.

Safi (Asfi)

On the Atlantic coast between Casablanca and Essaouira, Safi is a major port and industrial centre where phosphates, mined on the nearby phosphate plain, are shipped out. Safi also has a petrochemical processing plant. It offers interesting architectural sites from both the Arab and Portuguese epochs of its history, and it is the third of Morocco's three pottery centres (the others being Fez and Salé). There is a sizable foreign community, mostly French.

Meknes

Though steeped in as much history as nearby Fez, Meknes has managed to avoid being the kind of tourist trap that parts of Fez have become, perhaps because many travellers

Throwing a pot in Safi, a major pottery centre in Morocco.

are only getting through it to reach Fez. It has a modest *medina* and several fascinating historical sites, including an underground dungeon built by and for Christian slaves and prisoners, and the ruins of the stables of Moulay Ismaïl, said to have accommodated 12,000 horses. There is also a most pleasant new town where foreigners are pretty well left to their own devices. In summer, Meknes tends to be marginally cooler than Fez (which is an oven), and thus may prove a more attractive destination for those seeking a city break in the Middle Atlas region.

Agadir

Located in the far south on the Atlantic coast, Agadir is the tourist trap par excellence, and is the destination of many package holidaymakers from Europe, especially Germans, who seem to thrive there. It was destroyed by an earthquake in 1960 and built up again. There is nothing very old there, and everything is new, including multistorey beachfront hotels. It is very little like the Morocco one finds anywhere else in the country; indeed, it is in many ways very little like Morocco at all, and thus may serve as an escape for those who need one.

Beni Mellal

On the Tadla Plain, a large agricultural area in central Morocco, Beni Mellal can probably claim to be Morocco's most up-and-coming city. It is an agricultural centre, it has a new university and there has recently been some development of light industry. It has no historical claims to fame, but there are scenic areas in the nearby countryside.

Tangier (Tanja)

Before and during the years of the protectorate, Tangier was an International Zone, administered by more than 20 foreign powers. This has left a legacy in the popular imagination as a place of mystery and intrigue. It is in fact not much more mysterious than any other Moroccan city. Standing at the Strait of Gibraltar, it is the point of entry to Morocco for nearly all tourists travelling by rail, and most European rail passes permit free travel in Morocco.

If you enter Tangier from Europe, be prepared for the guides that swarm around arriving ferries. If you arrive in Tangier by rail from elsewhere in Morocco, the onslaught is less daunting. A short walk from the rail station or the ferry port will bring you to dozens of hotels, so you needn't worry about finding one, despite what the guides may tell you. The guide plague aside, Tangier is a charming city to walk around in and it has an exotic but manageable *medina*. The climate is pleasant most of the year round, though winters can be damp and cool.

With the exception of Agadir, Beni Mellal and Tetouan, all of the cities profiled here are reachable by rail. All of them contain universities where Morocco's burgeoning student population is educated.

The Desert

Few people live in the desert and you probably won't either, but don't pass up an opportunity to visit there. You'll find some of the most fantastic scenery and exotic architecture on offer in Morocco. *Qsars*, which are fortified, walled villages somewhat reminiscent of castles, are a regular feature of river valleys and oases. The best months to visit the desert are February and March. The further south you go in Morocco, the hotter and more arid it gets.

Ceuta and Melilla (Sebta and Melilia)

On the subject of getaways, these two cities on the north coast of Morocco deserve mention. They are geographically in Morocco, but politically they belong to Spain. You cross an international border when you enter either city from the

The *qsar*, or fortified villages, like this one at Aït Benhaddou, is typical of architecture in southern Morocco. A stork's nest sits on the corner.

Moroccan side. Ceuta, north of Tetouan, is quite small and crowded, really just a shopping strip with nowhere to park. Melilla, near Nador, is larger and more accommodating, with several good hotels, restaurants and parks.

Though Moroccans are often hassled by border guards at the crossings, foreigners can enter Ceuta and Melilla easily. They are popular destinations for a number of reasons. They are tax- and duty-free ports offering excellent shopping, especially for electronic equipment and gadgets; both provide ferry service to the Spanish mainland with different boats serving Algeciras, Malaga and Almeira; and they offer a low-cost escape from Morocco, for once you cross the border, you really are in another country. The architecture, food, language and people are all different.

If you are in Morocco only on a tourist visa, you cannot stay longer than three months. A day trip to Ceuta or Melilla constitutes leaving Morocco, and when you re-enter, you have another three months as a legal tourist in Morocco. This is another popular reason for foreigners to visit these cities. However, if you have official residency in Morocco (a *carte de séjour*), it is not necessary for you to leave every three months.

Border crossings can be either quick and easy or slow and frustrating, depending entirely on the highly changeable moods of the border guards on the Moroccan side. There is also a large seasonal variation in traffic across these borders. August can be particularly slow, as many Moroccans who live in Europe return home for their holidays. Any time you go, you should be prepared for a long wait at the border, often an hour or more; then if you get through quickly, you can be very pleasantly surprised. Before you can even think of getting through, you must fill out an exit visa form. On good days, you will find a stack of these at the border crossing enquiry window. If you don't see any about, and find no one at the window, make your presence known and try to get things under way. After you have filled out the card, you must surrender it along with your passport to the person at the window. The stamped passport will come back to you after an interval of a few minutes or a couple of hours, again depending on how the guards feel that day. Take a good book to read! Officials on the Spanish side usually ask only to see your documentation, and then wave you on.

If you return to Morocco quite heavily laden with goods you bought in Spain, you may find your load lightened on the way back in by the aforementioned guards. Let this be a caution to you as you feast your eyes on the many wonderful things to buy in Ceuta and Melilla. There doesn't seem to be any official information on exactly what and how much of anything you can bring in. If you are carrrying what seems to be an ordinary amount of luggage, chances are you will be waved through.

Guides

Tourist guides are a kind of plague in Morocco, sometimes infesting even the tiniest hamlet where foreigners appear. The typical guide professes to be a student, usually a university student (one wonders when they ever attended classes), must be in need of your cash to buy books and the like. They are all purported natives of the places they offer to show you around, and usually they are friends of the shopkeepers whose emporia they steer you into. They are all very eager to practise their English and to make a foreign friend. They are all males.

Foreigners' general experience of tourist guides is unfortunately somewhat negative. Thus you are urged to respond to the guides in a way that will not leave you feeling abused and abandoned. Here are a few tips:

- Don't be bothered by guides in the town or city where you live. They may trouble you at first, but they will very soon get to know who you are and leave you alone. News of foreign residents seems to fly through the guide circuit, and it may surprise you how fast you go from hopeful target to old furniture.

- If you want the services of a guide in a city or town where you are not a resident, wait for one whom you feel comfortable with to approach you, and engage him on very specific terms: that is, let him know what you want, and what you'll pay. If you wish to use English, don't settle for a guide who doesn't speak it that well unless you wish to provide English lessons as well as his salary. Don't pay him until you are finished, and pay him exactly what you agreed upon, along with a tip if you are pleased with his services.

- If you do not want the services of a guide who approaches you in a city or town where you don't reside, dismiss him as politely but as insistently as you can. Bombard him with logical reasons why you don't require his services, and repeat them as many times as necessary to drive home your point. Do not be rude or aggressive with guides, or your manner will very likely be returned to you with interest.

- Another tactic that may diminish a guide's interest in you is to make it known that you intend to do no shopping. You will be a much less attractive mark for a guide who stands to make no commissions from your purchases.

- There are many advantages to going about with one or more Moroccan friends. You will be approached by guides much less frequently, and your Moroccan friend will probably be able to dismiss those that do approach much more effectively and skillfully than you could dream of doing.

- If you are being relentlessly hassled by a guide and are unable to shake him off, you can approach a policeman with your problem, but be aware that you are probably putting the guide in for some pretty rough treatment at the hands of the authorities. Because of the economic importance of tourism, the government takes a dim view of guides who hassle tourists.

LEISURE TIME IN MOROCCO

So far we've concentrated on physically getting away from it all, but most of your leisure time in Morocco will probably be spent closer to home, if not actually in it. Here is a rundown of what foreigners and Moroccans find to do with themselves when they are not working.

Café Society

One of the great pleasures of visiting or living in Morocco is its cafés. Happily, café life is available to both men and women, for though Moroccan women do not frequent cafés (this is starting to change in cities), foreign women are not out of place there. A foreign woman alone in a café will attract unwanted attention, but in the company of a friend or friends of either sex, chances are she will be left alone.

Nearly every settlement in Morocco from small village to thriving metropolis includes cafés. Modelled very much on the French style, they offer tables both inside and on the street when weather permits. Unlike French cafés, only a small number of those in Morocco serve alcoholic drinks. All of them serve espresso coffee, mint tea, and other drinks (see Chapter Six: Food and Beverages on page 173 for a discussion of these). Moroccan men like to go to cafés alone or with their friends. Most tend to have a favourite where they hang out regularly and are well known.

It is usual for café patrons to spend a great deal of time nursing a single cup of coffee or small pot of tea. The beverage seems not to be the *sine qua non* of a café visit, rather the ambience is. Moroccans also make what Westerners think are excessive demands on the waiter: calling him over to bring water, being quite picky about the temperature or quality of drinks, snapping their fingers peremptorily when service is needed—but this is all part of the game of social stratification, and waiters, though generally a rather dour-faced lot, don't protest. It is customary to tip café waiters. Ten percent is thought quite generous, and if you visit a particular café frequently, regular tipping will assure you of good service.

Though many cafés offer some kind of food service, especially in the morning when fresh croissants and *petit pain* are available, it is acceptable in some cafés to bring food with you to eat along with the beverage you order. Thus you may want to pick up a *sfenj* (doughnut) or some other food for your breakfast and take it along to the café. It is not advisable, however, to do this at a posh pastry and coffee shop on a smart boulevard in a city.

The Evening Promenade

When weather permits, Moroccans love to go for a stroll in the evening hours, sometime between 5:00 and 9:00 pm or so. (During Ramadan, the promenade slot starts right after breakfast and may go on till late at night). The most popular places for walking are the tree-lined boulevards in a *ville nouvelle*, but even villages that were bypassed by French development have a main street for people to stroll up and down. Both men and women come out to enjoy the evening air, meet their friends, and perhaps enjoy a drink in a café. The promenade is a very social affair; people dress to look

The evening promenade: enjoying a pleasant stroll down Avenue Mohammed V in Rabat.

their best, and those that are unattached spend some time checking out others in similar circumstances.

The Public Baths (Hemmam)

Most Moroccans do not have bathtubs and showers in their homes. Even those who do make regular visits to the public baths. Moroccans feel, and quite rightly so, that this is the only place to get really clean. A visit to the public bath fulfils several needs—it gets you clean, it is very relaxing, it is a very satisfying ritual, and in the winter, it gets you warm. The public baths are also a very social place, particularly for women: it is one of the few places where they can enjoy each other's company in the absence of men, though women normally take their young children to the *hemmam* with them.

A *hemmam* may be for men only or for women only. More commonly, it is divided in two parts with completely separate entrances for women and men. As another option, men and women will use the same baths at different hours, typically women during the day, and men in the evening. Foreigners are something of a novelty in a *hemmam*, so you may want to go there first with a Moroccan, or with another foreigner who knows the ropes. If you visit the same *hemmam* regularly, you will become known there and even expected.

You'll need to take with you a towel and a change of clothes at least. Most people also take soap and shampoo, but many *hemmam* sell these in one-shot doses. It is also usual to take some device for scraping the skin, which may be a pumice stone, a loofah or any number of other devices used for this which are sold all over Morocco. A cup or small scoop is useful for dipping water out of buckets. Finally, you may want to take combs and hairbrushes, shaving accessories, a toothbrush or other toiletries. Women go to the *hemmam* laden with enough accessories to last a weekend by the look of it, but one is assured that everything they take has a purpose.

Behaviour in the *hemmam* is steeped in ritual and is perhaps more closely circumscribed by rules of propriety than any other activity you are likely to participate in in Morocco. It's probably not going too far to say that you oughtn't do anything in a *hemmam* you haven't seen someone else do first.

At some _hemmam_, tickets are sold at the door, which you then hand over to a person inside. At others, you pay when you finish. The price is quite nominal, about 100 riyals (5 dirhams), usually slightly more for women on the theory that they stay so much longer.

The first room inside the street door of a _hemmam_ is a changing room. There are usually benches to sit on and hooks for hanging up your clothes. Here you undress down to your underwear (DON'T take it off, complete nudity is taboo), leaving your clothes where others have done. Do not put your shoes on a bench, put them under it, or on the shoe rack provided. While your clothes will probably not be disturbed, don't tempt fate by leaving the pockets stuffed with riches—leave these at home or at your hotel.

If you see stacks of buckets in the changing room, grab a couple. If the _hemmam_ doesn't seem crowded, treat yourself to three or four, and proceed through the next door.

The business part of _hemmam_ consists of two or three rooms with tiled walls, floor, and ceiling. Each room has a different temperature, the innermost being the hottest, and also the one that has water for you to fill your buckets with. There are normally two cisterns, one of hot and one of cold water. Before you fill your buckets, however, it is customary to stake out your territory: this you do by putting your things down somewhere. This must be done with care, especially if the _hemmam_ is crowded. The main point to observe is, never sit 'downstream' from another bather. The floors of the inner rooms slant towards a drain, and you should sit where you are neither in someone's watershed, nor where your runoff will hit someone already seated. Again, this is a reflection of the pervasive distinction in Moroccan culture between public and private.

By the same token, you must observe propriety in filling your buckets from the cisterns. Water in the cisterns is public; in your buckets, it is private. Thus you should never pour water back into the cisterns from your bucket, as you would be polluting the common source. Similarly, you should not use your left hand to fill buckets from the cistern, or from a common bucket that is used to fill your individual buckets.

Now the buckets. Rinse them out first with a little water from the cistern and pour the water towards the drain. If someone is standing at the cisterns when you get there, they may well fill your buckets for you. This is a common courtesy that you should also extend if you are there when someone else comes. Take your filled buckets back to your bathing site, but before sitting down, rinse your floor space. Though it may not be visibly dirty, this is done as a ritual cleansing of the spot, to remove the residue of the previous bather and make it clean for you.

Now the hard part is over. Sit down and sweat for a while.

Most people do their initial sweat in the hottest room, but if you are unused to sauna or steambath-like temperatures, don't stay in too long. You will notice that people in the *hemmam* do various kinds of stretching exercises, and may give each other massages or help each other with stretching. For sedentary housewives or shopkeepers, this is a way of keeping muscles in tone, taking advantage of the warm temperatures that loosen the body up. Someone may offer to 'work you over' and there is no reason you shouldn't let them, and reciprocate if you wish. If it is another bather, this is offered as a courtesy, but be aware that most baths also have a professional, called a *kias*, who will do the whole massage-scrape-soap routine on you for a fee.

After you have sweated for some time, it is customary to scrape the skin, in order to remove the outermost layer of dead, soiled skin. It comes off in small spaghetti-like threads that can be rinsed off with water from your buckets.

Soap and shampoo come next. In some *hemmam*, you can apply these in whichever room you wish, but in others, soaping up is never done in the hottest room. See what others are doing. If you have to move, find and rinse off a spot in a different room, by the same procedure described earlier. Be careful not to splash anyone else with your suds or water. People who come to a *hemmam* together usually help each other wash as well, especially the hard-to-reach places.

When you are finished, you can return to the changing room, taking your buckets with you if you wish, though you

A man with a towel over his head has just come from the _ḥemmam,_ or public bath, in Sefrou.

needn't. Some people take a half-bucket of water with them to rinse their feet off just before putting on their socks.

After bathing, you will be greeted with _b-sehahatik_ (To your health). The response is _allah iyâtik s-sehah_ (God give you health).

The Cinema

Movie houses in Morocco are male spaces, except for a few posh cinemas in the big cities, usually showing European films, where women may enter unaccompanied by _ḥshuma._ Standard fare in Moroccan cinemas are Indian films, curiously not dubbed or subtitled in any language used in Morocco. There is also a large audience for the kind of international 'junk' films featuring car chases, big guns, martial arts, voluptuous heroines and the like. Low-budget, inane comedies from Europe, what we might call Eurotrash, are also popular. Audiences at these films tend to be young, boisterous males who talk and smoke during the entire feature.

Cinemas showing better quality European and American films, either originally in, dubbed in or subtitled in French, can be found in cities. Audiences in these are slightly more subdued, but smoking is still usually permitted.

A number of cities also offer cinéclubs, private clubs that use a commercial cinema once a week to show films that the club selects: usually Western films in or rendered in French. These clubs offer the best film viewing in Morocco. Membership is usually open to anyone, and fees are modest. The clubs may also offer you a way of meeting like-minded Moroccans. Women are usually as welcome in cinéclubs as men are.

Sports and Games

Rabid enthusiasm for sports, particularly football (soccer) is as common among males in Morocco as in any other country. Most of them follow European and international competitions keenly, especially in the run-up to World Cup competition; familiarity with various teams and even individual players is widespread. Matches are aired on television at least weekly in season. These are then rehashed endlessly in cafés until there is a new match to talk about. Foreign men interested in sports will find ample company in Morocco.

Moroccan boys and men also love to play football, and pick-up games can be found everywhere, particularly at the beach. Almost everyone plays barefoot when weather permits.

There are tennis courts and golf courses in or near most Moroccan cities. Few of them are public, but many have some policy for permitting non-members to use them. Your compatriots in Morocco are the best source of information about these places, as they tend to be heavily patronised by foreigners.

Women's Pastimes

What are the women doing while the men are out enjoying the world? To complete the stereotyped picture, the fact is that they are probably working at some domestic activity. As well as being expert in the expected household occupations—cooking, cleaning and child-rearing—Moroccan women are accomplished in a number of other domestic arts and crafts. Sewing, knitting, embroidery and crocheting are all popular. Foreign women who take an interest in these activities will find it easy to share them with Moroccan women.

Making Music

Accomplished amateur musicians abound in Morocco, and making music is a favourite activity wherever people are gathered, especially at home. Men and women participate equally in singing, although stringed instruments such as the three-stringed *loṭar*, the eleven-stringed *l-âoud*, or the *kamanja* (fiddle) are usually played by men. Men and women both play various percussion instruments resembling drums or tambourines, all made from skins stretched over ceramic or wooden frames. The most popular are the *derbouka*, the *ṭârija* and the *bendir*.

Folk dancing in groups very often accompanies music. Dancing in pairs is usually between members of the same sex. Men and women both perform a uniquely Moroccan hip-gyrating motion which is thought to be quite alluring. Moroccans are quite eager to initiate foreigners into their music and dancing, and it is a pleasant way to spend time together where music is the common language and no other is needed.

THE PRESS, TELEVISION AND RADIO

The Communication Age has definitely come to Morocco, and generally you will not want for printed and electronic information. Here is a summary of what's available.

Newspapers, Magazines and Reading Material

In cities you can buy the *International Herald Tribune* in the evening of the day it's published. The international editions of *Time*, *Newsweek*, and sometimes *The Economist* are also available. Daily newspapers from the English-speaking world are sporadically available at a couple of newsstands in Casablanca and Rabat; the kiosk in the Rabat train station has the best selection of English-language newspapers and magazines.

A monthly English-language newspaper, *The Messenger of Morocco*, written by and for the English-speaking community of Morocco, is published in Fez and is easy to find there, but a little more difficult elsewhere. It carries interesting articles on culture, tourism, leisure and sports.

A wider selection of French and Arabic dailies and weeklies can be found everywhere. Several newspapers in each language are published in Morocco, and newspapers from all over the Arab world, and the Paris dailies are widely available. Other European dailies can be found in large cities a day or so after publication.

There are American Bookstores, affiliated with American Language Centers, in Rabat, Casablanca and Marrakech. They offer a good selection of reference books, fiction

Magazines and newspapers in French, Arabic and the main European languages are widely available in Morocco.

and nonfiction, mostly in paperback. Other independent bookstores specialising in English- language books can be found in Fez, Oujda and Rabat. The English Book Shop on rue Al-Yamama in Rabat, behind the train station, has a good selection of used paperbacks at very reasonable prices.

Subscriptions from abroad are not reliable. If you must read something other than what is listed here, have someone send it to you, or if possible, receive it through your embassy or consulate.

Television

Morocco now boasts two television stations. One is state run, the other nominally independent. Both carry advertising. Programming is very wide-ranging and eclectic: you can study the beautiful calligraphy of the Koran on the screen while it is being chanted, or sample the latest rock videos from Britain and America. Films and soap operas from the Arab world (mostly from Egypt) figure prominently, and other internationally syndicated series, mostly American, are shown weekly. In addition, there are sports matches, nature programs, Moroccan music, news (always with an upbeat, pro-government slant) and all the other things you expect to find on television. There is a fairly even split between programming in French and Arabic. There is very little in English, except the occasionally subtitled film, and of course the rock and rap videos.

Satellite television, which is taking Morocco by storm, has a wide range of English-language programming. It carries the NBC Superchannel, MTV and several European and Middle Eastern channels that offer news and other programs in English.

Radio

A great listening selection is available if you've got a good radio. Either take with you or buy a good quality multi-band radio that has AM (also called medium wave, or MW), FM, long wave (LW) and especially short wave (SW). A wide variety of Moroccan stations broadcast many different programs on AM and FM featuring all the different kinds of Moroccan music (there are more than you would ever imagine) and music from elsewhere in the Arab world, as well as Western popular music. There is a little programming in English, but Arabic and French are the standards. On long wave and short wave, you can pick up stations from around the world, many of which broadcast in English, including Voice of America and the incomparable BBC World Service.

Photography

Islam frowns upon the use of representational images, especially as art. You will notice that no image of the prophet Mohammed exists anywhere. This fact may go some way towards explaining the aversion that Moroccans have to casual picture-taking by tourists. Moroccans don't generally own cameras or many photographs themselves, and the photos they do have are usually rather formal, commemorative shots of some special occasion.

If you wish to show some sensitivity to cultural norms, you shouldn't take someone's picture without asking them first. Doing so is considered rude and it may evoke an aggressive reaction. If you are on the tourist track, don't be surprised if your request to take someone's picture is answered by a request for money from you.

If you are off the beaten tourist track, be even more careful about taking pictures of people. You may arouse the suspicion of the local people, or worse, the authorities. Cameras are rare items in rural Morocco and the idea of taking souvenir photos of what for Moroccans are everyday affairs is very unfamiliar.

You should not photograph any public buildings in Morocco. This means any government buildings and offices, police stations, and offices of the Bank of Morocco. Doing so could result in the seizure of your camera, your film, yourself or the triple-whammy: all of the above. You may, however, photograph your friends and family with such buildings as Parliament or a post office in the background without causing a stir.

Film in widely available in Morocco, though you may not easily find film types used more by professional than casual photographers. Film processing is also available in cities, but is expensive and not always of good quality. Many foreigners choose to buy film with prepaid processing mailers, and send the film for development to laboratories in Europe.

MOROCCAN HOLIDAYS

Morocco celebrates the holidays of the Sunni Muslim calendar. During these holidays, schools and government offices close. Some businesses close, others don't, but any business that employs large numbers of Moroccans closes on the major Islamic holidays.

Morocco also has a few of its own holidays that entail the same closures. Additionally, the government has recently added other holidays to the calendar, most of them extolling its own accomplishments in various arenas. They vary in the extent to which they are observed, but all of them are days off for civil servants at least.

Islamic Holidays

Holidays celebrated by Muslims the world over are based on the Muslim calendar. Keep in mind that the Muslim year is shorter than the solar year, and so each year these holidays come 10 or 11 days earlier than the previous year; thus they gradually work their way through the seasons. All Islamic holidays begin officially at sundown on the evening before the official date of the holiday.

Âid aṣ-Ṣeghir

This is Arabic for 'little festival', which is celebrated on the first day after the month of Ramadan. Elsewhere in the Muslim world it is called *âid al-fṭir*, or 'breakfast festival'. It marks the end of the month of fasting.

Âid al-Kebir

This is Arabic for 'big festival' and it is the biggest holiday in Morocco. Elsewhere in the Muslim world, it is called *âid al-adha*. It is celebrated on the tenth day of the month of Du al-ḥijja, the month during which Muslims make a pilgrimage to Mecca. For reference, it occurs roughly two months and one week after the end of Ramadan. But if you're in Morocco, you'll know it's coming, because everyone will be talking about it. Âid al-kebir is to Moroccans what Christmas is in most Western countries: a time that everyone looks forward to spending with their families, to relax and enjoy each other's company. Normally, it is a two-day holiday, but not a lot gets done on the day before or the day after, because everyone is travelling to and from visits with their families. The holiday commemorates the sacrifice of a sheep by Ibrahim, who was directed to do so by Allah rather than sacrificing his son. This story from the Koran also occurs in the Bible, Ibrahim being none other than Abraham. For this holiday, every Moroccan family tries to buy a ram, which is ritually slaughtered then eaten over the next three days. The holiday is a carnivore's delight, but vegetarians would

Every Moroccan family aspires to slaughter a ram at Âid al-kebir, the main holiday of the Muslim calendar.

be well advised to make themselves scarce for this one, as many people eat virtually nothing but meat for the duration of the holiday.

Âid l-Mouloud

Called *mawlid an-nabi* elsewhere in the Muslim world, this two-day celebration marks the birthday of the prophet Mohammed. It falls on the 12th and 13th of Rabia I, three months after âid al-kebir.

Âshoura

This holiday, falling on the tenth day of Moharram, marks the day Ali, prophet Mohammed's son-in-law, was murdered in the mosque. It is primarily a Shi'a Muslim holiday, and is celebrated in Morocco as a gift-giving occasion for children. It is not a day off from work.

Moroccan Holidays

These holidays are observed according to the Western calendar, and thus fall on the same day every year. Except for Labour Day, they are all marked in grand style by the government, since they celebrate milestones in its history. Towns and cities are festooned in bunting and portraits of the king, and there are often public celebrations and ceremonies as well as extensive television and radio coverage.

Âid l-Ârsh

This is Arabic for coronation festival, and marks the anniversary of the coronation of King Hassan II. It falls on 3 March.

Âid sh-Shghoul

This is Labour Day, celebrated on 1 May, as in most parts of the world. Trade union members have the day off and there are rallies featuring slogan-chanting and the like. Otherwise, life goes on as normal.

Âid l-Massira l-Khedra

This is Green March Day, 6 November. It commemorates the 1975 march of 350,000 Moroccans, led by King Hassan II, into the Sahara to claim it for Morocco after it was relinquished by Spain. The holiday is an occasion for Moroccans to celebrate unity and patriotism.

Âid al-Istiqlal

This is Independence Day, 18 November. It marks the day on which Morocco declared its independence from France in 1956, when the protectorate ended.

Other holidays on the calendar are observed more by the government than anyone else and include New Year's Day, 1 January; National Day, 23 May; Youth Day, 9 July; Oued d-Dahab Day, 14 August; and something called 'Revolution of the King and the People' on 20 August.

Moussem

A *moussem* is the birth or death anniversary of a saint, i.e., a *murabit*. Depending on the saint's renown, these can be anything from low-key, hardly noticeable local affairs to major festivals. Some of them attract foreign tourists; many more of them attract Moroccan tourists, who may view them as opportunities for a sort of mini-pilgrimage. Among the most popular *moussem* are Moussem Moulay Abdellah in El-Jadida in August, Moussem Moulay Idriss in Meknes in September, and Moussem Moulay Idriss Al Ashar in Fez in October.

There are occasionally interesting festivities to watch or participate in at a *moussem*. These include folk dancing by *shikhat* (women dancers) or *genaoua*, a class of black dancer-musicians who travel about in small groups and play drums, dance, and excite crowds to frenzied gyrations. *Moussems* are usually accompanied by a *souq* as well that serves the needs of those attending. Country people often arrive with their tents to spend several days at the *moussem*.

Another regular feature of a *moussem* and other Moroccan celebrations is the *fantasia*: a group of horsemen in ceremonial dress line up at one end of a large field, and as they approach the other end at a gallop, rise up and fire their rifles into the air in unison. After they finish, the crowd oohs, aahs and applauds, and then the horsemen do it again. Despite the low-tech presentation of the spectacle in comparison to Western

Men and horses dress up for a *fantasia.*

diversions, it is very impressive entertainment, taken very seriously by the horsemen and their audience.

Western Holidays

There is no official recognition of Western holidays in Morocco except for New Year's Day. There is some awareness of Christmas, called *âid al-massih* (Messiah's festival) or *Nöel*, and Easter, usually known by its French name *Paque*. The school year is set up such that Christmas nearly always falls during the winter school holiday; Easter may or may not fall during the spring school holiday, which is usually around the last week in March.

Calendars and Dates

Though many Moroccan holidays are set by the Muslim calendar, the Gregorian calendar is by far in greatest use, with the French names of the months predominating over the Arabic ones. Moroccans write dates European-style when writing in French, i.e. day/month/year, and just the reverse of that when writing in Arabic, i.e. year/month/day.

FESTIVALS

Throughout Morocco, there are seasonal festivals that celebrate local events. The Moroccan National Tourist Office has begun capitalising on these, which in some cases has meant that they have lost their local flavour, but has also insured that there are better facilities for those visiting. It should be borne in mind, however, that where there is a conflict between the religious and the secular calendar, the religious one will usually prevail. This is worth keeping in mind if you are thinking of traveling great distances to experience local color: get confirmation of the festval's dates from the Tourist Office before you set off.

Those that take place with fair regularity and that are very much worth a visit are as follows:

Almond Blossom Festival, Tafraout, February (near Agadir)

This festival in the south of Morocco is a pleasant diversion from the swarming beaches of Agadir, lined with Europeans in search of a winter tan.

Honey Festival, Immouzer, May (near Agadir)

This remote village hosts an unusual collection of local-design beehives, made from split reed cylinders and clay. A little off the beaten path, but a must-see for beekeepers.

Festival of Roses, El Kelaâ des M'Gouna, May (near Ouarzazate)

The festival takes place around the time that cultivated Centifolia roses, used in the production of rosewater and perfumes, are harvested. A true feast for the senses.

Cherry Festival, Sefrou, June (south of Fez)

Cherry trees in blossom provide the backdrop for the usual sorts of Moroccan merry-making: a *fantasia*, sporting competitions, and lots of good food.

National Folklore Festival, Marrakech, June

This is now actually a transnational folklore festival, with musicians from across the Arab world and beyond. All the usual suspects accompany the crowds: folk singing and dancing, community events, crafts, costumes, jewelry, and of course, food.

National Sacred Music Festival, Fes, June
This festival attracts performers of sacred music from around the world, performed in mostly ancient venues.

Marriage Festival, Imilchil, September (near Midelt)
This colourful festival, featured in *National Geographic* and other outlets, is about to become a victim of its own success. Not so easy to get to, but worth the trek.

Date Festival, Erfoud, October (south desert)
A million date palms supply the subject of this festival in the south of Morocco. An opportunity to sample more kinds of dates than you knew existed.

Horse Festival, Tissa, October (near Fes)
Hundreds of horses mounted by riders in traditional garb compete in fantasias and other events. This is the one to hit if you miss the similar *fantasia* festival in Meknes in September.

COMMUNICATION

CHAPTER 8

'I picked up a book at random. "Master, it's not written!"
"What do you mean? I can see it's written.
What do you read?"
"I am not reading. There are not letters of the alphabet, and
it is not Greek. They look like worms, snails, fly dung ..."
"Ah, it's Arabic."'
—Umberto Eco, *The Name of the Rose*

'NEVER A DULL MOMENT' pretty well sums up the lively art of communication in Morocco. The average Moroccan speaks two languages fluently, and those who speak three or even four are not hard to come by. The foreigner who speaks one of Morocco's main languages may be frustrated initially with Moroccans' tendency to blend several languages into an ordinary conversation, and even into a single sentence. But communication is always the goal, and Moroccans are very concerned that you understand: they are willing to go to whatever lengths necessary to achieve this. *Fhemti*? means in Arabic, 'Do you understand?' and you will hear the word used often in all conversations,

WHO SPEAKS WHAT, WHERE AND TO WHOM

Education in both Arabic and French is universal in Moroccan schools. Children who grow up in Berber households have a Berber dialect as their first language. Spanish is spoken in the north of Morocco. English as a foreign language is available, and often required, in every secondary school in Morocco. However, the five languages are not on equal footing; each has its own arena that in some cases overlaps with and in some cases excludes the use of others.

Arabic

Arabic is the official language of Morocco. By this is meant Modern Standard Arabic, which is more or less the language of the Koran, with some very minor simplifications, and inevitable additions of vocabulary. Moroccans refer to it as *lugha ârabia*, Arabic language. It is the language used in such contexts as newspapers, newscasts, and official speeches. It is *not* the Arabic spoken in the street. That is Moroccan dialect, and Moroccans call that language *d-darija*. As in every Arab country, Morocco has its own dialect which differs in grammar and vocabulary from other dialects and from Modern Standard Arabic.

The Moroccan dialect of Arabic is the conversational language in all Moroccan cities, and even in most villages except where there are very high concentrations of Berbers. It is understood everywhere in Morocco, even though there are minor differences in the dialect among different regions of the country. Despite its prevalence, Moroccans tend to look down on their dialect as being an inferior language, especially in comparison to classical Arabic or French. It is regarded as fit only for everyday use, but not for any intelligent or sophisticated discourse. But attitudes notwithstanding, it is the single most useful language for a foreigner in Morocco to know. The practical benefits of mastering Moroccan dialect cannot be overemphasised.

Moroccan dialect is mutually comprehensible with Algerian, and to a slightly lesser extent, with Tunisian dialect. Further east than that, the differences become wider. Arabs the world over are usually conversant in Egyptian dialect because of the influence of Egyptian television programs. Native speakers of different Arab dialects can usually understand each other well enough for the purposes of casual conversation. Non-native speakers have more difficulty. If you know another Arabic dialect, or if you have studied Modern Standard Arabic, you will be able to learn Moroccan dialect fairly easily.

French

All Moroccans study French from the third year of primary school through the end of their education. It is a full-fledged second language in Morocco. It is the language of commerce, and to a large extent it is the language of the intelligentsia, or at least of those who are 'Westernised'. Until the mid-

1980s, French was the medium of instruction for science and mathematics from secondary school onwards, but now Arabic is used to teach all subjects except foreign languages. French is also the language of choice in the foreign community, and the one most Moroccans use in addressing foreigners unless they are clearly admonished to do otherwise. In urban Morocco, most signs and printed material appear in both Arabic and French, and there are daily newspapers in both languages.

To some degree, the use of French in Morocco still carries associations with the colonial period. This means that many Moroccans speak it with an attitude varying from simpering sweetness to pomposity to full-blown colonial imperiousness —as if by using French, the speaker in fact becomes French. Apart from its colonial associations, educated Moroccans value French for the access to modern and Western ideas that it provides, and most of them would feel quite handicapped in their conversation if they were limited to Arabic alone. Though Arabic is Morocco's only official language, all business contracts and commercial documentation are in French.

Berber

There are three separate Berber dialects spoken in Morocco which are largely unintelligible to each other, but share enough common features that speakers of different ones can communicate with difficulty. Rifi (also called Tarifit) is spoken in the north, Tamazight in the Middle Atlas region, and Shulha (also called Tashelhait, or Soussia) in the south. In Arabic, Shulha is used generally to refer to any Berber dialect, just as Shluh refers to any Berber.

For many years, the government forbade the use of Berber, including any written form of it, but recently restrictions have been loosened. Berber does not have a fixed alphabet; it can be written using either the Roman or Arabic alphabet, though it has some sounds that neither of them contains. It is primarily a language of the home, though it is used in Berber areas for commerce and on the street. Arabs, especially educated ones, tend to disdain all the Berber dialects, even though they may know nothing of them.

Unless you are working in a rural Berber area with uneducated Berbers, the rewards of learning a Berber dialect may not match the effort involved. There are no good pedagogical materials, no standard system of writing, and Berber is not related closely to any languages you are likely to know. (It is a separate subfamily of the Afro-Asiatic languages.) On the other hand, picking up a few words and using them whenever possible will endear you to the community.

English

English is rather a poor relation among languages in Morocco. Despite universal instruction in it at the secondary level, and the king's stated wish that it should become a firmly established third (or fourth or fifth) language in Morocco, it isn't making very fast headway. The quality of teaching is often poor, and Arabic and French are so firmly entrenched that nothing can displace them. Except in fairly specialised contexts such as development work, which is well represented by American and British aid agencies, or at top-level management in multinational firms, English is not a very practical language for everyday use in Morocco.

Looking on the brighter side, even in remote corners of Morocco, a person conversant in English can usually be found if there is no other way to communicate, and most Moroccans with a secondary school education know a handful of basic words and phrases. The Moroccan government and well-placed English speakers in Morocco are tireless in their support of English and some progress can be expected in coming years. The king himself is a fluent speaker, and there is an American-style university, called Al Akhawayn University, in the Middle Atlas town of Ifrane, in which English is the medium of instruction in all subjects. It offers graduate and post-graduate degree programs in many subjects.

Spanish

In the north of Morocco, the area formerly governed by Spain, Spanish functions as the second language on a par with French and is usually understood by traders and tourist guides in larger northern towns and cities. It is also available as a secondary school subject in the north, and in some larger schools elsewhere.

L-ârancia

Linguists have coined the term 'code-switching' to refer to the blending of two languages in conversation by people fluent in both. In Morocco, this practice is a fine art. The educated middle and upper classes of Morocco, especially in the Atlantic coastal cities, speak a hybrid language they call *l-ârancia*, a blend of Moroccan Arabic and French. The word itself is from the Arabic words for the two languages, *ârabia* and *francia*.

For the foreigner who knows only one of these languages, trying to decipher this mixture can be quite maddening, for there seem to be no fixed rules about which elements of grammar or vocabulary are drawn from which language, and parts of every sentence defy comprehension. Untrained ears may also find this language rather pretentious, a mere attempt to dress up street Arabic with fine-sounding French. But those who speak it are quite comfortable with it, and it is the first language of children of the bourgeoisie. It is an informal, conversational language, and not used in any official capacity, though it is often the language of spoken commerce among those fluent in it.

ARABIC: 30 MINUTES TO APPARENT FLUENCY

Lessons in Arabic are outside the scope of this book, but a smattering of knowledge about the language is both useful for the foreigner and impressive to Moroccans. Even being able to use a few phrases in the correct way makes a very favourable impression on Moroccans and shows them your interest in their language. As you read this section, keep in mind that the information here applies to Moroccan Arabic, and may well not hold true for Modern Standard Arabic or other dialects.

Sounds of Arabic

Even if you never learn to speak fluently, make every attempt to correctly pronounce the Arabic words you know. Arabic has several sounds that don't exist in English, and it uses the throat and the back of the mouth far more than English does. Don't hesitate to exaggerate the sounds until you've mastered them; this will be closer to the correct pronunciation than 'anglicising' them, which may well cause confusion: consider *qra*, read, *qrra*, teach, *kra*, rent, *khra*, excrement.

The following is a guide for pronouncing the Arabic words written in this book. It can also be used to pronounce any transliterated words you will see in Morocco. In cases where a commonly used form of writing a word differs from the system below, the commonly used form is followed to prevent confusion: thus Fez instead of Fas, Tetouan instead of Teṭwan. This system is designed to help you pronounce words the way they are pronounced in Morocco; it is not a letter-for-letter transcription key (i.e., one Arabic letter doesn't necessarily correspond to the same English letter in every word). There is no standard written form for Moroccan dialect, even using the Arabic alphabet, and many Moroccans will tell you that their dialect cannot be written at all. Letters not noted in this table are pronounced as in English.

Letter(s)	Arabic Pronunciation and Other Information
a	In the middle of a word, like the *a* in *father* or in *bat*, depending on surrounding consonants. At the end of a word, like the *a* at the end of *banana*
â	The Arabic consonant *âin* (ع). Voiced deep in the throat, like the sound people make when they imitate the snarling of animals. Ask a Moroccan to demonstrate
ai	Like *ai* in *bait*
(c)	Doesn't exist in Arabic. Hard *c* appears as *k*, soft *c* as *s*
ch	Equivalent to *sh*. Used in Morocco due to the influence of French

Letter(s)	Arabic Pronunciation and Other Information
d̲	Emphatic *d*: The Arabic letter *d̲ad* (ض). Flex your tongue. Has the effect of raising or shortening the vowels around it. Ask a Moroccan to demonstrate
e	Like the *e* in *bet*, or in an unaccented syllable, like the *e* in *blanket*
g	Doesn't exist in standard Arabic, but used in Moroccan Arabic and Berber. Always hard, like the *g* in *go*
gh	The Arabic letter *ghain* (غ). Like the sound you make when gargling, or like French *r* only more aspirated
h	The Arabic letter *ha* (ه). Comes from deeper in the throat than the English *h*. Ask a Moroccan to demonstrate
h̲	The Arabic letter *h̲a* (ح). Heavily aspirated at the back of the throat. Whisper 'hi' as loud as you can without voicing it. Ask a Moroccan to demonstrate
i	As in the word *Fiji*
j	The Arabic letter *jim*. Like the *g* in *mirage*. Never like the *j* in *judge*
k	As in English. Used in some French transliterations for *q* (*qaf*) as well
kh	The Arabic letter *kha* (خ). Like the sound of clearing the throat, vibrating the back of the tongue against the roof of the mouth. Ask a Moroccan to demonstrate
l	Often as in English, but in some words the tip of the tongue is brought further back in the mouth, especially in *Allah*
o	Like *o* in *dote*. Usually near emphatic consonants

Letter(s)	Arabic Pronunciation and Other Information
ou	Like *ou* in *soup*
p	Doesn't exist in Arabic, but may appear in loan words, where it is as in English
q	The Arabic letter *qaf* (ق). Like *k*, but pronounced all the way in the back of the throat, by stopping the tongue against the soft palate. Ask a Moroccan to demonstrate
r	Rolled, as in Spanish and Italian
s	Always as in English *kiss*. Never a *z* sound as in English *president*, *letters*
s̲	Emphatic *s*: Arabic *s̲ad* (ص). Flex your tongue. Has the effect of raising or shortening the vowels around it. Ask a Moroccan to demonstrate
t̲	Emphatic *t*: Arabic *t̲a* (ط). Flex your tongue. Has the effect of raising or shortening the vowels around it. Ask a Moroccan to demonstrate
(th)	Exists in Standard Arabic, but not in Moroccan Arabic. The *th* sound in *thing* becomes *t* in Moroccan; the *th* sound of *this* becomes *d* in Moroccan
u	Like *ou* but shorter; like *u* in *tube* (American pronunciation)
v	Doesn't exist in Arabic; may appear in loan words
w	As in English. Words or syllables beginning with this sound are usually transliterated by *ou* in Morocco, e.g., Ouarzazat and Tetouan, instead of Warzazat or Tetwan
x	Doesn't exist in Arabic; may appear in loan words (like taxi)

Letter(s)	Arabic Pronunciation and Other Information
y	As in English, but doesn't appear terminally, *i* is used instead
'	The Arabic letter *hamza* (ء). A glottal stop, achieved by closing off the air passage of the throat with the tongue. Like *tt* in Cockney *bottle*

There isn't a failsafe rule for where the accent falls in Moroccan words. In general it tends toward the end of a word, but never falls on a short vowel unless a word has only short vowels (e and u are always short, ou is always long, a and i can be short or long). Three-syllable words,which abound in Arabic, are usually accented on the middle syllable. Words ending in -a and -i are usually accented on the syllable just before.

Words to Watch Out For

Master the words in this list and you will be able to insert them with confidence in conversations and bring joy to Moroccans—or at the very least follow the drift of simple conversations. A Moroccan conversation that doesn't use most of them is hard to imagine. Greetings are treated separately in the next section.

Arabic	English
la	No
nâm	Yes (formal)
iya, wa	Yes (informal). Wa is used mostly in the north
bezzaf	Many, a lot, very, too much
shwia	A little, few, not much
mezian	Good
shnou? ash?	What?
shkoun?	Who?

Arabic	English
shhal?	How much? How many?
imta? foqash?	When?
fin? win?	Where? (Win is used in the north)
kif? kifash?	How?
âlash?	Why?
mashi	Not. Can be split up and clamped around a word: thus *mashi mezian* and *ma-meziansh* both mean 'not good'
kaien	There is
ma-kaiensh	There isn't
wakha	OK

The Art of Greeting

Moroccans put a lot of time and energy into greetings, whether they are speaking Arabic or not. Greetings may extend into minutes at the beginning of a conversation, with enquiries about family, friends, health, work, studies and so on being repeated over and over again. You can enquire about the well-being or progress of any subject common to you and the person you are greeting, but men should not enquire about the wives or other female relations of their Moroccan friends: this would be seen as expressing an inappropriate interest. You may, however, inquire about the health of someone whom you know to have been ill.

Foreigners very soon get the knack of the Moroccan greeting, for it is impossible to encounter Moroccans without one, but a few pointers in terms of behaviour and speech may be helpful at the outset. Very early on in a greeting, often before words are exchanged, there is some physical contact. The bare minimum is the handshake, and it usually lasts longer than a Western handshake, and may never end, or at least not until the greeting itself has ended. After shaking hands, either participant may hit his or her hand to the chest (showing affection for the other), or more rarely kiss his or her own hand (showing respect for the other).

Among those who know each other, hugs are common between members of the same sex. Accompanying these are kisses on the cheeks, one on each, although this can also go on for some time, especially among women, who make several passes back and forth from one cheek to the other.

Members of the opposite sex exchange handshakes and kisses on the cheek if they are well known to each other, but they don't usually hug unless they are of the same family. But of course mothers hug their sons, and fathers their young daughters. Men should not offer to shake the hand of a veiled or gloved woman, but may reciprocate if she offers her hand.

The spoken part of the greeting is usually fired off at top speed and is mostly ritual. The same phrases, with minor variations, are repeated over and over by each party, until the repertoire is not only exhausted but beaten to death. At that point, one or the other party will end the greeting by saying _hamdullah_, or more formally, _al-hamdu li-llah_, Praise God.

Common greetings you can easily master are:

Arabic	English Translation
s-salamu âlikum	Peace on you. Always said when entering a place where others are present. The response is _wa âlikum s-salam_
sbah l-khir	Good morning
mesa l-khir	Good afternoon or evening
tasbah âla khir	Good night. Literally, 'Get up happy'
Ahlan wa sahlan	(General friendly greeting)
la bas? la bas âlik?	General purpose expression for greeting or information. Literally, 'no harm.' May be a question or answer, with a meaning similar to 'How are you?' If uttered as a question, the answer is also _la bas_

Arabic	English Translation
la bas ...?/ ... la bas?	How is/are ...?
hani? (fem. hania?)	Are you well?
kif halak?	How are you doing?
ash khbarik?	What's new?

Godspeak

Arabic is overflowing with references to Allah, usually in set phrases that are associated with particular occasions. Many people say 'Allah' or '*erbbi*' (my Lord) for no obvious reason when sitting down, or as an expression of surprise; it does not have any connotation of profanity, as saying 'God' does to some in English. Following are the most common 'Allah' phrases, with translations and notes about usage. You can use these to great advantage even if you don't learn Arabic. Moroccans will appreciate your understanding of them.

Arabic	English Translation
bi-smillah	In the name of God. Said before beginning any activity, especially drinking, eating and driving
hamdullah *al-hamdu li-llah*	Thanks be to God. To express thanks or gratitude for any benefit or blessing
allah iâoun (ik)	God help (you). Said to those who are working or those who need help, especially if you aren't in a position to give help yourself
tbarak-allah âlik	God's *baraka* on you. A way of saying 'Congratulations' or 'Well done'
allah ibarek fik	God bless you. Response to the foregoing
barak' allahu fik	God's *baraka* on you. Usually a very polite or sincere 'Thank you'

Arabic	English Translation
allah iyerḥam walidin	God bless your parents. A desperate 'Please' or very grateful 'Thank you'
allah ijezik bikhir	God reward you with goodness. A thank you, sometimes used ironically, like the English 'Thanks a lot, buddy!'
allah iyâṭik s-sehah	God give you health. The response to *b-sehahatik*, said when one has acquired something new
allah iyâṭik s-ster	God give you protection. Usually a polite way of saying 'Please' to someone
allah ihennik	God leave you in peace. Usually 'Goodbye'. Sometimes 'Goodbye and good riddance'
allah ikhlef	God reward you. Used to indicate that you must decline an invitation
allah isalamik	God make you safe. The response to any of several phrases that have *salam* in them somewhere
allah ister	God protect (us)! Said in the presence of something threatening, and often used humorously, perhaps like 'Saints preserve us!' in English
in sha' allah	If God wills. Said in order to remove any certainty about the future

Numbers Game

Whether you intend to use Arabic, French or neither in Morocco, at least learn to recognise and use the numbers in both languages. Regardless of which language is being spoken, the names of the numbers may be used in either of them. It is especially common for an otherwise Arabic conversation to use French numbers.

The French numbers are spelled correctly here but with no advice on pronunciation—any number of phrasebooks can help you with that. The Arabic numbers are given as pronounced in Morocco, not as in the Arab world generally. Both French and Arabic decline the number one for masculine and feminine nouns; all other numbers are indeclinable.

Number	Arabic	French
one	*wahad, wahada*	*un, une*
two	*jouj* *	*deux*
three	*tlata*	*trois*
four	*ârba*	*quattre*
five	*khamsa*	*cinq*
six	*stta, setta*	*six*
seven	*sbâ*	*sept*
eight	*teminia*	*huit*
nine	*tsâud*	*neuf*
ten	*âshera*	*dix*
eleven	*hadâsh* #	*onze*
twelve	*tnâsh*	*douze*
thirteen	*tltâsh*	*treize*
fourteen	*ârbatâsh*	*quattorze*
fifteen	*khamstâsh*	*quinze*
sixteen	*settâsh*	*seize*
seventeen	*sbâtâsh*	*dix-sept*
eighteen	*temintâsh*	*dix-huit*
nineteen	*tsâtâsh*	*dix-neuf*
twenty	*âshrin*	*vingt*
twenty-one	*wahad u âshrin*	*vingt-un*
twenty-two	*etnin u âshrin*	*vingt-deux*
thirty	*tlatin*	*trente*
forty	*ârbain*	*quarante*
fifty	*khamsin*	*cinquante*

Number	Arabic	French
sixty	*sttin*	*soixante*
seventy	*sbâin*	*soixante-dix* §
eighty	*temenin*	*quattre-vingt* ‡
ninety	*tsâin*	*quattre-vingt-dix* †
one hundred	*mia, miat* Ω	*cent*
two hundred	*miatain*	*deux cent*
three hundred	*tltemia*	*trois cent*
nine hundred	*tsâmia*	*neuf cent*
one thousand	*alf*	*mille*
two thousand	*alfain*	*deux mille*

* This is a purely Moroccan word and occurs only as two (i.e., not in 22, 32, 42, etc.).

\# All Arabic numbers between 11 and 19 add an *-er* at the end when used in combination with another word, i.e., *hadâsh*, 11, *hadâsher alf*, 11 thousand.

§ In French, the terms for 71–79 are made by combining *soixante* with the names for 11–19.

‡ The terms for 81–89 are made in French by combining *quattre-vingt* with the names for 1 through 9.

† The terms for 91–99 are made in French by combining *quattre-vingt* with the names for 11 through 19.

Ω *miat* is used when used in combination with another word, i.e., *mia*, hundred, *miat alf*, one hundred thousand.

Hot Tips for the Arabic Student or Impostor

Whether you intend to make a sincere attempt to learn Moroccan Arabic, which is highly recommended, or whether you end up with only a handful of useful phrases, the following hints should make learning easier:

- Get yourself a tutor. Working with the few course materials available in Moroccan Arabic without a native speaker to guide you will prove very difficult. Language teachers abound in Morocco and you should have no difficulty finding one who is quite eager to pick up a little extra cash by giving private lessons. The best place to get one is on the recommendation of some other foreigner who is learning Arabic. If this doesn't work, inquire among the language teachers at a local school. This should not be expensive. An hourly rate of 50–75 dirhams will probably be acceptable.

- Learn the alphabet. Despite appearances, it is very logical, strictly rule-bound and has only a handful of shapes. It is the best mnemonic device for learning Arabic, because words related in meaning always contain the same letters. It is also strictly phonetic, so once you can read it, you can pronounce it properly. Buy one of the children's books used to teach the alphabet, available in any bookstore. They have pages to practise writing the various forms of the letters.

- When you have mastered the rudiments of the spoken language, record talk radio programs and listen to them with a native speaker. This will give you the rare opportunity to hear the same conversation more than once, and also to learn many common idiomatic expressions.

Here, also, are a couple of cheap tips that can rub a lot of the mystery off the sound of the language:

- The marker for feminine gender is *-a*. Words ending in this sound are feminine: Fati<u>h</u>a, Kenza, Mouna. Nouns and adjectives referring to living things can be made feminine by adding this sound.

- The definite article is *al-* (sometimes written *l-* or *el-*), and is used far more extensively in Arabic than we use 'the' in English. It is used more often than not with nouns.

- The letters of the alphabet are classified as either 'sun' or 'moon'. In words that begin with moon letters (which include all the vowels as well as some consonants), the *l* of the article is pronounced, and sounds like *al-*, *el-*, or simply *l-* at the beginning of a word. Thus, *l-qamra*, the moon; *l-yed*, hand; *l-mout*, death.

- Words that begin with sun letters (which are all consonants) absorb the sound of the *l* of the article into themselves, with the result that the *l* is not pronounced, but the initial consonant is doubled. Thus *sh-shims*, the sun; *n-na<u>s</u>r*, victory; *<u>t</u>-<u>t</u>req*, the road. In Moroccan Arabic, the letter *jim*, transliterated as *j*, is a sun letter in some words, a moon letter in others.

- Double consonants receive double duration in speech. You will not be understood if you don't linger over the double consonant for a moment. Consider *hemmam*, public bath, *hemam*, pigeon. Or *qra*, he read, *qrra*, he taught. This is also true for consonants doubled because of the addition of the article to a sun letter.

TALKING WITH MOROCCANS

Moroccans love to talk. This will be obvious to you within hours of your arrival in the country. Speech carries greater significance for Moroccans than it typically does in English-speaking countries. Curses and insults are much more consequential; profanity is regarded as far more terrible; and blessings are thought to carry actual benefits, they are more than merely kind words. To put it another way, there is no such thing as a 'throwaway remark' when you're speaking with Moroccans, whether in their language or in yours. This is helpful to keep in mind in any conversation you may have with them.

It is also useful to keep in mind that public and private speech, as already suggested in the last chapter, are two distinct acts. Public speech maintains appearances, and doesn't necessarily reflect facts that may be obvious to everyone; private speech is more forthright. A Moroccan's speech may seem as though it comes from two different people. In a sense, it does: the private persona, and the public one. Alone, neither represents the whole individual, and you will find it profitable to refrain from judgment until you have experienced both sides.

What you talk about with your Moroccan friends privately need not be limited in any way (though tread carefully with the subjects noted below). Moroccans are very quick (for some, even too quick) to develop trust and confidence in private relationships. There is also the added attraction for them of sharing their problems, thoughts and feelings with a foreigner. Young and educated Moroccans very often find that foreigners have a sympathetic ear for their difficulties, especially the ones that result from their bondage to traditions—so you may very well be hearing deep dark secrets very early on in your friendships with Moroccans. The important thing to remember is that if such information is divulged privately, it should only be referred to privately. It could be very embarrassing, and even socially damaging, for a Moroccan's private views on emotional, political or religious matters to be discussed among his or her peers.

As a foreigner, you would do well to regard the following topics as 'off-limits' in a group conversation. You may well feel that you want to avoid them even privately if your views are very much at odds with prevailing Moroccan ideas, as such topics tend very quickly to get out of hand and turn into heated debates.

- Sex and sexual mores
- Israel and Palestine
- The Prophet Mohammed
- The king of Morocco or his family
- The Western Sahara (see Chapter 1)
- Your religion, if it is not Christianity or Islam

On the other hand, there are a number of topics that Moroccans talk about with great interest and curiosity, and that are always a safe bet in striking up a conversation.

- Arabic or Berber language
- Your family
- Sports, especially football (i.e. soccer)
- What you are doing in Morocco
- What you think about Morocco
- Places you have visited in Morocco

It must be noted that many Moroccans, religious or not, will want to talk about Islam with you. They may ask if you have 'entered Islam' (converted) or if you 'know God' (believe in him). If you have strong views on these matters that are at odds with those of the locals you may wish to think about developing mild answers to such questions and thus avoid a protracted and probably one-sided discussion. Moroccans believe in the perfection of their religion rather fiercely, and disagreeing in either a particular or a general way can lead to lengthy sermons.

Conversational Style

A few features of Moroccan conversation may seem baffling without a bit of background understanding, but can be related directly to cultural themes we have already encountered, namely the contrast between private and public life, and Moroccans' great love for talking.

Repetition

Does it seem that you have the same conversation over and over again with the same person? Do people make a point to you repeatedly in the same conversation, even though you have indicated that you understand? You are not being subjected to this because of your primitive language skills. Moroccans are quite happy to repeat well-known views over and over, or to rehash conversations that have been successful in the past. Conversation is a way of bonding with people, and this kind of repetition is just cement for the bond.

Curiosity

Deep, probing questions about any aspect of your personal life, with or without apologies for their forwardness, may be thrown at you. Your family, your love life, your finances and your past are all open to inquiry. You don't have to answer, and it is not even thought rude to say 'none of your business' (*mashi shghoulik*) in a light-hearted way. Moroccans are forever asking 'why?' about anything you may say or do, but if they don't get an answer, they are usually happy to leave well enough alone.

Lying

Flagrant untruths are rampant in Moroccan speech, yet lying is actually disparaged as much as it is in other countries. How to reconcile the two? One reason that a Moroccan may be 'economical with the truth' is to save face, to avoid *hshuma*. In the presence of peers, a Moroccan may feel compelled to deny any number of blatant realities, if admitting to them would mean a loss of face. Lies of a lesser variety—white lies, or merely slippery language—are not really thought of as lies in the Moroccan value system. In public especially—and this means in any business transaction, or in any conversation among strangers—everyone is out for himself, and it is acceptable to see how much you can get away with.

If this speech habit is troublesome for you, the only antidote is to be as wily as the natives. Don't be gullible. Don't believe everything you hear. If you question very closely any suspected untruth, you will probably get to the bottom of it, because this kind of fabrication is usually spontaneous and artless.

Emotionalism

The range of emotion that is considered normal in public and private behaviour is very wide indeed. Fierce arguments erupt regularly, accompanied by shouting, gestures, threats and curses. Occasionally, one or more parties to an argument may completely 'lose it' and appear to go off the deep end. This is not out of the ordinary. You will notice that others do not respond to such displays with alarm, and that the storm soon passes. Remember the important role that speech plays in Morocco. In cases like these, words are often a safe alternative to action: the more antagonism that can be released in speech, the less likely that a confrontation will turn physical. By the same token, you generally need not fear dire threats made in angry speech—they are unlikely to be carried out.

Gestures to Use and Abuse

Experts tell us that speech makes up only 10 per cent of face-to-face communication. Gestures don't fill in the other 90 per cent, but in Morocco, they go a long way towards it. The hands are very active in conversation: when not touching you to drive home some point, they may well be flying all over the place. Here are a few standard gestures and what they mean.

Gesture	Meaning
Thumb held under the chin	(Of things) something is full or crowded, or (of persons), he/she is (too) rich

Gesture	Meaning
Waving the hand back over the shoulder	The past, or something in the past
Thumb upright over closed fist	Something good: 'Number One'
Flicking fingers against thumb towards someone or something	Appreciation for something new, bright, clean or pretty. Towards a person, it is a compliment on dress or appearance
Two index fingers held side by side	*Kif-kif* (Sameness, identity)
Index finger pulling down lower eyelid	<u>H</u>shuma. Sometimes used facetiously
Wagging index finger from side to side	No; never
Hand outstretched, palm down, fingers closing to palm in unison	*Aji* (Come here)
Hand outstretched, palm up, fingers closing to in unison	Give it to me
Upward motion of the forearm and hand under the other raised forearm	Departure. May mean 'he left', 'I'm going', 'Can I go?' etc., depending on context
Quickly turning up a downturned palm, one or both hands	What? Why? What's this? The gesturer needs more information
Finger pointing to temple	The person referred to is witty or intelligent
Finger pointing to forehead	The person referred to is crazy or stupid

The following gestures are obscene or offensive and should never be used:

- Clapping an open palm over a closed fist.
- Pointing a slightly lowered middle finger at someone.

- Pointing a slightly raised middle finger at someone.
- Forming a circle with the thumb and index finger (indicates 'zero' or bad results—and is not a sign for OK).

Sounds Like...

Finally, a note on some common English words that often raise chuckles in Morocco, especially among young people, because they sound like Arabic or Berber scatalogical terms and euphemisms. Of course you can't always avoid using them, but at least you will know that there is a cause for the laughter. 'Balloon', 'blew', 'blue', 'left', 'lift', 'zip' and 'zipper' all sound like various Berber and Arabic slang words for the male organ. 'Cosy', 'quiz', 'twenty', and 'zucchini' evoke images of female anatomy.

'Much of a Moroccan's time is spent in alliance-building and alliance-maintenance. He assumes, and rightly so, that most other Moroccans are doing the same thing, and that therefore he must be on his guard lest he be outmanoeuvred...In his dealings with others...the Moroccan takes for granted an element of conspiracy.'
—John Waterbury, *The Commander of the Faithful*

THIS CHAPTER DEALS WITH an area of life that is most likely a central one for the foreigners who live in Morocco: work. It is not a concern that is central for most Moroccans—a striking difference that manifests itself in many ways in the relations between the two groups. This is not to imply that Moroccans shy away from work. It merely reflects the fact that Moroccan culture is centred around family and family relations to a degree not seen in Western countries, where livelihood and careerism are held in greater esteem. Moreover, it reflects the fact that but for their work, most resident foreigners would not *be* in Morocco, whereas of course Moroccans would be, regardless of how they earned a living.

WORK IN THE CONTEXT OF LIFE

The ideas that work should be in some way personally fulfilling, that it should give meaning to your life and that it defines who you are in the world are foreign in Morocco. As we have seen in earlier chapters, a Moroccan's main concern in life is family; everything else is subordinate to this. Fulfilment through family life and personal relationships is much higher on the average Moroccan's agenda than satisfaction with work. A Moroccan's place in society is more determined by the circumstances of birth and family background than by livelihood. Thus, work for most Moroccans is merely a means of supporting and protecting the family, and if possible, of enhancing the family's prestige. Work is not expected to bring personal satisfaction.

Westerners also take for granted some other ideas about work that, while present in Morocco, are imports that have not fully taken root. Working for hourly wages and keeping dependable business hours are concepts foreign to Arab cultures generally, although Western-style businesses in Morocco have at least nominally adopted these practices. However, it is not at all unusual to find businesses closed unexpectedly or opened unpredictably, and for Moroccan workers to take what foreigners may consider a very casual attitude about keeping appointments and regular working hours. Likewise, the concept of a deadline is not one that jibes very well with the Moroccan way of life. Things happen when they are fated to happen; never sooner, never later.

Finally, the sort of personal ambition in work that is often respected in the West, the concept of 'career goals' and risk-taking in the interest of personal advancement are not much seen in the Moroccan workplace. The combination of fatalism, the relative lack of social mobility and the general insecurity that is part of life in the underdeveloped world have produced a Moroccan worker who is much more concerned with holding onto and protecting what he's got, rather than risking anything in an attempt to get something better. 'Little and lasting is better than much and passing,' goes a Moroccan proverb.

Doing as the Romans Do

If the foregoing paints a bleak picture for someone trying to 'get things done' in Morocco, it needn't. But foreigners who work with, report to, or employ Moroccans need to be aware of cultural differences in the concept of work. The most disastrous work scenarios involving foreigners in Morocco are those in which the outsiders come in and attempt to manage, negotiate and produce using an unmodified Western approach. The most successful projects are those that study Moroccans' ways of working and structure the work environment in such a way that honest and dependable work is meaningfully rewarded. For example,

- Cultivate good personal relationships with all the Moroccans you work with. Nothing is impersonal to them, and the idea of *professionalism*, in so far as it means separating personal from business concerns, doesn't hold water.

- Be careful to maintain the social divisions implicit in your work relationships with any Moroccan colleagues you meet outside of work. Or more to the point, don't get too chummy with people you employ, and don't act too familiar with your work superiors. Doing either could compromise the effectiveness of your working relationships.

- If at all possible, do not impose threatening ultimatums and strict deadlines on people, unless you are purposefully trying to force a situation towards a negative outcome.

- An authoritative style of management gets respect and works effectively with Moroccans; an authoritarian one does not. This means that whoever is in charge should be fully capable, decisive and sympathetic to but not indulgent of subordinates' points of view. But if you try to govern in a too heavy-handed way, you are inviting subordinates to unite and conspire against you.

- If you must reprimand a worker or colleague, do so privately and discreetly. Use an intermediary if you are unable to approach a situation without an angry confrontation. In brief, do not humiliate a Moroccan before his or her peers; you will be judged as the bad guy by all sides and probably won't accomplish anything positive.

- Anything Moroccans do to separate themselves from the group is more likely to attract disrespect and suspicion than admiration from their peers. So do not expect a great deal of personal initiative or ambition in Moroccan employees. These attributes may be valued in the West, but in fact are often viewed negatively in Morocco. By the same token, do not put people 'on the spot' in a situation where they are expected to break ranks with their peers, because they probably won't, even if you think it would be in their interest to do so.

- Everything takes longer in Morocco than you hope, think or expect it will, and this is as true in the workplace as

anywhere. Delays of every kind are endemic. It is a fact of life, so try not to let it be a source of stress. Just count on things taking longer.

A Man's World?

A casual look around the street on a working day can easily give the impression that it is overwhelmingly men who work in professional positions in Morocco, but this is an appearance that deceives. It would be more accurate to say it is overwhelmingly men who leave their offices to visit cafés and stroll around. In fact, a third of all doctors, lawyers and university professors in Morocco are women. A walk through the offices of banks and corporations would reveal a greater number of working women than might be expected, not only in clerical positions, but also in middle and upper management.

But women's progress notwithstanding, the world of paid work, especially professional work, is very much dominated by men in Morocco. As in all other respects of Moroccan society, women are afforded unequal treatment and respect in the working world, and they have to work for—and sometimes fight for—many considerations that men may take for granted.

BUREAUCRACY AND CORRUPTION

The word *bureaucracy* comes from French. They invented and perfected this method of controlling and accounting for the interactions of the individuals with institutions, especially government institutions. When the French left Morocco, they took with them three times the number of bureaucrats that the English had used to rule India, which had eight times the population. Moroccans took over this top-heavy system created by the French, modifying it only where it was possible to make it slower, more unwieldy, more cumbersome, more frustrating and generally more inefficient—or so it will seem to anyone having to deal with it! So it rolls on, heedless of the victims in its path.

Ordinary mortals can only cower in the face of this intractable behemoth. But there always arise situations where it is desirable, even expedient, to get things done, and so a time-honoured, parallel system of administration runs alongside the bureaucracy, which Westerners normally think of as corruption.

Moroccans accept as a fact of life many sorts of transactions that most Westerners view as corrupt. It is important to understand that for Moroccans, these ways of doing business do not always carry the negative connotations that they do in the West. Commerce in Arab cultures generally takes for granted the necessity of exploiting family and personal contacts for accomplishing ends, and the inseparability of personal and professional interest. In Morocco, the level of corruption of government ministers in the pre-colonial period was legendary, and times have not changed all that much since then. The king has made occasional pronouncements against corruption, but secret deals in high places are still a regular feature of Moroccan life. This means that circumventing established channels is often the rule, not the exception, for effective dealing.

Favours, Bribes and Kickbacks

The most effective method of interacting with an institution in Morocco where the goal is getting something done or making something happen is to find a contact and service it. Reciprocal favours are one method, the 'you scratch my back, I'll scratch yours' approach. Offering money (i.e., a bribe) to achieve a particular result is another. The promise of later reward for granting a request (a kickback) is a third.

There are hundreds of instances where these ways of dealing are used: a civil servant trying to arrange a transfer to be nearer her family may offer money or favours to see that her application is favourably reviewed; anyone may offer a bribe to get a passport issued in a matter of weeks, rather than months; a teacher may be approached with enticements by a father to grant a favourable grade to his child; a large contract may be awarded to a company that has the best contacts in a certain ministry.

These widespread practices are a dilemma for nearly all foreigners living in Morocco, not only those who are doing business. There is no easy solution to the problem. If you stand aloof from all such practices, waiting with quiet confidence to obtain results using the proper channels and methods, you may well achieve nothing and be viewed as something of a fool. Yet many foreigners come from backgrounds where such practices are viewed as unethical and wrong, and thus cannot be expected to take them up for the sake of expediency.

If there is a solution, it is to meet the system halfway. Certainly you should make whatever useful contacts you can in all the Moroccan institutions you deal with, whether in your work or just in the ordinary process of living in Morocco. It is useful, even necessary, to develop good personal relations with all your institutional contacts, particularly 'people in high places'. Try to be attentive to ways that you can help them before they ask for it. If you can develop social relations with them (by inviting them to your home, for example), all the better. This ensures that you will be able to get their attention and assistance when you need it. But it also means that you may be called on to help them, and quite possibly in ways that you are not comfortable with, at some point.

Everything is in your favour if you present yourself as—and actually are—a person of incorruptible integrity. This means not participating in unethical practices (such as bribery, either on the taking or giving end) and making it clear that you have no intention of doing so. If you once begin, you are marked as one who is ready to do this kind of business and there is no easy way out. If you are in a situation where progress appears impossible without unprincipled action, then you have already come too far down the wrong road.

Nevertheless, if you are asked or called upon to do something to further your own goals that is ethically unacceptable to you, outright refusal will probably not bring you any closer to a solution. Try to find a compromise, wherein you can offer something useful that does not violate your principles. This may well mean involving yourself in a situation in a way that is foreign and novel to you; but remember that foreign and novel is one thing, and wrong and immoral another.

Consider, for example, a range of requests that might be made to you in your capacity as a colleague or business associate. At one extreme, you might be asked quite directly to cough up a particular sum in order to effect a desired action. This is an unusually direct approach, but it happens occasionally, and of course you should refuse. Somewhere in the middle range of unusual requests, you may be asked if you can provide a private meeting place in your home for a male colleague and his female companion; or you might be asked to purchase goods that are unavailable to a Moroccan associate (such as merchandise from your commissary, from abroad or alcohol during Ramadan). Whether you cooperate in schemes such as these is a matter for your own judgment. At the harmless end of the favour trade, you may be asked only for simple things of a kind that you would happily grant to any friend: lending small household items or small sums of money for short periods of time.

In all these cases, you will note that what you may think of as the boundary between professional and private life is breached. Since, generally speaking, Moroccans do not perceive this boundary, success in your dealings will depend on your ability to regularly and willingly overlook that boundary as well.

Moroccans like to maintain good personal relationships with everyone. They do not like to close doors on anyone, because today's ally could well be tomorrow's adversary and vice versa. Remember that a Moroccan's identity and sense of well-being are largely based on the quality, nature and even quantity of interpersonal contacts; the more of these they have, the better. So if you are unable to arrive at a comfortable agreement with a Moroccan, it is better to back off gracefully and with goodwill than to erect a barricade between yourself and someone who is in a position to help you, whether now or in the future. Unless you are convinced that you wish eternal and complete separation from a Moroccan you are dealing with, leave negotiations with that person in a way that will enable you to resume them easily later on.

INVESTMENT IN MOROCCO

With these many caveats as introduction, it can now be said that doing business in Morocco offers many rewards for the entrepreneur, and the outlook for the future is very bright indeed. The Moroccan government is actively courting foreign investment, and Morocco has a great deal to offer companies looking for a foreign base or production centre. Cheap labour, a growing population and its proximity to Europe all suggest that Morocco is well poised to develop the sort of economic relationship with Europe that Mexico has with the United States. It is unlikely that Morocco will ever find its way into the European Union (although it is currently an associate member), but there has been talk of establishing a free trade zone with Europe by 2010, analogous to the North American Free Trade Agreement that links Canada, the United States and Mexico.

Several new laws concerning banking and investments were promulgated in the 1990s to coax foreign capital into Morocco. A number of enterprise zones have been established offering investment incentives, including exemption from various taxes and import duties for a fixed period of time. By offering various substantial incentives, the government is trying to some degree to steer potential investors away from Casablanca, which now enjoys the greatest share of foreign business presence in Morocco, to other areas more in need of development. Administrative procedures for investing and setting up a business have also been streamlined recently, to cut the red tape involved in establishing a commercial presence.

Foreign investment rose fourfold in Morocco in the five years to 1992. It has been growing even faster since then, mostly as a result of European investment attracted to labour costs that are at least 25 per cent lower than those in the European Union. Textiles, clothing manufacturing and agribusiness are in the vanguard of investment. At present, there is a large privatisation program under way in Morocco that is expected to raise US$ 2.2 billion. A wide range of Moroccan concerns in all sectors—service, industry, manufacturing and finance—are up for sale.

As a result of privatisation and other offerings, the Casablanca Stock Exchange has been growing with capitalisation increases in double-digit percentages in recent years; the main checks on growth are the still heavily rainfall-dependent economy and bureaucratic obstacles to free trade.

SETTING UP A BUSINESS IN MOROCCO

Besides encouraging investment in the form of pure capital, the Moroccan government and industry are especially interested in attracting job-creating enterprises to Morocco. It is not an undertaking for the fainthearted, but great rewards await those with determination and tenacity.

Foreign business people and those who advise them in Morocco stress several points repeatedly. They are:

- Thorough and up-to-date market research is a necessity. While statistical data is not as readily available in Morocco as it is in more technologically developed countries, it can be found, and it must be examined before any serious project development begins.

- You've got to know the country, and you've got to know people in the country. Nothing gets done in Morocco without contacts, and contacts require time to develop and nurture. One adviser goes so far as to say that you should live in Morocco for two years before you even try to set up your own business.

- To start a successful enterprise in Morocco, you must be physically present to make it happen, or have a proxy who fully shares your knowledge, authority, vision and commitment to the project. Moroccans like their business dealings to be vivid, here and now. Everything is personal. Remote management via telephone, fax, mail and occasional meetings will not set a fire under anyone.

- Patience is the virtue that counts most of all. If you are inclined to walk away when the chips are down, you won't have much success. Remember that time is not a commodity here. It is not measured or traded off against anything else. It just rolls on.

The Details

How do you get a handle on all of the foregoing expertise without putting in the time required? You can't, but you can use any of several resources available to the aspiring entrepreneur in Morocco to set you on the right road.

There are two useful initial points of contact for those wishing to set up shop in Morocco. One is the consulate of your embassy. It should have up-to-date information about any number of economic, business and labour issues in Morocco, and can serve as a referral service for many practical aspects of setting up a business.

Two Chambers of Commerce operate in Morocco for English speakers, both with offices in Casablanca. The American Chamber of Commerce assists US enterprises getting established in Morocco, and the British Chamber of Commerce aids British and Commonwealth business people.

For those going in at the high end of business development in Morocco, all of the 'Big Six' accounting firms offer services for setting up a new enterprise from start to finish. For those with smaller visions or resources, the consulates and Chambers of Commerce can usually make referrals to the Moroccan officials—lawyers, *fiduciaires*, and *expert comptables*—who can direct and babysit the administrative process of becoming a legally established business entity in Morocco.

In the world of Moroccan business, it is essential to either speak French, or have a completely trusted partner who is able to do so. Without French in the Moroccan business world, you will always be slightly in the dark about what is actually going on.

THE MOROCCAN WORK FORCE

A significant percentage of the potential Moroccan workforce is unemployed, or only marginally employed, and this is due to nothing other than the relatively undeveloped state of the economy. Unemployment is a problem for those who complete secondary and higher education, and a much bigger problem for those largely unskilled, who have either no education or leave education early.

The greatest single sector of the available Moroccan workforce is unskilled, but trainable. Training in particular work skills can be carried out in French, provided that workers have completed at least primary education. Training conducted in Moroccan Arabic can reach all elements of the potential work force.

Skilled Craftsmen

An ancient tradition of apprenticeship to highly skilled craftsmen still exists in Fez and Marrakech, and to a lesser extent in other cities. The idea of mastering a single skill and practising it for a lifetime is very familiar in Morocco—in fact, more familiar than the Western practices of career changing, or being a jack of all trades, or 'serial polymath'. This means that an investment in training Moroccans is very likely to bear lasting fruit; the idea of a stable job based on the exploitation of a mastered skill is one that would appeal very strongly to the average Moroccan in search of work.

Unionisation

Labour unions represent just over half a million workers in Morocco, or about five percent of the full-time work force. Moroccan workers have a constitutional right to unionise, and labour laws provide a number of safeguards and benefits for workers, including various grades of guaranteed minimum wage, paid holidays and a statutory work week. Some labour

Among the many trades developed to a fine art in Morocco is stone carving, such as this at the tomb of Mohammed V in Rabat.

unions and union federations participate in political activity that is sometimes at odds with the government. This led to public disorder and rioting in 1990, but there has not been any major trouble since then. Organised labour has a token number of designated seats in the Moroccan parliament.

THE MUHAJERIN

A very significant factor in Morocco's economy and work force are a group called collectively the *Muhajerin*, literally, emigrants. They are the nearly two million Moroccans who live abroad. France is home to the largest number, followed by the Netherlands, Belgium, Italy, Libya and Canada. These Moroccans remit a portion of their wages to their families in Morocco, usually in the form of postal money orders, in the gray market of cash exchanges with moneychangers in border towns or directly given to their friends and compatriots travelling to and from Morocco. This is Morocco's largest single source of foreign currency, amounting to US$ 2 billion per year.

Many of the *Muhajerin* try to spend some time in Morocco each year. Homes that they own in Morocco form a significant proportion of the available rental market. While many of the *Muhajerin* still consider Morocco their home and talk of retiring there, the generation now growing up are really immigrants in foreign countries, and foreigners in Morocco.

The Moroccan government actively courts the favours of the *Muhajerin*. A special ministry caters to their needs, and Moroccan banks operate in countries where they live to facilitate the exchange of capital. A monthly television program in Morocco follows their success abroad.

It is not known yet whether the influence of the *Muhajerin* will decline in coming years, as the first generation retires and the second generation becomes more assimilated into their host cultures. But for the present, they are a sophisticated lot who are often most receptive to foreigners. They have had the experience of culture shock going in the other direction, trying to adapt to a Western society, and they will be in many cases more understanding of 'where you're coming from' than Moroccans who have not travelled. More pertinent to the subject of this chapter, the *Muhajerin* are well acquainted with the ins and outs of doing business inside Morocco and between Morocco and other countries. So don't overlook their expertise when you are seeking advice about your own work, investment or financial dealings in Morocco.

FAST FACTS

CHAPTER 10

'The intelligent man knows by seeing;
the educated man, by explanation.'
—Moroccan proverb

Official Name
Kingdom of Morocco

Capital
Rabat

Flag
Red background with a green five-pointed outlined star known as Solomon's seal in the centre

National Anthem
'Hymne Cherifien'

Time
The same as Greenwich Mean Time

Telephone Country Code
212

Area
total: 446,550 sq km (172,413.9 sq miles)
land: 446,300 sq km (172,317.4 sq miles)
water : 250 sq km (96.5 sq miles)

Highest Point
Jebel Toubkal (4,165 m / 13,664.7 ft)

Land
Located in northern Africa, Morocco is bordered by Algeria and the Western Sahara to its east and south. The North Atlantic Ocean is to the west and the Mediterranean Sea to the north separates it from Spain

Climate
Mediterranean climate

Natural Resources
Fish, iron ore, lead, manganese, phosphates, salt and zinc

Population
32,725,847 (July 2005 est)

Ethnic Groups
Arab-Berber (99.1 per cent), other (0.7 per cent), Jewish (0.2 per cent)

Religion
Muslim (98.7 per cent), Christian (1.1 per cent), Jewish (0.2 per cent)

Official Languages
Arabic

Government Structure
Constitutional monarchy

Adminstrative Divisions
14 regions: Grand Casablanca, Chaouia-Ouardigha, Doukkala-Abda, Fes-Boulemane, Gharb-Chrarda-Beni Hssen, Guelmim-Es Smara, Marrakech-Tensift-Al Haouz, Meknes-Tafilalet, Oriental, Rabat-Sale-Zemmour-Zaer, Souss-Massa-Draa, Tadla-Azilal, Tanger-Tetouan, Taza-Al Hoceima-Taounate

Currency
Moroccan dirham (DH)

Gross Domestic Product (GDP)
US$ 134.6 billion (2004 est.)

Agricultural Products
Barley, citrus fruits, olives, vegetables, wheat and wine

Other Products
Livestock

Industries
Construction, food processing, leather goods, phosphate rock mining and processing, textiles as well as tourism

Exports
Clothing, crude minerals, fertilisers (including phosphates), fish, fruits, inorganic chemicals, petroleum products, transistors and vegetables

Imports
Crude petroleum, fabrics, gas and electricity, plastics, telecommunication equipment, transistors and wheat

Airports
Estimated total of 63, of which 25 have paved runways. The main international airport is Aeroport de Casablanca Mohammed V

FAMOUS PEOPLE
Ibn Battutah (1304–1368)
Travel writer from the medieval ages who's renowned for his work entitled *Rihlah* ('Travels').

Abd al-Karim (1882–1963)
Of Berber descent, he fought for Moroccan independence from Spain and France during the 1920s.

Samira Said
Singing sensation whose most famous song is 'Maghlouba'.

Mohammed Khaïr Eddine

French-language poet and editor whose controversial works have raised many political and sociological questions.

Fatima Mernissi

Award-winning author whose many books and articles about Moroccan culture have shed light on the changing role of women in the Muslim and Arab world.

Hicham El Guerrouj

Olympic Gold Medalist from Berkane, Morocco, who has set world records in 1,500 m, 2,000 m and one-mile races.

CULTURE QUIZ

The situations below are drawn from real life. They could happen to you! And even if they don't, you will no doubt acquire your own list of cross-cultural events in which your mental multiple-choice list of responses doesn't always contain the right answer. The best approach to these small lessons in life is one that includes a sense of humour!

SITUATION 1

You are walking through a narrow passageway of a *medina* and you hear someone shouting behind you *"Balak, balak."* Immediately you:

Ⓐ Reply *"Allah iâṭik al-bal."*
Ⓑ Get out of the way.
Ⓒ Stop and have a look at the *balaks* on offer.
Ⓓ Reply "*Balak* to you too, buddy."

Comments

The correct response is **Ⓑ**. The literal translation is 'Your attention' but what it really means is 'Gangway'. The other responses will get you nowhere, except maybe run over.

SITUATION 2

A Moroccan friend in a position of influence has just cut through heaps of red tape for you in order to get something accomplished that would have taken you ages to do without him. When you are next at his house, he asks you very politely if you will give his cousin a job. You have a job available but you've met the cousin and you have no intention of taking him on. Therefore you:

Ⓐ Politely refuse.
Ⓑ Say you will discuss the matter with the cousin.
Ⓒ Point out the cousin's known shortcomings.
Ⓓ Dodge the question and change the subject.

Comments

Any of the responses will make your feelings known. **Ⓐ** is the western approach, which is much too direct. **Ⓑ** postpones the matter needlessly. **Ⓒ** should be avoided at all costs, as it would be a real face-destorying act for both your host and his cousin. The truly Moroccan response is **Ⓓ**, which makes it clear that you can't say yes and don't wish to say no.

SITUATION 3

You are standing at the kerb of a busy city street, about to enter the pedestrian crossing. A car is approaching but you surmise it will stop because the light is yellow, about to go red. You catch the eye of the driver. Do you:

Ⓐ Confidently step into the street.
Ⓑ Freeze until you see what the driver is going to do.
Ⓒ Run across the street so as to cross before the car can reach the intersection.
Ⓓ Gesticulate wildly at the driver to indicate that he should stop.

Comments

The safest response is **Ⓑ**. Pedestrians are not routinely deferred to in Morocco, and so responses **Ⓐ** and **Ⓒ** are both daredevil stunts. **Ⓓ** probably serves no useful purpose, but may be amusing for the driver or other pedestrians.

SITUATION 4

You are in the home of a Moroccan friend for the first time. He introduces you to his charming young son, a handsome boy of three or four years. You:

Ⓐ Praise the child's looks and manner profusely.
Ⓑ Acknowledge the boy briefly, then ignore him.
Ⓒ Shake hands with the boy, or give him a kiss.
Ⓓ Offer the child a small gift of money.

Comments

Ⓑ and **Ⓒ** are acceptable; **Ⓐ** and **Ⓓ** are not. Excessive praise of a child, especially a boy, is thought to attract attention of the

Evil Eye which will bring the child no end of harm. Offering money to the child would insult your host. It is appropriate to acknowledge the introduction kindly and politely, but don't go over the top.

SITUATION 5

You are nearing the end, you think, of a multi-course meal at the home of your Moroccan friends. You are so stuffed you can't possibly eat another bite. But everyone is saying "Eat, eat!" and continues to put choice morsels in front of you. You:

Ⓐ Feign illness and sit back from the food.
Ⓑ Praise the food, praise your host, say you're full and insist you can't eat any more.
Ⓒ Continue to shovel it in for the sake of propriety.
Ⓓ Redistribute the morsels placed in front of you to other diners.

Comments

Your hosts would be happy for you to choose **Ⓒ**, but **Ⓑ** is probably your best bet. **Ⓐ** would cause alarm and invite shame on the family; **Ⓓ** would be considered rude.

SITUATION 6

Whenever you accompany your Moroccan friend to a café he always picks up the tab. You have insisted that you be allowed to pay the bill sometimes, but so far without success. So you:

Ⓐ Give up and enjoy the free ride.
Ⓑ Conspire with the waiter in advance to let you pay.
Ⓒ Decline further invitations to the café.
Ⓓ Let your friend continue to pay, and find some other way to reciprocate.

Comments

Ⓑ and **Ⓒ** will serve no purpose. You will probably not be comfortable with **Ⓐ**, though it won't bother your friend. **Ⓓ** is probably the best response. Chances are that your friend doesn't want to be seen by his peers as someone sponging off a foreigner.

SITUATION 7

You are a female on a crowded bus where there is standing room only. You notice that something rubbing your leg is not just the casual contact of a crowded place, but a hand with definite intentions. You look around to find attached to the hand a male passenger who is smiling at you broadly. Do you:

Ⓐ Scream and point at him.
Ⓑ Deliver a knee to his groin and a swift uppercut to his jaw.
Ⓒ Inform the conductor.
Ⓓ Grimace disapprovingly and step away as much as possible.

Comments

Responding with **Ⓐ**,**Ⓑ** and **Ⓒ** in turn would make for an interesting anecdote later, but **Ⓓ** alone is the best way to extricate yourself from the situation without complicating it. Moroccans love a scene, and if you do too, go ahead and make one, but be aware that you are at a distinct disadvantage in that many would not take your side, and unless you can rant in French or Arabic, anything you say would only cause amusement.

SITUATION 8

You are a male at a wedding party where all have been enjoying themselves and making music. Some time after the dancing begins, another male party guest approaches you and asks you to dance with him. Do you:

Ⓐ Demur sheepishly.
Ⓑ Tell him in no uncertain terms that you're not that kind of guy.
Ⓒ Dance with him.
Ⓓ Slug him.

Comments

The only winning answer is **Ⓒ**. It is usual for people of the same sex to dance with each other, less ususal for opposite sex couples to dance. It requires no special talent—just do what everyone else is doing.

SITUATION 9

You are a remote country *souq*, enjoying all the interesting exotic merchandise on sale. You come upon an old woman selling herbs, animal parts, odd-looking stones and minerals and various unidentifiable objects. You whip out your camera to get a snap of this very unusual sight. Immediately, people nearby start pointing at you and shouting. Do you:

Ⓐ Snap your picture and run.
Ⓑ Put your camera away and act innocent.
Ⓒ Shout back at the people.
Ⓓ Snap your picture and face the music.

Comments

None of these answers is very good, because you've already make a major blunder by thrusting a camera in someone's face without asking permission. Especially when you are off the beaten tourist track, you must be very careful about photographing people; they are not used to it and often distrust foreigners with cameras.

SITUATION 10

You are seated at a pleasant outdoor café when you are approached by a very ragged beggar, holding out her hand to you. The only money you have is a 50 dirham note. Your reaction is:

Ⓐ Hand it over.
Ⓑ Dismiss the beggar with *"Allah isehhal."*
Ⓒ Ignore the beggar.
Ⓓ Hold up your hands, palms forwards, indicating that you are unable to help.

Comments

Any of the responses is acceptable. Anything other than these is probably not.

DO'S AND DON'TS

Gaffes to avoid and pleasantries to observe have been noted in passing throughout this book. Here collected in one place are pointers for social conduct that will help you to blend in seamlessly with the locals.

DO'S

- Shake hands with people on every possible occasion, even people you know well and people whom you have already seen once that day or that week.
- Kiss people of the same sex on both cheeks when greeting, multiple times if you wish, if they make a gesture to do so.
- Invite Moroccans to your home as a way of returning hospitality. This is more suitable than taking a 'hospitality gift' with you to their house.
- Take the time to exchange lengthy greetings with your Moroccan friends, inquiring about everything you can think of and answering all of their questions.
- Plan to stay for some time—a couple of hours at the very least—when you are invited to a Moroccan's home.
- Be assertive, forthright and confident in all of your dealings with merchants, vendors, clerks, officials and others you meet in public. Otherwise, you'll be regarded as a pushover.
- Wear modest clothing at all times. This is particularly important for young women who want to avoid unwanted attention from men in public.
- Take off your shoes when you enter a room with a carpet on the floor, and leave them where others have left their shoes.

DON'TS

- Inquire about the health or well-being of your male friend's wife or marriageable daughter, if you are a male. It is not suitable to express interest in this way.
- Touch anyone on the face; it is inviolable personal space.

- Offer food to guests or companions after you have eaten from it. Offer it before you have eaten from it.
- Use your left hand to touch people, to hand over money or to touch merchandise (especially food). Do not put your left hand anywhere that is for the common use of people, such as a fountain or spring. Use your right hand instead.
- Enter a mosque unless you are a Muslim.
- Treat beggars rudely or confrontationally.
- Reprimand or criticise a Moroccan who is your social equal in a group or public setting. If there is a problem, deal with it personally or indirectly, using other people as go-betweens.
- By the same token, don't tolerate rude or disrespectful behavior from children or from anyone who is your social inferior; this will seriously compromise your dignity.
- Eat or drink in public during Ramadan.
- Offer your hand to shake the hand of a gloved or veiled woman; but if she offers first it is okay to shake hands.
- Sit with your legs outstretched pointing at another person. If you are sitting on the floor or on low cushions, it is best to sit cross-legged, with your legs folded under you, or with your knees drawn up.

GLOSSARY

This section is not intended as a substitute for a phrasebook or a language course, but you may find useful words and phrases here for situations that you are likely to encounter. Variant forms are given where there is a difference according to the gender or number of people spoken to. Refer to the pronunciation guide on pages 222–225 for the following words and phrases. See also pages 226–231.

:

Polite Phrases and Words Used in Greetings	
English	**Arabic**
Excuse me	
(to a man)	*smha-li*
(to a woman)	*smhai-li*
(to more than one person)	*smhou-li*
Please	*âafak*
After you!	
(to a man)	*tfudl*
(to a woman)	*tfudli*
(to more than one person)	*tfudlou*
To your health! (said to anyone who is wearing something new, has a new haircut, has completed a meal etc.)	*besahatek*
Welcome to you	
(one person)	*marhebabik*
(two or more people)	*marhebabikum*
Thank you	*shukran*
No, thank you	*la, shukran*
Come in!	
(to a man)	*dekhel*
(to a woman)	*dakhli*
(to a group)	*dakhlou*

Prelimaries of Introductions	
English	**Arabic**
We are honoured (a polite response when you are introduced to someone)	*metsharfin*
What's your name?	*smitek? shnoo smouk?*
Where are you from? (to a man) (to a woman)	*mnin nta?* *mnin nti?*
My name is Mary	*smi Mary*
I'm from England	*ana mn inglaterra*

Shopping and Ordering	
English	**Arabic**
Bring me a café au lait, please	*Ara qahua ou <u>h</u>alib, âafek*
Give me two kilos of oranges, please	*Ara jooj kilo diel limoun, âafek*
How much are those dates?	*Be-sh<u>h</u>al had-ttmar?*
That's really expensive!	*Ghali bizzaf!*
Bring the bill, please	*Ara l-<u>h</u>isab, âafak*

Here are the names of some common foods that you may want to order in a restaurant or buy to prepare yourself. To find out whether a shopkeeper (or waiter) has something, prefix '*wesh ândek*' to the item: thus, *wesh ândek djaj* means 'have you got chicken?' To ask how much something is, prefix '*Be-shhal*' to the item: *Be-sh<u>h</u>al khebza* (how much is a loaf of bread?)

To order something, prefix '*Ara*' to a number or quantity (if required), followed by the name of the item: *ara della<u>h</u>a, aâfak* (give me a watermelon, please), *ara kilo diel aâneb, aâfak* (give me a kilo of grapes, please). '*Diel*' corresponds more or less to English 'of'. All Arabic words are the collective name. To singularise (i.e., to order only one of something), add terminal 'a'.

Fruits

apples	*tefah*
apricots	*mishmash*
bananas	*banan*
cherries	*heblemuluk*
dates	*temar*
figs	*kermous*
grapes	*aâneb*
lemons	*sitron*
oranges	*limon*
peaches	*khokh*
pears	*bouâwid*
plums	*berqoq*
strawberries	*toot*
watermelon	*dellah*
yellow melons	*bestekh*

Vegetables

artichokes	*qoq*
beans (dried)	*loubiya*
beans (fava)	*fool*
beans (green)	*loubiya khedra*
cabbage	*kromb*
carrots	*khayzou*
eggplant	*denjel*
garlic	*toum*
olives	*zitoon*
onions	*besla*
peppers	*fulfla*
potatoes	*betata*
tomatoes	*matisha*
turnips	*luft*
zucchini	*qraâ*

For the following staple foods, the collective name is given in Arabic. Where two forms are given, it is the collective followed by the plural. To indicate a single item of one of these, add 'a' to the end of the word. Thus, *khebz* means bread, and *khebza* means a loaf of bread.

beef	*begri*
bread	*khebz, khebzat*
butter	*zibda*
chicken	*djaj, djajat*
cous-cous	*tâm*
eggs	*biḏ, biḏat*
fish	*ḥut*
flour	*ṭeḥen*
ground beef	*kefta*
milk	*ḥalib*
mutton	*ghenmi*
rice	*roz*
salt	*melḥ*
yeast	*khamira*

Phrases to Bail You Out and for Emergencies	
English	**Arabic**
I don't understand	*ma-feḥemtsh*
Is there someone (here) who speaks English?	*kayen shi-wahad (hena) lli aârf l-inglizia?*
Do you speak English? Addressed to a man (to a woman)	*wesh taârf(i) l-inglizia?*
I need a doctor	*khṣni ṭṭabib*
Call a doctor!	*aâyyet aâla ṭṭabib!*
Call the fire department!	*aâyyet aâla l-bumbiya!*
Repeat, please	*âouwed/âouwdi, âafak*
Impossible!	*ma-imkinsh!*

Phrases to Bail You Out and for Emergencies

I don't know	*ma-nâarf*
Speak slowly, please Addressed to a man (to a woman)	*tkillem(i) bshwia, âafak*

Phrases to Ward Off Unwelcome Intrusions

English	Arabic
Remove your hand!	*ḥayyed yedk!*
Go away! Addressed to a man (to a woman)	*sir (siri) f-ḥalik!*
Get away from me!	*bâad mn-ni!*
None of your business!	*mashi shghoulik!*
I'm happy where I am (to politely refuse an offer from someone to sit next to them)	*ana gals b-khir*
Tend to your own affairs! Addressed to a man (to a woman)	*dekhel (dakhli) f-souq rasek!*
What do you want?	*ash bghiti?*

USEFUL PHRASES AND EXPRESSIONS

This is a list of some of the commonest phrases and expressions in Moroccan Arabic. It is not by any means a substitute for a good phrase book or for language lessons, but it should help you to find a few handles on the stream of words flying by you. The arrangement is alphabetical by transcription, on the theory that you may be able to locate something here that you have heard. Multiple forms are given for person and number where appropriate. Where two forms are given without explanation, these are the masculine (used for addressing a man) followed by the feminine (used for addressing a woman).

If you know neither French nor Arabic, it is probably more practical for you to learn 'emergency' language (Where is there a toilet/hospital/policeman etc.) in French; it is the language that Moroccans expect foreigners to speak, resources for it are much more widely available and for the average speaker of English, it presents fewer obstacles than the Moroccan dialect of Arabic. Don't hesitate to try English first; it is gradually catching on.

English	Arabic
Repeat, please	*âouwed/âouwdi, âafak*
Two kilos, please	*arra jooj kilo, âafak*
A black coffee, please	*arra qhua kehela, âafak*
What do you want?	*ash bghiti?*
What did he/she/they say?	*ash gal/galt/galou?*
At what time?	*ashmin waqt?*
I want X	*bghit X*
Good-bye	*bissalama*
What time is it?	*chhal (hadi) f-ssaâ?*
Come in!	*dekhel/dakhli!*
Where did he/she/you/ they go?	*fin msha/mshat/mshiti/ mshaou?*
Sit down	*glis/glisi*
Get out (of a car, train, bus, etc.)	*hbet/hbti*
Maybe, possibly	*imkin, mumkin*
I didn't understand anything	*ma-fhemt waloo*
(It's) impossible	*ma-imkinsh, meshi mumkin*
No problem	*makaien mushkil*
What's wrong with him/ her/you/them?	*mâ-luh/lha/lek/lhum?*
I don't know	*ma-nâarf*
Welcome (addressing one/ multiple persons)	*marhababik/marhababikum*
None of your business	*mashi sghoulik*
In a little while	*min daba shwia*

Go away (firm but not necessarily rude)	*seer f-halek*
Look	*shoof/shoofi*
Listen	*smâ/smâi*
Excuse me! (when you've jostled someone, etc.)	*smah-li/smahai-li!*
What do you call this in Arabic?	*smeet hada f-lârabia?*
After you (or otherwise to show deference)	*tefddel/tefddli*
Speak slowly, please	*tkillem/tkillmi bshwia, âafak*
Get in (a car, train, bus, etc.)	*tlâ/ tlâi*
Have you got any X? (to a shopkeeper)	*wesh ândek X?*
Can I...?	*wesh imkin-li...?*

RESOURCE GUIDE

This section contains general information to make your stay in Morocco more comfortable. For topics not treated here, consult the index.

ACCOMMODATION

Tips about obtaining long-term accommodation can be found in Chapter Five. For short term accommodation—that is, hotels for those vacationing in Morocco, or for residents traveling within Morocco—the choice is limitless. Morocco has benefited from its long association with France to offer a wide range of hotel accommodations, rated according to a reliable star system. Any settlement of more than 10,000 or so people in Morocco usually has a hotel of some sort; larger towns have a selection.

It is probably safe to say that unless you are young, flexible and adventurous, you will not be comfortable in Moroccan accommodations that rate fewer than three stars. Below this level, you will encounter any number of shocking surprises in your room, which may happen upon arrival, or not until the middle of the night. All hotels are required to post their star rating and their rates. The rates are usually not negotiable. Hotels may offer two rates, one for the room only, and one denoted as *demipension* or 1/2-pension. The latter includes breakfast, but inquire whether it also includes another meal (typically lunch), and survey whether the place is likely to serve a lunch you would like to eat. Breakfast, when included, is likely to consist of coffee or tea, croissants or bread, butter and jam (usually apricot).

Hotels rating four and five stars are of a similar standard to those you would find in Europe; in fact, many international chains operate four- and five-star hotels in Morocco. You can, however, acquire very comfortable accommodation in native 3-star hotels, and these are likely to provide a more interesting experience than the international hotels.

Always ask to see a room before you agree to take it. If anything is not acceptable to you, ask to see other rooms.

This is the time for you to practice assertiveness! Hotel clerks are always eager to rent the most undesirable rooms first to anyone who will settle for them.

A number of websites offer lists of hotels; an Internet search on 'hotels in Morocco' or 'Morocco hotels' will turn up links mostly to four- and five-star hotels, and better three-star hotels. For more timely and less commercial information, try the same search in Usenet groups (accessible through Google); this may elicit responses from people who have recently travelled in Morocco.

Except during peak holiday periods, and very occasionally on weekends in the larger cities, it is easy to secure hotel accommodation in Morocco on a walk-in basis, without booking in advance.

CHILDCARE

The best choice for at-home childcare in households where both parents work outside the home is a nanny. For engaging one, the same guidelines apply as for hiring maids (see Chapter Five). A Moroccan nanny should not be expected to provide any instruction for children, but they provide an excellent opportunity for your child to learn to speak Moroccan Arabic (or possibly Berber) in a natural way. You can instruct your maid to use French with your children, but you should be aware that this could result in your child learning a somewhat fractured version of that language.

Countries whose citizens are represented in adequate numbers in Morocco—at the very least, French and American—have organised preschools and playgroups for young children. For information about these, contact the French or American private schools in Morocco, or your embassy or consulate.

CHURCHES

Christian churches and other non-Islamic places of worship are few and far between in Morocco; your embassy or consulate is the best place to start if you are looking for a religious group with ties to your homeland. All of the major cities in Morocco have Catholic churches or cathedrals that are relics of the French colonial era, and most of these are still active today. A number of Christian organisations do charitable work in Morocco, along with back-burner proselytising.

EMERGENCIES AND HEALTHCARE

The ability of existing Moroccan institutions to deal with sudden and unexpected crises may fall far short of what you are used to. Whether you are travelling in Morocco as a tourist or you are resident there, it is wise to have at the back of your mind a plan to deal with disastrous turns of events. Whether travelling or at home, always have a well-stocked First Aid kit, and insure that you are confidently up-to-date on administering standard first aid procedures, such as CPR, treatment for shock and the like. Do not assume that any Moroccans in your vicinity will be familiar with these, or will be able to summon professionals to intervene.

There are nearly 50 hospitals in Morocco, including some in Rabat and Casablanca that offer a level of expertise and care that competes on a European standard. These latter are the exception rather than the rule. Hospitals in provincial towns are usually underfunded and observe a standard of sanitation that most people would find wanting. For emergency care, there is no alternative, and the existing resources do the job as well as they can. For routine medical care, you are best advised to consult your compatriots, employer, or your embassy to get a referral.

HANDICAPPED FACILITIES

There is virtually no accommodation for people with physical disabilities in Morocco. Moroccans with such disabilities are typically beggars. If you require a wheelchair, it is probably not advisable to travel in Morocco without taking all required facilities, including attendants, with you.

INSURANCE
Health Insurance

You should not live or travel in Morocco without some form of health insurance, and you should provide for this before you get there. For tourists, a standard travel insurance policy that includes health coverage is adequate in most cases. For those staying longer, consult your employer or compatriots, or your embassy or consulate.

Real Estate Insurance

Real estate or insuring the contents of your house can be done through any of the regular insurance companies with offices in all cities in Morocco; many of these have links to French companies and are associated with banks, such as Wafabank. Arrangements for all of these matters is strictly a French-language affair (look for assurance immobilier or *assurance de biens*), and you should have any documents translated that you don't completely understand. It is important that you understand and abide by your responsibilities for the security of your property, as specified in the insurance contract.

Automobile Insurance

It is recommended that you get full coverage from the renter, unless you are sure that some policy you already hold will cover you. For car insurance on a car that you own, consult the same companies that sell property insurance.

MEASUREMENTS AND SIZES

Morocco uses the metric system for all practical purposes: the temperature scale, travelling distances and everyday measurements of objects. For clothing, shoe sizes follow the European standard, with women's shoe sizes ranging from 34 to 42 and men's shoes from 38 to 47. Keep in mind, however, that these sizes apply only to standard manufactured shoes. Moroccan style footwear such as sandals and *bilgha* should always be tried on before buying; the vendors of these will be happy to help you find the right size, or you may have shoes manufactured to fit your feet.

Imported clothing and Moroccan-manufactured clothing for export is usually sized according to general international standards, e.g., small, medium and large. Some men's shirts and women's dresses are sized according to the European metric system. Local clothing is sized according to varying or no standards. In all cases, there is no substitute for trying on the clothes before you buy them. You can have tailored clothing made in Morocco for a fraction of what it would cost you in a developed country; this includes both traditional Moroccan garments and Western-style suits. Tailors are relatively easy to spot by the display of fabrics in their shop windows, and by the boys who are attached to one end of decorative thread that is being braided some distance away by a tailor in his shop.

SCHOOLS

For information about public and private education for children in Morocco, see Chapter Five, pages 151-152. Opportunities for higher education study in Morocco are limited and not generally of interest to foreigners, except those whose area of study includes some aspect of Morocco or its history and institutions. Fluency in French is more or less mandatory for study at university level in Morocco, and familiarity with Arabic is extremely useful. An exception to this rule is Al Akhawayn University in Ifrane (website: http://www.alakhawayn.ma/index.htm).

There are numerous opportunities for language study in Morocco: Arabic, French and English. For a listing of schools, see http://www.worldwide.edu/ci/morocco/flschools_adult.html.

SPORTS AND FITNESS FACILITIES

There are no American- or European-style fitness clubs or gyms in Morocco, but some embassies and private companies may offer limited facilities. The national passion is soccer; if you have a taste for it, you will find no shortage of people to play with. With its extensive coastline, Morocco also offers many opportunities for swimmers. There are public beaches on all coasts, though it is advisable to avoid those directly adjacent to cities, such as Rabat and Salé, because of sewage effluent that is put directly into the sea. Casablanca and Rabat have swimming clubs, some of which have private seawater swimming pools.

It is recommended that you avoid swimming in any inland freshwater lakes, streams, or rivers, because of the risk of schistosomiasis, a parasitic infection spread by the skin-boring larvae of liver flukes.

Morocco is rapidly emerging as a destination for golf tourism and in 1999 was voted the Emerging Golf Destination of the Year. Those travelling to Morocco for the golf can easily organise tours through companies that specialise in this. Search the Internet for 'golf in Morocco' for a sampling.

SOME USEFUL WEBSITES

The following web addresses can be used to find up-to-date information about travelling in Morocco:

- http://www.1stmaroc.com/index_uk.shtml
  The English version of the mainly French-language site 1stMaroc, a business and tourism portal. Many useful links, including one to a directory of real estate agents.
- http://www.britain.org.ma
  The official website of the British Embassy in Morocco. Of interest mainly to Britons for official business; links provided are mostly to other UK government sites.
- http://www.amcham-morocco.com
  The official site of the American Chamber of Commerce in Morocco, mainly of interest to Americans wishing to invest or do business.
- http://www.casanet.net.ma
  A categorised hierarchical directory. In French only. Useful if you know the name of a specific business or institution and need contact details.
- http://www.cdc.gov
  The US government Centers for Disease Control site. It has a 'traveller's health' area with up-to-date health alerts about all regions of the world.
- http://www.embassyworld.com/embassy/morocco.htm
  The Morocco page of Embassyworld, a directory of embassy locations around the world. The selection for Morocco is somewhat spotty, but you may find the one you're looking for here.
- http://www.mincom.gov.ma
  The official government site, packed with official and other spin-doctored information. On the 'Moroccans Abroad'

link, you can find the addresses and email contacts for Moroccan embassies, consulates and missions around the world. The 'Morocco on the Net' link is a very useful portal to dozens of Moroccan websites.

- http://www.morocco.com
  A mainly commercial site that serves as a portal to hundreds of other websites with some Moroccan content. Navigation is occasionally tiresome, but perseverance will usually lead you to the information you seek.
- http://www.oncf.ma/
  The official website of the Moroccan railroads. Available only in French and Arabic, but it's not so hard to navigate the French site even if you only speak English in order to find the current train schedules.
- http://www.uktradeinvest.gov.uk
  A UK government site that examines different countries for the benefit of Britons wishing to do business there, but there is a lot of good practical information and links, even for the ordinary person. Go to the top-level address and choose 'Morocco'.
- http://www.usembassy.ma/
  The official website of the US embassy in Morocco; up-to-date information for tourists and residents alike.

FURTHER READING

The list here does not pretend to be comprehensive, scholarly or objective, but it is hoped that the remarks offered will enable you to decide whether you want to get your hands on a particular book or not. Apologies to all worthy authors whose books on Morocco do not appear here owing to my ignorance of them or lack of time to consult them.

BUSINESS

The five publications listed here provide basically the same information, from different points of view. Each has some information not found in the others, and each puts its particular spin on the information provided, so if you are serious about doing business in Morocco, you should consult as many of them as you can. All are free; all are updated regularly; except for the Price Waterhouse book, all are translations of French editions.

Doing Business in Morocco
- Price Waterhouse, 4 Rue Colbert, Casablanca, or any office of Price Waterhouse

A Guide for Investors
- Office for Industrial Development, 10 zankat Ghandi, B P 211, Rabat

Investing in Morocco
- Groupement Professionnel des Banques du Maroc, 71 Avenue des FAR, Casablanca

Investing in Morocco
- Ministry of Foreign Trade, Foreign Investment and Handicrafts, 63 Avenue Moulay Youssef, Rabat

Investing in Morocco—Why and How
- Banque Commerciale du Maroc, 2 blvd. Moulay Youssef, B.P. 11 141, Casablanca

CROSS-CULTURAL TOOLS

The Art of Crossing Cultures. Craig Storti. Boston, MA, US: Nicholas Brealey Publishing, 2001.

- The best book for the novice or aspiring expatriate bound for Morocco or any country. Even those who have lived abroad for many years may gain very useful insights into their adaptation from this book. It analyses intelligently and convincingly the phenomenon of culture shock and discusses how to treat it. It is also chock full of delightful quotations from travel writers ancient and modern. As a bonus, Storti has both lived and worked in Morocco.

Understanding Arabs, A Guide for Westerners. Margaret K Nydell. Boston, MA, US: Intercultural Press, 2002.

- A short, practical how-to book for personal and business dealing with people from Arab cultures. Occasionally, the author goes rather too far in suggesting the concessions Westerners should make to avoid offending Arabs—as if Arabs themselves need take on none of the work of effective cross-cultural communication—but it is nonetheless a very practical and useful book with lots of good advice.

FIRST-HAND ACCOUNTS

Travel writers have always found rich pickings in Morocco. There are fascinating accounts dating from the mid-19th century from English speakers who visited Morocco at critical and not-so-critical periods in its history and reported on what they found. All of these make fascinating reading for anyone on their way to, in, or feeling nostalgic about Morocco.

Mogreb-el-Acksa. R B Cunninghame-Graham. US: Long Riders' Guild Press, 2004.

- R B Cunninghame-Graham's account of his adventures in Morocco. In the autumn of 1897, this Scottish eccentric set out, disguised as a Turkish doctor, to visit Taroudant, a walled city in the south of Morocco which no foreigner had ever seen. He never got there, owing to an endless series of complications and setbacks, but the story of these makes one of the most fascinating accounts of Morocco ever written. He saw the country as the intrigues of the European powers were about to topple the sultanate and establish the protectorate, and his perceptions about what would follow proved to be quite prescient. Out of print for many years, this quite original book is now reissued.

Morocco That Was. Walter Harris. Arizona, US: Elan Press, 2003.
- Walter Harris was the correspondent for the *Times* of London from the turn of the century up through the early years of the protectorate. When he wasn't dispatching reports, he was off having adventures with Moroccans, which he relates in this book in a self-aggrandising style that is occasionally off-putting, but always interesting. His account of the politics of the Sherfa (descendants of the Prophet) in Morocco still holds up quite well today. Also long out of print, the 1921 book is now reissued in paperback.

In Morocco. Edith Wharton. London, UK: Tauris Parke Paperbacks, 2005.
- The American novelist visited Morocco in 1919 as a guest of the newly established French government there and recorded her observations in her book. The combination of acute observation and fine writing is irresistible. As a woman and a high-ranking guest, Ms. Wharton had access to the harems of the movers and shakers in Morocco, and her observations on the condition of Moroccan women at the time are a fascinating look behind closed doors that have hardly been opened since. First published in 1920, the book is now reissued in the Century Travellers series.

Behind Moroccan Walls. Henriette Celarie. Constance Lily Morris. Montana, US: Kessinger Publishing, 2003.
- A treasure of a book if you can ever get your hands on it, produced in the days when typesetting was an art and not

a computer program. It is in fact a translation of Henriette Celarié's *Amours Marocaines* and *La Vie Mysterieuse des Harems*, which are both accounts of a highly-placed French colonial lady who took a great interest in all that she saw around herself in the early years of the Moroccan protectorate and wrote about it in fictionalised vignettes. These stories will also be of special interest to women.

Journey Into Barbary. Wyndham Lewis. California, US: Black Sparrow Press, 1984.
- In 1931, the English writer and artist spent several months travelling in Morocco. His trenchant observations of characters, largely foreigners, whom he met along the way are collected in this book, which if not the best eyewitness account of Morocco, contains some of the finest writing of its kind. His occasionally withering but always witty descriptions of what he found give a vivid psychological picture of the times.

Dreams of Trespass: Tales of a Harem Girlhood. Fatima Mernissi. Boston, MA, US: Addison Wesley Publishing Company, 1995.
- Fatima Mernissi, who is Morocco's, if not the Arab world's leading feminist, gives an engaging first person account of her privileged but shackled upbringing. Ms. Mernissi documents the arcane—and now largely obsolete—system of female seclusion that was the environment of her childhood, and in so doing provides rich insights into the mentality of Morocco's adult population today.

Their Heads Are Green and Their Hands are Blue. Paul Bowles. New Jersey, US: The Ecco Press, 1994.
- A collection of Paul Bowles travel writings, a good portion of which are about Morocco, including accounts of his adventures recording tribal music in the Rif, and travels in the desert.

A Year in Marrakesh. Peter Mayne. Arizona, US: Elan Press, 2003.

- Perhaps the most enjoyable of the what-I-did-in-Morocco books. An Englishman leaving an unsuccessful posting in colonial India, Mayne went to Marrakech in the waning years of the protectorate with the express purpose of having a colourful life. In no time, he ingratiated himself into the local culture, while always maintaining an ironic and amusing distance from it. Forty years after the fact, much of what he observed of Moroccan mores rings true.

Honor to the Bride. Jane Kramer. New York, US: Penguin USA, 1991.

- While her husband Vincent Crapanzano was vivisecting the psyche of Tuhami, writer Jane Kramer was taking notes for this book. It is a short, lively account of the summer of a family in a poor quarter of Meknes in the late 1960s. Over the course of two months, their daughter was kidnapped, deflowered, found in a brothel and then successfully married off to a stranger. The author, using a simple narrative style, manages to convey with uncanny accuracy the chaos of everyday Moroccan life, in which everything eventually has its moment of making sense.

A Street in Marrakesh. Elizabeth Warnock Fernea. Illinois, US: Waveland Press, 1988.

- An American woman's account of her family's year of living in the *medina* of Marrakech. The author has the outlook and narrative skill of a novelist and quickly draws the reader into her domestic drama. The book is of special interest to women for its attention to their lives in Morocco.

Morocco, The Traveller's Companion/Margaret and Robin Bidwell. New York, US: Tauris Parke Paperbacks, 2005.

- Margaret and Robin Bidwell have read through most of the foregoing works, and dozens of others to compile this book. In 17 thematic chapters, they survey the literature of Morocco seen through foreigners' eyes from classical times to the present. It is an excellent source of information and a delightful read for the aspiring or established Moroccophile.

FOOD

Couscous and other Good Foods from Morocco. Paula Wolfert. New York, US: HarperCollins, 1987.

- A labour of love by food writer Paula Wolfert. She has done the culinary world a great service by making known many of the secrets of Moroccan cooking, including an analysis of that mysterious spice *ras al-hanut*. Also very useful is a listing of common and not-so-common Moroccan spices, giving their Arabic, English and Latin species names. For anyone who wants to cook Moroccan food outside of Morocco and still have it taste as good, this is the book to use.

Moroccan Cooking, the Best Recipes. Fettouma Benkirane. J P Taillandie, 1983.

- A good English-language cookbook available in Morocco. Simplified versions of a number of traditional dishes are described.

HEALTH

Les plantes médicinales du Maroc. Abdelhaï Sijelmassi, Casablanca: Editions Le Fennec, 1993.

- A wonderful guide through the wild plants of Morocco and their uses in folk medicine. Though the book isn't published in English (there is an Arabic edition), English speakers with even a smattering of French will be able to make sense of most of it, and all plants are identified by black and white line drawings, as well as by their French, Latin, Berber, classical Arabic and Moroccan Arabic names.

The World Traveller's Manual of Homeopathy. Dr. Colin Lessell. Essex, UK: C W Daniel Co Ltd, 2004.

- A monument of practical scholarship and worth its

weight in prescription drugs for anyone off the beaten path where there is no (dependable) doctor. The different chapters cover the various ailments likely to be encountered by travellers and how they can be treated homeopathically.

LANGUAGE

No French language materials are listed here. The French spoken in Morocco is good textbook French because that's the way they learn it, and any coursebooks or phrasebooks will serve you as well in Morocco as they will in France. You will not get much use out of the generic Arabic language phrasebooks available; they contain mostly vocabulary and structures that are not used in Morocco.

There is a book-and-cassette based course in conversational Moroccan Arabic available from ATS, Glen Ridge, NJ, USA, Telephone (201) 748 5673.

A Dictionary of Moroccan Arabic. Ed. Richard S Harrell and Harvey Sobelman. Washington, US: Georgetown University Press, 2004.

- Would benefit greatly from a revision and expansion that it has never received. It is sometimes infuriating for its abstruse system of transliteration and for the number of ordinary words it doesn't contain, but it is still a good (and the only) dictionary of the language available to English speakers. The Moroccan-English and English-Moroccan sides are published in one hardbound, reasonably-priced volume. If you aspire to become conversant in Moroccan Arabic, it is nearly indispensable. Two related books that you may find useful are *A Basic Course in Moroccan Arabic* and *A Short Reference Grammar of Moroccan Arabic*. The first should be used with a native teacher to ensure correct pronunciation, and to provide a first-hand source of information about standard speech in your area that may differ from that given in the book. *The Reference Grammar* is a useful adjunct to learning the language.

Moroccan Arabic Phrasebook. Dan Bacon and Bichr Andjar. Victoria, Australia: Lonely Planet Publications, 1999.

- A quick but limited way into the language. It is a very ingenious compilation of useful sentences arranged by subject and context. It also provides some information about grammar that can start you off on the road to self-styled sentences.

MOROCCAN AND MIDDLE EASTERN HISTORY AND POLITICS

The French have 'done' Moroccan history in a way that no one else has. If you want to delve deeper into this area and you read French, consult the bibliographies in Abun-Nasr, Geertz, Munson, Porch or Waterbury; their books are noted below and in the following section. Only works in original English are given here.

A History of the Maghrib. Jamil Abun-Nasr. Cambridge, UK: Cambridge University Press, 1987.

- For those who like their history in big books with small print, this is a good place to start. It is an English language original and has the virtue of being written by an Arab, rather than a later colonialist (for surely everyone other than the Berbers are colonialists of sorts!). Taking in the history of the entire Maghrib, i.e. what is today Morocco, Algeria, Tunisia and Libya, it provides an important regional perspective that is missing in some Morocco-specific histories.

The Conquest of Morocco. Douglas Porch. New York, US: Farrar, Straus and Giroux, 2005.

- Douglas Porch gives a blow-by-blow account of how the French took over. Mostly a military history, but with interesting insights into pre-colonial politics.

Lords of the Atlas. Gavin Maxwell. London, UK: Eland Books, 2004; US, Gardners Books, 2004.

- A very lively account of the Glaoua, the pre-eminent political family of southern Morocco during the waning days of the French protectorate in Morocco. It includes a riveting narrative of the final days of colonial rule. Out of print for many years, it is now available in the excellent Century Travellers Series.

The Commander of the Faithful. John Waterbury. New York, US: Columbia University Press, 1970.
- In this book, it is difficult to discern where the history stops and the politics begins. In essence, it is an analysis of the Moroccan political animal, based on an examination of motivating forces in Moroccan history that have resulted in the political scene prevailing there today. Author John Waterbury offers useful insights and warnings for anyone who would wheel and deal in Morocco.

Religion and Power in Morocco. Henry Munson. London, UK: Yale University Press, 1993.
- An argumentative book that is mostly intent on refuting the major theses of other writers on Morocco, principally Clifford Geertz (whose book *Islam Observe*d is discussed in the following pages). Munson's is more a street-level than an ivory tower view of Moroccan history, and so is convincing in that respect, but his writing is occasionally polemical to the point of being off-putting. Still, his book offers an essential updating on Moroccan politics and religion during the last 20 years that Geertz's and Waterbury's books have no account of.

MOROCCAN AND MIDDLE EASTERN SOCIOLOGY AND PSYCHOLOGY

Caravan: The Story of the Middle East. Carleton Coon. Florida, US: Krieger Publishing, 1976.
- Straddles the divide between history and sociology, being most properly a social history of the people of the Middle East. Though more than 40 years old and out of print, it holds its own as a convincing interpretation of the peoples, cultures, and civilisations of the Middle East, including a thought-provoking account of the historical economic

factors that influenced Islamic precepts. The author spent a good deal of time in Morocco and was well acquainted with the country.

Language Attitudes Among Arabic-French Bilinguals in Morocco. Abdelali Bentahila. Clevedon, UK: Multilingual Matters, 1983.

- A very meaty digest of the results of a number of tests and surveys conducted on Moroccans to elicit their responses to the use of languages in their country. You could live years in Morocco and probably come to the same conclusions on the basis of observation, but reading this book is a faster way to get at the politics of speaking French and Arabic in Morocco, and why the use of each language is so laden with extra-linguistic messages.

The Arab Mind. Raphael Patai. New York, US: Hatherleigh Press, 2002.

- A controversial work that analyses the Arab mentality and gets to the roots of Arab values by showing the connections of Arabs' thought and behaviour with their desert heritage and child-rearing practices. Derided in some circles as quite politically incorrect, it is nevertheless a very convincing and intelligent psychological portrait of Arab cultural patterns. You will probably find it more compelling reading after you have been in Morocco for a while, rather than before you go.

Tuhami, Portrait of a Moroccan. Vincent Crapanzano. Chicago, US: University of Chicago Press, 1986.

- Professor Vincent Crapanzano plies his Western, psychoanalytical mind on the hapless Tuhami, a Moroccan tile maker who lives a great deal in the spirit world, thinking mostly of sex and rarely having it. You will probably never meet a Moroccan like Tuhami, but you may see bits of him in every Moroccan man you meet. As for the author's psychologising, decide for yourself whether it is more real than the experience it attempts to pigeonhole.

Wit and Wisdom in Morocco: A Study in Native Proverbs. Edward Westermarck. MT, US: Kessinger Publishing, 2003.

- Edward Westermarck was a Finnish philosopher best remembered for his work on the history of marriage, but he spent a total of seven years in Morocco and did a great service to all who would know about the place by studying the natives and culture with dedication and intelligence. In this book, he seems to have rounded up every proverb, cliché and fixed expression ever uttered in the country, categorised it according to subject, and analysed it for meaning.

Ritual and Belief in Morocco. Edward Westermarck. US: University Books, 1968.

- In this book, he tries to get at the root of conceptions about the world that guide Moroccans' behaviour, and though somewhat dated now, it remains a monument of dedicated scholarship that provides essential background information about what makes Moroccans tick. Unfortunately, both of Mr. Westermarck's books are out of print, but they can be obtained from good academic libraries.

Islam Observed. Clifford Geertz. Chicago, US: University of Chicago Press, 1971.

- Takes a look at the development and adaptation of Islam in two cultures: Moroccan and Indonesian. It will probably be more meaningful and interesting to you after you've been in Morocco for a while, but it is a good introduction to how Islam has been tailored to fit Morocco without losing any of its original shape.

Beyond the Veil. Fatima Mernissi. London, UK: Saqi Books, 2003.

- Lays bare the psychology of male-female relations in Muslim society, particularly in Morocco. For anyone who wants to understand why Moroccan men and women treat each other as they do, the book is indispensable. Short of the perilous hotbed of experience, it may well be the only way to find out what really goes on between the sexes both behind closed doors and on the street in Morocco.

MISCELLANY

- The US Government publishes a series of Country Studies, mostly for the use of its personnel living abroad. These are very good one-volume compilations covering history, politics, culture, economics, and the like. Most also contain annotated bibliographies. *Morocco, A Country Study* is the predictable title of the series volume about Morocco. (Latest edition, US Government Printing Office, Washington.)

- If you can own only one coffee-table book about Morocco, it should be *Morocco* with photos by Barry Brukoff and text by Paul Bowles (US, New York: Harry N. Abrams, 1993). The pictures are good enough to make you want to retire your camera, assured that the best shots of Morocco have already been taken. And Paul Bowles, a continuous resident of Tangier since 1947, has insights into the country deeper than some readers will wish to dive.

- The Society for Moroccan Studies welcomes membership from anyone who takes an interest in the study of Morocco. Membership entitles you to notice of lectures (most of which happen in London) and to *Morocco*, a yearly journal of interesting and scholarly articles about Morocco. Their address is:
The Society for Moroccan Studies
Centre of Near and Middle Eastern Studies
SOAS, Thornhaugh Street
Russell Square
London WC1H 0XG

ABOUT THE AUTHOR

Orin Hargraves grew up in the mountains of south-western Colorado and graduated from the University of Chicago. His association with Morocco dates from 1980, when he began his service as a US Peace Corps volunteer there. Now he divides his time between rural Maryland, where he caretakes and cooks at a Buddhist retreat centre, and London, where he works as a freelance writer and lexicographer. His email address is orinkh@carr.org.

INDEX

Titles in the CULTURE**SHOCK**! series:

Argentina	Hawaii	Pakistan
Australia	Hong Kong	Paris
Austria	Hungary	Philippines
Bahrain	India	Portugal
Barcelona	Indonesia	San Francisco
Beijing	Iran	Saudi Arabia
Belgium	Ireland	Scotland
Bolivia	Israel	Sri Lanka
Borneo	Italy	Shanghai
Brazil	Jakarta	Singapore
Britain	Japan	South Africa
Cambodia	Korea	Spain
Canada	Laos	Sweden
Chicago	London	Switzerland
Chile	Malaysia	Syria
China	Mauritius	Taiwan
Costa Rica	Mexico	Thailand
Cuba	Morocco	Tokyo
Czech Republic	Moscow	Turkey
Denmark	Munich	Ukraine
Ecuador	Myanmar	United Arab
Egypt	Nepal	Emirates
Finland	Netherlands	USA
France	New York	Vancouver
Germany	New Zealand	Venezuela
Greece	Norway	Vietnam

For more information about any of these titles, please contact any of our Marshall Cavendish offices around the world (listed on page ii) or visit our website at:
www.marshallcavendish.com/genref